P9-CMX-965

CORPORATIONS AND THEIR CRITICS

Issues and Answers to the Problems of Corporate Social Responsibility

Edited by
Thornton Bradshaw
and
David Vogel

McGraw-Hill Book Company

New York   St. Louis   San Francisco   Auckland   Bogotá
Hamburg   Johannesburg   London   Madrid   Mexico
Montreal   New Delhi   Panama   Paris   São Paulo
Singapore   Sydney   Tokyo   Toronto

CONTENTS

iii

Library of Congress Cataloging in Publication Data
Main entry under title:

Corporations and their critics.

Includes index.
1. Industry—Social aspects—Addresses, essays,
lectures. 2. Corporations—Addresses, essays,
lectures. I. Bradshaw, Thornton F. II. Vogel,
David, date.
HD60.C7   658.4″08   80-11393
ISBN 0-07-007075-X

    34567890   DODO   8987654321

The editors for this book were William R. Newton and Beatrice E.
Eckes; the designer was Mark E. Safran, and the production
supervisor was Thomas G. Kowalczyk. It was set in Garamond by
Datapage.

Printed and bound by R. R. Donnelley & Sons Company.

FOREWORD

This book demonstrates that corporations vary as much in their social performance as they do in their economic performance. Without doubt, corporations are essentially economic institutions with primary responsibility for maximizing the long-term welfare of their shareholders. This observation, however, does not conclude the debate over the appropriate social role of corporations; it merely inaugurates it. For there exist an infinite variety of ways in which corporations can go about making profits. They range from marketing products that are unsafe to discovering products that help prolong lives, from bribing officials in foreign governments to creating labor-intensive technologies appropriate for underdeveloped nations, from cooperating with trade unions to attempting to prevent their emergence, and from seeking to comply with government regulations to attempting to circumvent their enforcement.

Just as the governments of the fifty states differ in their administrative competence, concern for the less fortunate, and degree of corruption, so do the nation's large private governments—its corporations—vary in their treatment of their employees, relationship to surrounding communities, and concern for the environment. In short, corporate officials, like elected ones, are not uniformly corrupt or virtuous; business, like government, is not a monolith. On the contrary, executives have considerable discretion in how they conduct the enterprises they manage—at least as much as many governmental officials do.

Corporations and Their Critics consists of twenty-three original essays;

twelve are by senior corporate managers, including nine chief executive officers. The business contributors are not representative of business thinking or corporate behavior. On the contrary, they were selected precisely because they were atypical. Thornton Bradshaw and I invited contributions from executives who, by virtue of either their own pronouncements or the conduct of their companies, had made a distinctive contribution in the field of corporate social performance. We asked them to explain what they had done and why. By providing a forum for those firms whose executives had demonstrated creative efforts to reconcile economic imperatives with legitimate social expectations, we hope to encourage others in the business community to think more imaginatively about the potential social role of the corporation.

Our list does not claim to be definitive. Several executives from whom we solicited contributions were unable to complete them, while there were other companies which surely deserved inclusion. We also confined our selections to the largest enterprises. Even more important, once one goes beyond the bottom line in evaluating corporate performance, subjective judgments invariably intrude. The selections from the business community included in this volume reflect the personal views of the editors as to what constitutes the appropriate social role of the corporation. Those who share different biases would undoubtedly make different selections.

The remaining eleven essays are by persons who either individually or through their organizations have been closely involved in scrutinizing the social performance of business in the 1970s. Although we did not receive essays from all those from whom we sought contributions, this volume does include a sampling of those whose perspectives reflect many of the public's principal concerns with the corporation. While this book is not organized as a dialogue, our aim in soliciting these essays was to help clarify the nature of public debate over corporate social performance. We asked the nonbusiness contributors to formulate, as explicitly as possible, what they actually expected of corporations in those areas in which they were knowledgeable and then to specify which firms had come closest to meeting their expectations.

CORPORATE SOCIAL PERFORMANCE

The social performance of a large corporation comprises three dimensions: corporate philanthropy, corporate responsibility, and corporate policy. Corporate philanthropy includes charitable efforts undertaken by a firm that are not directly related to its normal business activities. Corporate responsibility refers to the way in which a corporation behaves while it is pursuing its goal of making profits. The final category, corporate policy, encompasses the position of a firm on issues of public policy that affect both business and society as a whole.

Corporations differ widely in the way in which they approach philanthropy. On the average, they tend to give away approximately 1 percent of their pretax earnings. However, a small group of major companies, including those of two of our contributors, Dayton Hudson Corporation and Cummins Engine Company, regularly allocate the maximum deduction of 5 percent allowed by the tax laws. Most firms tend to administer their giving through professional staffs located at company headquarters. A few, however, most notably Levi Strauss & Co., have a more decentralized program involving employees throughout the firm in the allocation of funds to organizations and institutions wherever Levi Strauss maintains plants, including locations overseas. Firms also vary in the amount of initiative they exercise. While most firms commonly write a large number of relatively small checks in response to requests from established institutions, others are more enterprising. They are willing to find new and somewhat controversial organizations and to solicit recipients actively in accordance with some overall plan or purpose. In a particularly innovative effort, one company, Control Data Corporation, has decided to take a portion of the funds that it would normally dispense through its foundation and use these moneys to subsidize the development of plants in inner-city areas. Aetna Life & Casualty, Levi Strauss, and Dayton Hudson are among companies that encourage their executives to play a more active role in civic affairs.

Much of what has traditionally come under the heading of corporate social responsibility falls within our second category, corporate responsibility. The degree of responsibility with which a corporation conducts its business is defined by two parameters: (1) the minimum requirements for responsible social conduct are established by the law, largely through government regulations; and (2) the outer constraints on corporate responsibility are economic. However well intentioned, a firm's managers or owners cannot be expected to conduct its business in a way that impairs its competitive economic position. It is within the parameters of the law and the marketplace that firms conduct their business with varying degrees of responsibility.

These constraints are neither ambiguous nor static. Thus, the more profitable a company or the more secure its market position, the more able are its managers to consider the impact of the company on the welfare of its various constituencies. From this perspective, profitability can be regarded as a necessary condition of responsible social performance. But it is by no means a sufficient one. Some firms have compiled records of outstanding economic performance while remaining remarkably insensitive to social concerns. On the other hand, while no company has ever shown a loss because of extensive social commitments, certainly compliance with government regulations has adversely affected the profits of many enterprises. Responsible social performance is thus neither identical with profitability nor incompatible with it, but it is significantly influenced by it.

Nor is the law a rigid boundary; its application and interpretation vary over time. As government regulation has steadily increased, the boundaries of managerial discretion have progressively narrowed. Thus, while Levi Strauss's decision in the 1950s to integrate its plants in the South represented an outstanding example of corporate responsibility, after 1965 providing equal opportunity for all employees was not responsible; it was simply obeying the law. This example could be multiplied many times.

Moreover, firms vary considerably in how they cooperate with government regulatory requirements. At one end of the continuum, companies may view compliance with regulatory statutes and rules in strictly cost-benefit terms; they violate the law whenever the benefits of noncompliance appear to exceed the costs of compliance. These companies are likely to regard managers found guilty of disobeying government directives as fall guys whose only sin was getting caught rather than as individuals who violated the trust of both the company and the public. Examples of such corporations can be found by scanning the headlines of the 1970s. Other companies, however, while perhaps skeptical of the appropriateness of particular regulations, accept the legitimacy of the government's role to place restrictions on corporate behavior. Regarding compliance with regulations as a challenge rather than an obstacle, they make their best efforts to formulate policies that conform to the public's preferences as expressed by the political process.

The companies whose activities are described in this volume fall into the latter category. E. I. du Pont de Nemours & Co.'s policies in the area of occupational health and safety, the programs of Aetna, Dow Chemical Company, Control Data, and Levi Strauss in the area of equal employment opportunity, and Dow Chemical's and Cummins Engine's policies in the area of environmental protection are examples of constructive efforts to employ management skills and corporate resources consistent with both the letter and spirit of the law. Still other companies have attempted to address pressing social problems on their own initiative even in the absence of regulatory requirements. The efforts of the Equitable Life Assurance Society of the United States and Control Data to encourage minority economic development are notable examples of this approach, as is the wide variety of corporate programs to increase the hiring of the hard-core unemployed that the Committee for Economic Development has encouraged and publicized. In addition, Cummins Engine and Aetna have taken the initiative to develop policies designed to protect the privacy of their employees and consumers. In a similar spirit, Harvey Kapnick, formerly of Arthur Andersen & Co., has urged corporations to strengthen voluntarily the role of their boards, while

J. Wilson Newman of Dun & Bradstreet Companies describes how the accounting profession can more effectively help corporations monitor their social performance.

The volume's nonbusiness contributors provide additional illustrations of the diversity of corporate responses to social pressures and government regulations. Herbert E. Alexander, an expert on campaign financing, summarizes the variety of ways in which firms reacted to pressures from fund raisers from Nixon's reelection campaign, while Timothy Smith of the Interfaith Center on Corporate Responsibility describes which companies have attempted to consider the impact of their trade and investment decisions on the welfare of citizens in the less developed nations. Similarly, the extensive research of the Council on Economic Priorities and INFORM reveal considerable diversity of corporate performance in the areas of land development, occupational health and safety, environmental protection, and equal employment. The syndicated columnist Milton Moskowitz offers a comparative analysis of corporate behavior in the area of affirmative action and urban renewal, and Sandra L. Willett of the National Consumers League examines the conduct of particular corporations in her organization's area of expertise. Finally, Donald E. Schwartz of the Georgetown University Law Center and David W. Ewing of the *Harvard Business Review* describe how corporations vary in their willingness to reform their governance structures and establish procedures that protect the civil liberties of their employees.

The most controversial dimension of corporate social performance involves business-government relations. Mainstream corporate opinion has become highly critical of government regulation. It is blamed for promoting inflation, retarding technological innovation, reducing productivity, and increasing economic concentration. This perspective, however, is not shared by all corporate executives. There is recognition on the part of some members of the business community that regulations are attempting, however imperfectly, to address real social problems and that much of the pressure for increased regulation is in response to previous corporate abuses. Rather than automatically oppose any new regulation, those executives have instead sought to promote constructive alternatives. Accepting the goals of regulation, they then seek to draw upon their own experience to offer suggestions about how it can be made more effective. Still others have engaged in voluntary efforts to improve the quality of public debate about business-government relations.

The role of Cummins Engine in shaping public policy in the areas of employee privacy and emission controls is particularly distinctive in this connection. Similarly, the Bank of America has committed itself to a voluntary disclosure policy in an effort to improve public understanding of its activities. L. William Seidman of Phelps Dodge Corporation has advocated that a similar policy be adopted by all corporations as a means of enhancing the ability of business to participate constructively in the political arena. In his essay Mark Green, the director of Congress Watch, lists firms that have lobbied in favor of legislation supported by the consumer movement, while Michael C. Jensen of NBC News contrasts the relationship of various corporations with the press.

CONCLUSION

Implicit in our decision to invite chief executive officers to discuss particular dimensions of their firms' social conduct is the assumption that these dimensions vary from category to category and from issue to issue. Thus, a corporation which displays considerable initiative in integrating various social objectives into its economic activities may also have an uninspired program of philanthropy or automatically oppose all new regulatory proposals regardless of their merits.

But those who make decisions throughout a corporate institution do not operate in a vacuum. For many firms, their overall record of social performance appears to be either significantly better or significantly worse than that of other firms with relatively similar economic characteristics. What might account for these overall differences?

The single most important factor is the orientation of the individual or individuals who are at the apex of the corporate hierarchy. If any one generalization emerges from these essays, it is the absolutely critical role that the corporation's top leadership plays in establishing the social values of the institution. The popular notion that modern corporations are managed by anonymous and interchangeable bureaucrats is misinformed. Most obviously, a significant number of corporations remain essentially family enterprises. That is, they are headed either by an entrepreneur or his or her descendant or by someone personally chosen by members of the family that controls the company. Many of these individuals have strongly held social convictions, and they are in a position to have their convictions reflected in the way in which the company they manage conducts its business. It may not be coincidental that a disproportionate number of the corporations cited by students of business as having outstanding overall records of corporate social performance tend to be dominated by a family or its representatives.

However, even professional managers are far from alike. As these essays clearly reveal, a significant minority of the individuals who head the major economic institutions of the United States have developed a sophisticated perspective on the social role of the corporation, and their attitudes do have a measurable impact on the policies and positions of the organizations they manage. We should not underestimate the impact of particular executives on the social and ethical values of a company, although we need to learn more about how this process works.

Nonetheless, there are decided limits to what social efforts we can expect of business. The most important of these is the nature of our economic system: many of the most critical social problems confronting our economy are not subject to the discretion of senior management; they involve issues of government policy that are outside the control of any individual firm. Nor is it realistic to expect the business community to assume a leadership role in balancing social needs with economic imperatives on a national scale. For at least a century, the overwhelming majority of the business community has held political and social views located well on the right of the political spectrum. This has been true not only in the United States but in every other capitalist democracy, and there is no reason to assume that this pattern will change. Indeed, the nation's current economic difficulties are likely to make most business executives even more conservative. The social reforms whose enactment have so dramatically improved the lot of the average American over the last 75 years mostly were adopted in spite of business lobbying, not because of it. Our nonbusiness contributors were included not to make this volume appear balanced, but because of our recognition that it has been outside pressures—by journalists, academics, trade unionists, and public-interest organizations—that have played an absolutely indispensable role in challenging corporate complacency. The corporate role is inherently a conservative one; if business is to perform as well as it can, it requires pressure from those outside it.

ACKNOWLEDGMENTS

We would like to acknowledge the generous assistance and financial support given by the Aspen Institute for Humanistic Studies in the preparation of this book. We are particularly grateful to Waldemar Nielsen, of the Aspen Institute, for his advice and encouragement. The Aspen Institute's support of this project reflects its long-standing commitment to promote constructive dialogue about the role of the corporation in society.

DAVID VOGEL

INTRODUCTION

For many years, the business executive who made a profit, provided an acceptable place of work, paid a going wage, and obeyed the law was considered to have done the job. Although standards varied from time to time, they were generally easily recognized. The executive who met or surpassed the standards was a success. One who did not meet the standards went out of business.

The system was rather simple both in its operation and in the way people saw it working. The able business executive was a pillar of the community because business achievement was considered a high form of success, worthy in itself and crucial to social well-being. Smoke pouring from factory stacks was regarded as a symbol of prosperity. Americans brought up on the stories of Horatio Alger valued material success and were confident that free enterprise was the high road to the good life, open to all, even "Nick the bootblack." Of course, even in its heyday the image of the successful business executive engendered a certain amount of mistrust and suspicion. Most Americans disliked and feared concentrated power whether in government or in business; the strain of populism ran deep. And the power of business was exercised in ways only dimly perceived by most people.

CHANGING STATUS OF BUSINESS

The status of business in American society has undergone a remarkable transformation in recent years. Standards governing business conduct are no longer pegged solely to the bottom line. Much more is expected, particularly of those who manage large corporations, but just what is not always clear. And as old certitudes have faded, latent mistrust has grown to the point at which lack of confidence in business's motives has become the overwhelming popular response to the role of the large corporation in the United States.

Faced by uncertainty and hostility on every hand, today's large business enterprise is forced to confront deeply disturbing issues. Just what is expected of the management of large corporations? And if the expectations can be separated and defined, can the corporation hope to meet them? Is it a matter of an adjustment here and there that will leave the basic structure of the business enterprise intact and still get the job done in the time-honored sense? Or are basic changes in the corporation and its governance needed to produce an institution adaptable to changing social mores? And what part should government play in the restructuring of corporate goals and ways of attaining them?

These questions are addressed in this book. They are not answered, of course, in an absolute sense. How can they be when we are still deep in the process of change? Yet the process itself must be better understood, and an attitude which permits business management to respond to some of the changes and lead in others must be formed. That in brief is our purpose. Through the eyes of our critics, we have tried to present a view of business that calls it to a broader scope of activity in contemporary life. Through the ideas of practitioners of the art of management, we examine some of the faltering steps by which some corporations are attempting to meet these new expectations.

Make no mistake: the issues are important. It is a truism to say that institutions are born, grow, change, and die as they answer or fail to answer the needs of people. If people expect more from a corporation than an adequate return on investment and if the corporation does not deliver that "more," then it will change or die.

Many years ago, Paul T. Cherington, the first professor of marketing in the United States and probably in the world, wrote a book entitled *People's Wants and How to Satisfy Them* (1935). Nothing has changed except the definition of what a "want" is. What expanded wants and needs may be and how to meet them is what this book is about.

To put the matter in perspective, it might be useful to attempt to place the corporation in the context of the large social changes taking place in the United States and to identify some of the demands that will be made of the corporation over the next few decades. Business managements are accustomed to aiming at moving targets, but an understanding of the direction of social changes is crucial if corporations are to meet the demands of the future.

Something of the future can be anticipated by examining facts of the past and present—demographic changes, patterns of household mobility, increased or decreased affluence, the rise of the two–wage-earner family, the aging of the society—although the results of such speculation should be viewed skeptically. People have a way of changing their minds without notifying the chart gazers in advance, as in those Third World countries where birthrates have plummeted in defiance of all conventional forecasts.

But of one thing we may be certain: whatever form social change takes over the next few decades, whatever the trends in population, wealth, creativity, etc., turn out to be, the corporation will be strongly affected. So will all our institutions, since the heart of social philosophy is the relationship between individuals and their institutions. Not much has changed since Socrates talked under the plane trees in ancient Athens.

EXPECTATIONS FOR THE FUTURE

Well, then, what can we expect? Will the United States resume its vigorous economic growth? Can we count on the pie expanding rapidly enough to satisfy everyone: those who want a more nearly equal distribution and those who simply want more?

Will the apparent shift to fiscal conservatism prove transitory or a definite break with the spending philosophy of the past 50 years?

Will our untidy democratic process meet the challenges of a new age, through its contentious forums producing solutions to major problems such as energy, inflation, employment, transportation, health care, housing, and race relations?

Will world tensions abate, permitting corporation managements a longer view of options in international business, a better feel for the future of the transnational corporation?

Each reader will answer these questions in his or her own way, providing an individual view of the unfolding world in which corporations will operate. Our assumptions are pessimistic.

In the United States we anticipate continuing strong inflationary pressures and slower economic growth with all the accompanying economic, social, and political tensions. The pie will not expand quickly enough to continue to ameliorate the pressures for changes in the distribution of wealth.

Underlying this slower economic growth, we believe, will be a vastly increased real cost of basic energy and many raw materials and a continuing decline in worker productivity, though nothing is inevitable or invincible about these two factors. Both can be dealt with, given time and political will.

The shift to fiscal conservatism and the discipline of the marketplace will be, we feel, short-lived. As economic growth slows, inflation continues, and social tensions increase, pressure for renewed government intervention will become irresistible. The social programs of the 1930s, 1950s, and 1960s will not be revisited, but the 1980s will be characterized by their own attempt to satisfy the ever-rising expectations of the people. The emerging revolution in communications will add a new dimension to people's wants and a new and powerful mechanism for immediate political feedback.

Will we learn in the next decades how to cope with specific social problems in time to avert crises? Regrettably, we think not, although it's obviously better to live with crises and struggle than to weaken individual freedom in the search for orderly solutions. We seem fated to conduct our political discourse at the top of our lungs.

Finally, we would anticipate a period of deep international uncertainty with continuing balance-of-payments problems, further tensions with the Soviet Union, intensified Third World social and economic distress, continuing anxiety about the Middle East, and uncertainty about the role of China.

These assumptions, should they prove correct, mean that the corporations of the 1980s will operate in an environment of increased social tensions and steadily escalating possibilities for conflict. They also suggest that more and more people will look to the corporation as a visible, powerful institution to help resolve the tensions and avoid the conflicts. The corporation would then have several roles to play:

1. THE ECONOMIC ROLE

First and foremost, the corporation must be an effective economic institution or it can be nothing at all. Wherever else the future may take it, the corporation must continue to respond to the marketplace, producing quality goods at the lowest possible cost, allocating resources efficiently, distributing its products, and earning an acceptable profit for its shareholders. This is merely a restatement of the classic definition of the corporation.

It may be too obvious to dwell upon, but if there is no bottom line, then there is no opportunity to go beyond it. The creation of wealth is the foundation on which all else rests.

The first and overriding role of corporate management is to meet people's needs with professional skill. But professionalism is not the whole of it, now or in the future. The corporation has other roles which we believe will be of growing importance in the days ahead.

2. INNOVATION

The genius of business has always been its capacity to innovate. As business executives saw a need, they turned their minds and hands to the provision of new products or services that would fill it. (Henry J. Kaiser said that he saw problems as opportunities "in work clothes.") Today, the need for innovation is larger than ever, but the supply seems smaller. As productivity lags, more innovation is needed. As raw materials become scarce, imagination must give us substitutes. At a time when the United States appears to have lost its edge in global business competition, only innovation and entrepreneurship will restore it.

But can the corporation innovate? We believe that it can and must. The fact is that innovation these days isn't coming as often as before from primitive laboratories or backroom operations. It is coming increasingly from large corporations and other private and public institutions that have the money and human resources to conceive and incubate new ideas and convert them into products and services that are meaningful and beneficial for humanity.

Agreed, there are forces within the corporation which blunt the edge of innovation: pockets of bureaucratized employees indistinguishable from their much-maligned counterparts in government offices; the unrelenting pressure to accomplish massive numbers of transactions in an orderly fashion; and the equally pressing need to protect oneself from mistakes, since the price of mistakes can be high and the reward for innovative change low.

After all, corporations are organized to produce goods and services, not ideas. The management pecking order usually reflects one thing: the number of employees supervised. Even company laboratories, centers of corporate scientific creativity, are often organized as rigidly as the accounts payable department.

And yet, faced by the growing realization that without innovation the corporation cannot survive, ways are being found to overcome conservatism and resistance and block the natural drift of the large institution into musclebound impotence. For example, many companies today are being organized into relatively autonomous profit centers to encourage the entrepreneurial spirit. The objective is to push the responsibility for profit as far down in the corporation as possible. Innovation generally follows because without innovation profits fade.

Some companies facing new challenges acquire small companies with proven innovative results. Major oil companies, for instance, acquire small solar businesses, not for their earning assets, which are usually minuscule, but for their innovative capability. This can raise the problem of how to keep the innovative spirit alive and well in the newly acquired assets. How can innovators be rewarded? In their own small companies they take the risk and, if they win, reap the reward (subject to sharing with the tax collector). What can a large company offer them?

The corporation will be increasingly called upon to demonstrate that it can innovate in this and many other areas. Corporations will have to struggle to overcome their internal resistance to change in organizational matters, performance rewards, and the practice of risk taking itself. Their survival may depend on their success.

3. SOCIAL EXPECTATIONS

Up to this point we have dealt with the traditional roles of the corporation: innovating, providing products and services, making a profit. What are some of the new demands which will be placed on the corporation? A few examples will help.

People and Work

In the 1950s an industrial psychologist said to me, "There are more stupid jobs than there are stupid people." He went on to describe a consulting assignment that he had recently completed. He had been called in to look at a plant situation in which worker dissatisfaction was high, absenteeism high, and output low. The consultant observed the work process and stated to the plant manager, "Your problem is easy. Any moron could do this work." The plant manager disagreed. The consultant persisted, brought in a group of patients from a nearby mental institution, and proved his point. His "morons" were happy and never left the job until the whistle blew; productivity increased markedly. The solution in this case was redesign of the job itself to provide more variety and challenge to normal workers. Today Daniel Yankelovich, the pollster and sociologist, talks of much the same thing but uses somewhat more elegant language: "the growing mismatch between employees and jobs."

One of the most compelling expectations of people today is the desire for personal fulfillment. Since much of our time is spent in working, a major part of that expectation must be met in the workplace.

Part of this desire stems from the changed composition of the workforce. For one thing, employees are likely to be far better educated than they were in previous eras. There is also more leisure time and more ways to use it. There are more women in the workforce: about half of all women of working age now hold jobs. Many women with children are working: 40 percent of all women with children aged 6 or younger and 55 percent of all women with children aged from 6 to 17. A large proportion of workers are from two–wage-earner families. The growing importance of the job for these millions of Americans means that their expectations increasingly come to focus on the workplace, which for better or worse provides much of the social structure formerly filled by family, church, and community.

Corporate managers are experimenting with new ways to meet these enlarged expectations. Some companies offer job enrichment: attempts to redesign jobs to fit the needs of people as opposed to the needs of companies. Others vary hours of work ("flextime") or organized husband-and-wife work teams. As pressures mount in the future, other innovative approaches must be tried.

Hard-Core Unemployed

One critical, and thus far intractable, problem area of natural concern to corporate managers is that of the hard-core unemployed. Experience with business involvement to date is mixed. One company tried, with the help of a university and a number of professional social workers, to retrieve a carefully selected group of unemployables. None had ever worked before, none could obtain driver's licenses, most had a drug or a drinking problem, most had parents who had never worked, all were early school dropouts, and none had hopes of ever entering the mainstream of society. The program was meticulously planned, sensitively administered, and amply funded, but few of those included lasted the course, and even fewer entered the workforce although jobs were guaranteed. Those who were employed eventually dropped out. A failure? Perhaps, although it seems to me that a social experiment of this kind fails totally only when it does not provide knowledge useful for the next experiment. In that sense, this social experiment was a success.

But the question remains: To what extent should a corporation devote its resources (funds of its shareholders and talents of its management) to social experiments which can have only an indirect impact on the corporation?

Governing the Corporation

If the purpose of the corporation is more than simply producing a healthy return on investment, does it not then serve more masters than the shareholders alone? Does it not serve consumers, environmentalists, employees, retirees? Should each of these groups be represented on the board of directors? This is the approach proposed by Ralph Nader and incorporated in incipient legislation.

Or should the various interests be served by public directors selected from government-approved lists? This is an approach favored by George Lodge of Harvard University. Some corporations have been forced by the government to appoint public directors. In each instance this has come about as part of a settlement with the government over alleged breaches of accepted corporate behavior.

Or can a board of directors, elected by the shareholders in the traditional fashion, expand its area of surveillance to include all the interests affected by the corporation? Some boards, for instance, have appointed social responsibility committees which, as the name suggests, have the task of ensuring that the corporation fulfills a wide range of social responsibilities. Should employees have specific board representation as in West Germany and Sweden and as has been proposed in the United Kingdom?

There has been considerable action in the area of recognition of the problems of governing the corporation in view of its expanded impact on all segments of our society. There will be more.

Judging the Corporation

If corporations are to provide services other than making and selling things, by what standards can they be judged? What kind of financial reporting should be expected?

Judging economic results is difficult enough, but it is simplicity itself compared with the problems of judging social performance. No corporate executive who deals with the accounting profession, the Financial Accounting Standards Board, the Securities and Exchange Commission, or the New York Stock Exchange can claim that standards of economic judgment are precise and unalterable. But how can corporate actions in communities, especially projects such as the retrieval of hard-core unemployed or various environmental activities, be judged? How can the good citizens among the corporations be identified?

One company issues an annual social responsibility report which includes a balance sheet of the year's activities (both debits and credits) prepared by a business writer–social activist. The arrangement precludes editing by the corporation and guarantees publication. This may be a startling departure by some corporate standards, but it is really a small step and hardly scratches the surface of the problem.

Some who have reflected on the problem lean toward yearly issuance of so-called social responsibility audits, but little has been done beyond a few brief descriptions in annual reports. However, a widening recognition that people will judge corporations by poor standards if better ones are not available may lead to the development of better reporting in the future.

Corporate Philanthropy

As private-sector needs grow and private foundations diminish, business philanthropy becomes more important, and, indeed, corporate foundations are growing rapidly in size and scope of giving. How should the corporate foundation be administered? What purpose should it serve?

Corporate philanthropy has become large only in recent years. When it was in its infancy, it could easily be administered by an inside board of corporate officers and a secretary. The contribution program was largely one of responding to an appeal by a local hospital or to a fund drive by a technical college which supplied graduates to the corporation or of providing support for the chairman's or the president's favorite cultural activities.

But corporate officers are not chosen for their skills in judging private-sector needs or in giving away money—quite the contrary. Also, the large size of many corporate foundations makes response giving entirely inappropriate as a sole endeavor. A program of financial contributions based on clearly perceived long-range objectives is in order.

Should outside boards of trustees experienced in the needs of the not-for-profit sector be appointed to accomplish this purpose? Should specific objectives be determined for the corporate foundation? Should areas of interest be delineated? Should experimental projects be set in motion? Should follow-up appraisals be made?

There will be considerable movement and change in corporate philanthropy in the next few decades as funds available for giving grow and corporate managers become practiced in this new and challenging area of their responsibility.

Responsibility for Employees' Families

What kinds of responsibilities does the corporation have for the families of its employees?

As the corporation claims more time and more dedication from the rising executive, less of each is left for the family. The family tends to become matriarchal. With the father isolated, the father as model disappears, and family bonds are loosened.

As the corporate world broadens, the world of wife and mother narrows and the distance between the two increases, producing a destabilizing pressure on the family structure. It is true that the prototype family—the father who works, the wife who stays home and takes care of the children—is becoming the exception rather than the rule, but it is still common, particularly among senior and middle managers. Maintaining and strengthening its integrity in the face of today's social upheavals is clearly a paramount concern. But is it an important corporate concern as well? We believe so, but each corporation must decide the issue in principle and design its program accordingly.

The dominant American family these days is the two–wage-earner or two-salary family, raising a new issue of polarized loyalties. Will the corporation be able to move its executives with the same abandon as it did in the past, or is this a matter between working wife and husband and of no concern to the corporation? It seems to us that all affected parties will inevitably become involved.

At any rate, the changed composition of the workforce has clearly brought an entirely new set of family problems. The extent to which they become the responsibility of the corporation remains to be seen.

The problems of people and work, hard-core unemployed, governing the corporation, judging the corporation, the corporate foundation, and responsibility for the families of employees illustrate the range of challenges faced by the corporation when it begins to respond to the new expectations of its various publics. The lives of corporate executives would be simpler and more comfortable if they did not have to venture beyond the relative certainties of the bottom line. But they no longer have that choice.

4. COPING WITH GOVERNMENT REGULATION

Fourth on our list of new roles for the corporation is uninvited but inevitable: coping with proliferating government regulations. As certain as death and taxes is the growth of government regulations. Everyone close to the issue— business executives, college administrators, and even government employees —recognizes the high cost of regulations and their stifling impact. But regulations will continue to beget regulations; new regulatory offices will spawn counterregulatory offices in business organizations and other targets of the government's heavy thumb.

Business may chafe under the restraints and expense of the regulatory process, but the plain fact is that regulation is a less harmful way to inject the public interest into private institutions than the likeliest alternatives, those largely associated with the overall planning of authoritarian states. Consumer interests, environmental protection, health, and safety all require standards, and standards require monitoring. Thus, regulation grows with every extension of the public interest.

All aspects of a business operation—hiring, firing, providing a workplace, determining health and retirement benefits, installing a new manufacturing process, and so forth—are controlled to one degree or another by government. A crude-oil pipeline can be planned, engineered, and financed in a relatively short time. Slogging through the swampland of government regulations and permits connected with the project can and usually does take many times as long. Yet coping with regulations as one form of response to social demands is as essential to corporate survival as making a profit. We must slog on.

5. MEETING THE MEDIA

Most senior executives can remember when, in the not too distant past, corporate doors were shut to the press. The corporation simply wasn't any of journalists' business, except, of course, when it wanted to introduce a new product or boast about a particularly good year. On those occasions, a press handout would do.

That world has gone the way of the dinosaurs, and yet the dinosaurs' tracks remain. The press and the electronic media search out dramatic stories because the public interest is at stake. Business executives often try to manipulate stories because the shareholder interest (sometimes just the management interest) is at stake. Neither business nor the press trusts each other, and the basic confrontation is set up.

Examples abound. An engineering-trained plant manager faces the television cameras to explain a serious plant accident. He is less than frank and does not come across as a credible representative of corporate management. He fails as a manager and must be withdrawn from his job.

A representative of a public-interest group testifies before a Senate committee on a popular issue. The room is filled with television cameras and reporters. After a blistering attack on industry, a short recess is declared, during which the television crews dismantle the equipment and most reporters leave. An industry executive then testifies in a room empty except for a few committee members and visitors to the nation's capital.

An incident occurs at a nuclear plant which appears to have the potential for an uncontrolled meltdown—a catastrophe. Neither government representatives nor management can assure the media that there is no danger from escaping radioactive gases or that the chain of events set in motion by a stuck valve can be safely controlled. This is the stuff of high drama, and no reporter worth his or her salt would want to be anywhere but at the front, in this case the plant itself.

Something other than the unfolding of a story is at stake, and that is the determination of national policy on nuclear energy. Can national opinion, and therefore national policy, be forged under these circumstances? What is the responsibility of the media? Of government? Of industrial managers?

The relationship of the media and business is difficult and, to a degree, must be antagonistic. Corporations will survive only if people approve of what they do. What people think they do is largely shaped by the media. Public acceptance must be earned by doing the right things, but people must think that corporations are doing the right things.

The media are as important to the survival of corporations as they are to the survival of our democracy.

6. THE CORPORATION AND POLITICS

The more the corporation is expected to expand its functions beyond the economic and the more its total environment is determined by the actions of government, the more pressure there will be for it to act as a political activist. The line between government and business, once sharp and clear, has become more and more shadowy. Economic decisions are no longer clearly distinguished from political ones.

Should the manager who has corporate constituencies to satisfy organize these constituencies to further the goals of the corporation or try to bring to bear the power of the corporation's publics in the political arena? Public-interest groups organize to achieve their objectives. If the corporation is expected to achieve social ends, should it not then behave as a political institution?

Many corporations are doing this: organizing employees, retirees, suppliers, and shareholders, informing them on matters of interest to the corporation, and asking them to write their members of Congress on important matters of legislation. Some corporations form and support political clubs. Others organize speakers' bureaus. Many take advantage of recent legislation to set up political action funds and support candidates who are sympathetic to the objectives of the corporation.

All this is a long way from the narrowly defined economic functions of the corporation. But if people expect more than economic results from the corporation and if the corporation has to deal with a wealth of government regulations arising from that expectation, then it is forced into becoming a political institution as well as an economic institution, like it or not.

The widened expectations of people would indeed seem to require new definitions of the role of corporate managements. The traditional economic functions—profit making, entrepreneurial innovation, job creation—remain. A profitless corporation cannot survive.

But now we also recognize that profit alone is not enough for corporate survival, and that's something new. All in all, the corporation is being perceived as a social institution, an influential determiner of how people live. At least in part, the corporation is forced into a broadened role by the decline of other institutions: family, community, and church.

To what extent can the corporation fulfill these new expectations? How successfully can it navigate in the uncertain waters beyond the familiar bottom line? If the corporation strives to fulfill this new and difficult role, does it weaken its ability to carry out its economic function? Yet if it does not try to define and act upon these new demands, does it not then jeopardize its franchise altogether.

The corporate world, in a word, has become complex and uncertain where it had been merely clear-cut and difficult. The years before us will be trying ones. Old formulas must give way to new as corporate managements come to terms with this dilemma before their franchise is withdrawn and before the nation is tempted to turn to other means of fulfilling social expectations.

Americans do not distrust business because they oppose the capitalistic system. Their unhappiness stems from legitimate grievances with business's performance in recent years and from what the public perceives to be a lack of corporate accountability.

The issues are clear: fairness to employees and customers, freedom from shortages and pollutants, products of good quality, prudent use of natural resources, equitable conditions of employment, a healthful workplace, and many more. Those issues must be dealt with fairly and directly and to the satisfaction of American society, or large corporations will invite increasingly strident reform efforts that will serve the purposes of neither business nor society. Those who believe, as I do, in the intrinsic value of the decentralized market system must act now to develop a more humanistic, responsible, and innovative form of capitalism to meet society's demands as well as satisfying its needs. Accomplishing that difficult but necessary objective will be central to any intelligent discussion of American business for the foreseeable future.

THORNTON BRADSHAW

Part 1

BUSINESS AND THE POLITICAL ENVIRONMENT

Lobbying, Disclosure, and Corporate Ethics

The political role of the large business corporation has long been a subject of considerable controversy. Critics of business contend that corporations enjoy too much influence over the decisions of both American and foreign governments, while many executives have become concerned about the inability of business to communicate its views successfully to both the public and government officials. The essays in Part 1 examine several contemporary dimensions of the political role of the large corporation.

The first two essays focus on the objectives of corporate political participation. Mark Green, who directs a well-established public-interest lobbying organization, argues that business has a responsibility to consider the impact of public policies on the welfare of the consumer in determining its political stance. While lobbyists for consumer organizations and corporations usually find themselves on opposing sides, Green argues that this pattern of conflict is not inevitable. Discussing a number of recent political controversies, including federal no-fault automobile insurance, the establishment of a Consumer Protection Agency, and airline deregulation, he reports that on several occasions corporations and consumer organizations have supported similar positions. However, Green concludes that, with the exception of a few unusually public-spirited companies, it is unrealistic to expect corporations to support progressive causes unless such a stand complements their economic interests. He would be happy to settle for corporations that obey the law and preserve the integrity of markets.

1

Among the firms Green cites as relatively public-spirited are Levi Strauss & Co., Atlantic Richfield Company, J. C. Penney Company, and Cummins Engine Company. In their essay, "Business Responsibility and the Public Policy Process," Henry B. Schacht, the chief executive officer of Cummins Engine, and Charles W. Powers, the company's director of public policy, seek to articulate the principles that govern their company's political involvement. They contend that a corporation has an obligation to establish a constructive and responsible relationship with each of the constituencies, or "stakeholders," whose welfare its decisions affect. The process of defining the optimal policy that effectively responds to the public's legitimate expectations is, however, very difficult and time-consuming. Analyzing three public policy controversies that have affected Cummins—the construction of a new company headquarters in Columbus, Indiana, the establishment of emission controls for diesel engines, and the issue of employee privacy—Schacht and Powers describe the process by which Cummins was able to adjust successfully to the public's rapidly shifting expectations of business. They conclude that if corporations are to participate both effectively and responsibly in the policy process, they must first acknowledge the public's right to define the parameters in which a corporation conducts its business.

Herbert E. Alexander is the director of a nationally prominent research organization specializing in the monitoring of corporate political behavior. His essay focuses not so much on how corporations decide which political position to endorse as on the diverse means they employ to advance their political views. Concentrating on the "corporate Watergate" and the federal election-reform laws that followed the widely publicized revelations of illegal corporate campaign contributions, Alexander discusses the ways in which corporations have attempted to respond to one of the most important political developments of the 1970s: extensive government regulation of corporate political participation. He predicts that corporations can look forward to intensive public scrutiny of the methods by which they seek to influence the political process.

Business-press relations have also changed dramatically since the 1960s. Many executives have become upset about the quality of press coverage of economic affairs; they blame the media for encouraging public suspicion of business. Michael C. Jensen, one of the nation's most prominent business reporters, argues that business itself is responsible for much of the suspicion that has developed between these two central national institutions. Citing several examples of corporations which have mishandled their relations with the press, Jensen offers a number of guidelines to assist executives in improving the quality of business reporting. While Jensen does not regard a rapprochement between executives and journalists as likely in the near future, he is encouraged by the increasing willingness of the press to devote the resources necessary to give the reporting of business affairs the prominence it deserves.

Underlying much of the strain between business and the press has been the issue of disclosure: to what extent should the corporation consider its business the public's business? While federal and local regulations have increasingly restricted the corporation's right to privacy, firms still enjoy considerable discretion as to what and how much information they make public. A. W. Clausen, the president of the Bank of America, and L. William Seidman, a businessman who was formerly economic adviser to President Ford, argue that it is in the enlightened self-interest of business to maximize the amount of information that they are willing to disclose voluntarily.

In 1974 the Bank of America adopted a disclosure policy based on the rather innovative premise that the bank's constituencies have the right to know about bank policies that affect them; all information is to be revealed unless the company can demonstrate that disclosure would impair its competitive position or the privacy of its employees or clients. The bank is pleased with the results of its disclosure policy, and Clausen's essay summarizes the many benefits that it has produced. Clausen, however, emphasizes that the bank's policies are not appropriate for every corporation: each firm must determine for itself which disclosures are appropriate. Seidman argues that if the corporation is to compete effectively in the political process, its credibility must be restored. The way to do this, Seidman suggests in his essay, "Corporate Political Responsibility," is for industry voluntarily to adopt its own "sunshine" legislation. Such a step would enable those affected by business decisions to understand the complex factors that underlie them. It is hoped that this would then improve the quality of public decision making.

Among the most controversial dimensions of business political activity is the relationship between United States–based multinational corporations and foreign governments. Reflecting widespread public concern with the social and political impact of American multinationals, a number of church organizations have strongly criticized various corporate investment and marketing decisions. They have been particularly concerned with two issues: the political impact of corporate investments in South Africa and the social consequences of the marketing of infant formulas to mothers in underdeveloped nations. Timothy Smith, who has spearheaded the churches' challenges to corporate policies in these and other areas, describes what he regards as the appropriate social responsibility of corporations involved in international commerce. While critical of the social performance of most companies, he does cite several corporations, including Control Data Corporation, Abbott Laboratories, Polaroid Corp., the Chase Manhattan Bank,

Irving Trust Co., and the Mellon Bank, which have responded to the churches' criticisms in a constructive manner.

WHEN CORPORATIONS BECOME CONSUMER LOBBYISTS

On Conscience and Profits

MARK GREEN

Mark Green is the director of Public Citizen's Congress Watch, Ralph Nader's lobbying organization in Washington. He is a graduate of Cornell University and Harvard Law School, where he was editor in chief of the Harvard Civil Rights–Civil Liberties Law Review. *Between 1970 and 1975 he directed Nader's Corporate Accountability Research Group. In 1974 he was the research director of Ramsey Clark's Senate campaign, and in 1976 he served as Clark's campaign manager.*

He has written or edited numerous books, including The Closed Enterprise System *(1972),* Who Runs Congress? *(1972),* The Other Government: The Unseen Power of Washington Lawyers *(1975), and, most recently,* Taming the Giant Corporation *(1976). He has also published widely in many periodicals, including the* Yale Law Journal, New York Review of Books, The New York Times, The Washington Post, The New Republic, The Nation, *and* New York.

What constitutes responsible corporate behavior, especially in the political arena, and what companies have achieved it?

Of course, there are those who would give a one-line answer to this question. The business of America is business, or the only responsibility of business is to maximize profits, to paraphrase Calvin Coolidge and Milton Friedman. But their succinct philosophies, though internally consistent, have about as much relevance to this question as did John D. Rockefeller's observation: "The good Lord gave me my money." Today, in the era of corporate good citizenship, major executives would as soon be caught lunching with Ralph Nader as admitting that *all* they care about is profits. And they would be correct for reasons beyond the imperatives of public relations.

Most chief executive officers would agree that their goal is, as some economists have expressed it, profit *satisfaction* rather than profit *maximization*. Given the competing obligations of companies to their affected constituencies—shareholders, workers, communities, consumers—this equilibrium function is gaining acceptance. In addition, the University of Chicago catechism of the Friedman school of economists notwithstanding, it is clear that our large corporations have a large noneconomic impact. Since major firms undeniably affect their local communities, the environment, consumer health and safety, patterns of employment discrimination, inflation, the balance of trade, foreign disputes, political elections, and legislation, it seems rigid and unrealistic to judge a company merely by its profit and loss statement. One may not enjoy sleeping next to an elephant, but reality requires accommodating that fact, not denying it. So, too, with the political and social impact of elephantine corporations.

Finally, it is true that profit is a brilliant measurement because it is concrete, understandable, and unarguable and permits useful comparisons. It is apparent why this measurement has preempted the attention of those who seek to judge the impact of corporations. But what is immeasurable is not unimportant. And a corporation's impact on its community and country can be substantial even though it is not currently reducible to comparative numbers and analyses.

While the impact can be substantial, it is not always socially responsible. This brings us back to the question: When and why do companies engage in socially responsible behavior, independent of the marketplace, affecting either their local communities or national politics?

Because much has been written about what constitutes socially responsible *local* behavior, it need not be extensively discussed here. Once one overcomes the conceptual barrier that a company has no responsibility other than to maximize profits to shareholders, there are several areas of consensus. A few of them, with some examples of each, follow:

1. *Minority affairs.* Racial or sex discrimination is morally wrong and legally can be very expensive, as back-pay awards have indicated. Aetna Life &

Casualty has 12 percent nonwhite employees; Cummins Engine Company has 100 black managers and executive trainees. Going somewhat further, Jewell Electrical Instruments purposefully stays in black communities and supports minority-owned suppliers. Levi Strauss & Co., not for economic reasons, deliberately spared a factory in a poor black Alabama county.

2. *Diversity on boards.* It is an anachronism for such influential societal organs as boards of directors to exclude nonwhites or women. Aetna and Jewell, however, each had blacks and women on their boards by the mid-1970s.

3. *Corporate contributions.* Although the tax code permits charitable deductions of up to 5 percent of a company's pretax profits, corporate gifts overall total only about 1 percent. But Cummins Engine gives 5 percent, and Levi Strauss from 3 to 5 percent. Xerox Corp. is a major supporter of the United Negro College Fund.

4. *Environment.* A company's costs and hence its profits ought to reflect *all* the costs of production, which include pollution. Owens-Illinois, Inc., was rated first in pollution-control equipment in the paper industry by the Council on Economic Priorities.

5. *Safe products and technology.* Because prevention is preferable to compensation for both ethical and economic reasons companies would do well to sell products that they know won't injure people or the planet. S. C. Johnson & Son of Racine, Wisconsin, announced its own ban on fluorocarbons in aerosol-spray cans well before the Food and Drug Administration (FDA) did. Their actions were unlike those of the Ford Motor Co. with its Pinto and Firestone Tire & Rubber Co. with its 500 tire.

6. *Adequate disclosure.* Market capitalism can work only if consumers have substantial knowledge of the comparative values of offered goods or services. Informational advertising is still too rare. Exceptions include information initially developed by government, such as Environmental Protection Agency (EPA) mileage ratings or Federal Trade Commission (FTC) data on the tar and nicotine content of cigarettes. Under a voluntary code of disclosure the Bank of America reportedly gives more information than other financial institutions about banking practices.

CORPORATE LOBBYING TECHNIQUES

All the activities described above are laudable though modest. Not discriminating or polluting or injuring consumers is hardly an exceptional aspiration for corporations. More controversial and difficult are the adoption and promotion of consumer-oriented positions on national legislative issues. But trying to discover consumer-oriented corporate lobbying resembles mining for silver in the late 1880s in Colorado: one knows that some silver is there, but there isn't much.

Historically, of course, corporate lobbying merely sought to enhance profits, either by keeping government out of the economy (the drug companies fought food and drug legislation in 1938) or by having government help manage part of an industry (the infant airline industry lobbied for and helped to write the 1938 Civil Aeronautics Act). Among the various techniques, three stood out.

First, there was what one could call the Chicken Little approach. In the early 1930s, Richard Whitney, president of the New York Stock Exchange, predicted that passage of pending securities acts would destroy the securities market. At about the same time, Henry Ford warned that unemployment compensation would destroy the work incentive. Wall Street lawyer and corporate executive Wendell Willkie predicted that passage of the Public Utility Holding Company Act of 1935 would destroy the utility industry. These men, history will report, proved to be better capitalists than seers.

Second, there is "the jingle of cash," as one dairy lobbyist inelegantly put it during the Nixon years. The technique was most bluntly explained by Sen. Boies Penrose of Pennsylvania at the turn of the twentieth century, when he told a group of business supporters, "I believe in a division of labor. You send us to Congress; we pass laws under which you make money; . . . and out of your profits you further contribute to our campaign funds to send us back again to pass more laws to enable you to make more money."[1] Hence the aphorism that a corporation is known by the politicians it keeps. More genteel versions of this sort of thing are company political action committees (PACs), now permitted by law, which are proliferating; between 1974 and 1979 they increased tenfold.

Third, companies often employ teams of analysts and lobbyists who prevail by inundation. Or as the late Rep. Allard K. Lowenstein once put it, "How much can anyone do with limited staff and all the mail and what not to cope with? . . . That's one reason why the lobbies are so influential. They have people who are able to spend all their time collecting data on why pollution is good for River X. What Congressmen can match that?"[2]

These corporate lobbying techniques have traditionally been invested in the status quo, in keeping with business's *idée fixe* that the less government the better. So major parts of the business community opposed the creation of the National Highway Traffic Safety Administration, the Environmental Protection Agency, the Consumer Product Safety Commission, the Occupa-

---

[1] Mark Green, *Who Runs Congress?* 3d ed., The Viking Press, Inc., New York, 1979, p. 2.
[2] Ibid., pp. 26–27.

tional Safety and Health Administration, and the Consumer Protection Agency. They also opposed the Clean Air Act, the Toxic Substances Control Act, the 1976 amendments to the Sherman Antitrust Act, and the Labor Law Reform bill of 1977.

Sometimes, however, trade groups will lobby against their *idée fixe* if this stance means money; business supported the Overseas Private Investment Corporation of the early 1970s, a federal insurer for large multinationals; and airlines supported the Noisy Aircraft bill of 1978, which would have required the federal government to collect from $2 to $4 billion from airline consumers and give it to the airlines to pay for noise-abatement devices. When profits and laissez faire collide, the business sector will unflinchingly surrender the latter.

This is the corporate lobbying that is a staple of Washington and of Jack Anderson's columns, but occasionally large companies and trade groups advocate reforms that appear to promote consumer welfare. Leading consumer and labor lobbyists, in interviews, mentioned seven such instances in the past few years. A closer look at such potentially responsible corporate behavior can help illuminate when and why companies engage in good works.

CONSUMER PROTECTION AGENCY (CPA)

The bill that attracted the most contentious business-versus-consumer lobbying in the past few years would have created a $15 million nonregulatory office of consumer representation to advocate consumer interests before federal agencies and courts. Opposed were the Chamber of Commerce of the United States, the Business Roundtable, the National Association of Manufacturers (NAM), the National Federation of Independent Business, and hundreds of trade groups and companies. According to House Speaker Thomas P. (Tip) O'Neill, speaking shortly before the final vote, "I have been around here for 25 years and never seen such extensive [business] lobbying."

Arrayed on the other side were 150 consumer, labor, senior, and environmental groups, the Carter administration, and more than 100 business firms. Among these firms were such companies as Kings Supermarkets, Atlantic Richfield Company, and Cummins Engine. A disproportionate number of the firms were retailers or companies with name brands that sold directly to retailers. Their motives were mixed: they acted partly to generate a good image to the consumers with whom they had to deal every day, partly to deter abusive business practices which sullied the entire business community, and partly through an instinct for good government. To be sure, these firms were greatly outnumbered by those in opposition, but business supporters did usefully demonstrate that the business community was split on the issue.

Supporting companies were painstakingly solicited by consumer and business leaders during the 8 years in which the bill was pending. By 1977, when the legislation appeared to be in trouble, these companies banded together into the Ad Hoc Coalition. Launched at a White House meeting with President Carter, consumer adviser Esther Peterson, and several Cabinet secretaries, the Ad Hoc Coalition established a small office in Washington. One of the group's leaders was Peter T. Jones, then general counsel at Levi Strauss and previously an executive at Montgomery Ward & Co., Inc. Since both firms were part of the coalition, Jones's observations on them deserve quotation at length:

> In 1972 Tom Brooker was head of Marcor–Montgomery Ward. Because the CPA bill had a reasonably good chance of becoming law, it seemed sensible for us to try to improve it. Brooker readily agreed. After our major recommendations were accepted by its Senate sponsors, we agreed to support the bill. When Mobil acquired control of Marcor–Montgomery Ward, both Mobil and its new subsidiary, Wards, continued to support CPA, but on a much less active basis.
>
> I then joined Levi Strauss & Co. and got a call from Esther Peterson in the White House asking if Levi Strauss & Co. would support the bill. I went to Walter and Peter Haas, Chairman and Chief Executive Officer of Levi Strauss & Co., and discussed the history and pros and cons as to the merits of the bill. I also told them, if you decide to support this bill you will get some criticism from some members of the business community and no kudos from most of the others. But the Haas' just said, well, it won't be the first time and it won't deter us. It sounds like we should support it and therefore we will.[3]

Jones got the go-ahead. He attributes this to the fact that the Haases were very independent in mind, spirit, and means, with a long history of corporate social responsibility. "I really am a believer in the key man theory of corporate responsibility," he added, reflecting Ralph Waldo Emerson's view that a successful institution is usually the lengthened shadow of one man. If one or two people at the top are indifferent or opposed, the institution will be indifferent or opposed, but if the people at the top strongly favor proconsumer measures, the institution will reflect that sentiment. Corroborating his theory was his own prior experience at Montgomery Ward. Tom Brooker favored the CPA for several reasons, and Montgomery Ward was therefore an active supporter. The top leadership of Mobil Corporation was unenthusiastic and thus did little to aid the bill's passage. (When the writer of this

---

[3] Personal interview with Daniel Becker of Congress Watch.

essay called Herbert Schmertz, Mobil's media representative, to ask him to devote one of his editorial advertisements to the bill, he demurred.)

Some of the supporting companies did more than lend their names to this legislation. Kings Supermarkets, Giant Food Inc., and Dart Drug Corp. took out full-page advertisements on its behalf; Cummins Engine called the wavering member of Congress from its home district in Indiana. Ultimately, though, these firms and the coalition had only a negligible impact on Congress. While their corporate opponents were spending substantial time and money to defeat the bill,[4] the proconsumer firms gave little time and almost no money. The reasons appear to be twofold. First, since no profits were likely to accrue to a supporting firm as a result of its advocacy, there was little incentive to spend company funds; on legislation at least, profitability is far more energizing a motivator than public-spiritedness. Second, peer pressure from the overwhelming bulk of the business community cooled the ardor of the supporters.

Consider, for example, the agony of J. C. Penney Company. For 2 years the company had been courted by Esther Peterson and consumer groups. It had an in-house consumer supporter, David Schoenfeld, who vigorously advocated the legislation to corporate officials. Their only major objection to early versions of the legislation was that it permitted the CPA to issue interrogatories to business (this provision was dropped in the final version). Despite a very conservative Washington liaison office, J. C. Penney had a chairman, Donald V. Seibert, who was open-minded, politically moderate, and very sympathetic to the representational component of a consumer office. But he was also a leading member of the Business Roundtable, a major opponent of the legislation. When I asked Seibert a few months after the bill's defeat why he hadn't finally supported it, he spoke vaguely and unpersuasively about how late and inconsequential his firm's support would have been. More to the point was the comment of one business executive knowledgeable about the episode: "There was just no way he was going to go against the Roundtable on this one."

PUBLIC PARTICIPATION

Perhaps to compensate for its loss of nerve on the CPA, J. C. Penney has been the leading company in favor of the concept of public participation. As implemented at the FTC, small amounts of public participation funds go to citizen groups and small businesses so that they can afford to appear in agency proceedings where they can make a contribution.

---

[4] See *The Nation,* issue of Feb. 25, 1978; *Fortune,* issue of Mar. 27, 1978.

Initially, it was David Schoenfeld, previously with the Consumers Union of the United States, who got interested in the issue:

> I came across the concept in the course of reviewing all bills and legislation. I'm a consumer advocate and I thought it was important for the consumers' interest to be heard. Business lobbies protect their own interest. But I want consumers to lobby to protect *their* interests.[5]

Schoenfeld then began a series of meetings between consumer leaders and representatives of J. C. Penney:

> The original bill came out of [Edward M.] Kennedy's office and looked pretty good but had vague and general language. The Legal and Governmental relations people [at Penney] wanted to tighten it up a bit. I spoke with Carol Foreman who set up a series of meetings with Joan Claybrook, and I brought Charlie Lotter [Penney's lawyer] and we met over a series of months and hammered out a compromise. The language was tight and specific—something which the company could support, and Joan and Carol sent the proposal to Sens. Kennedy and [Charles] Mathias who bought it, and S. 270 came out with our language. Senator Kennedy held hearings on it and I testified in support.[6]

J. C. Penney's devotion to the bill may be tested. Although several federal agencies are in the process of instituting public participation programs, the general legislation to apply the approach governmentwide, Senate bill 270, never passed the Ninety-Fifth Congress. It has been reintroduced in the Ninety-Sixth Congress, but by this time it has been around long enough to have attracted big-business attention and hostility. A representative of the NAM has said privately that his organization has no principled objection to the measure but will oppose it nonetheless. And some members of the Business Roundtable have decided to exploit the current political mood and attack public participation as inflationary even though they realize that only someone economically illiterate could argue that a $10 million program within a $500 billion budget could affect the rate of inflation. The point is that these two business lobbies don't like consumer advocates in agency proceedings that they now dominate, and they don't need well-grounded reasons to promote their continued hegemony. This time, it is hoped that J. C. Penney will not capitulate to peer pressure.

---

[5] Personal interview with Daniel Becker of Congress Watch.

[6] Ibid.

NO-FAULT AUTOMOBILE
INSURANCE AND PASSIVE
RESTRAINTS

No-fault automobile insurance, which promises to increase the speed and size of compensation claims by eliminating the cost of lawyers from the process, has been seriously considered by the past two Congresses. Lawyers say that it unfairly denies victims the right to go to court, but most consumer groups say that it is necessary to make the tort system work efficiently for crash victims. The American Trial Lawyers Association, many of whose members stand to lose as much as one-fourth of their incomes from no-fault insurance, have vigorously opposed the measure. They have massively lobbied the Congress and have made substantial campaign contributions.

The leading advocates of the measure have been the insurance companies, especially Allstate Insurance Co., State Farm Mutual Automobile Insurance Co., Aetna, and Nationwide Corp., which anticipate lower costs and possibly lower premiums from the measure. They were joined by the American Insurance Association, the Ford Motor Co., the Car and Truck Renting and Leasing Association, and the National Automobile Dealers Association. "But they weren't doing it out of the goodness of their hearts," observed Sallie Adams, the staff aide to the Senate Commerce Committee who worked on this legislation. "They were relieved to be in favor of what they saw to be a good piece of public policy, and they also saw it as good business. It looked like good PR, and they would not lose money on it." In an interview Adams elaborated on what she believed to be the reasons for the insurance companies' enthusiasm and effort:

> The insurance industry is in an adversary relationship with its customers [policyholders]. The policyholders pay big and increasing premiums, but are fought when they want to get paid. . . . The result is that the companies overpay minor injuries and nickel and dime the serious ones. It doesn't pay for them to go to court on small claims, so they end up paying about four times the actual losses. The companies realized that for the same money they could pay the policyholders and not have to fight them. The problem for the companies was that the bill now provided for immediate payouts. Thus the companies no longer had the use of the monies which they delayed sending out. . . .
>
> Some companies opposed the bill, and others were hesitant about it, because if the federal government became involved, they feared further federal regulation. Also, some of the earlier supporters, notably Firemen's Fund, felt that they would lose too much money through immediate payout.[7]

The insurance companies' support for no-fault insurance paralleled their

---

7 Ibid.

work on behalf of passive-restraint systems in cars, which the Department of Transportation (DOT) has mandated for 1982–1983 vehicles. Such systems, including air bags, can save 9000 lives and 63,000 injuries a year, which is good for drivers and for insurance firms, which thus avoid paying money on claims. There was a key congressional vote in 1977 to approve or disapprove of the DOT regulation, with the Senate approving by a 2 to 1 margin. A lawyer for the insurance firms thought that "the corporations' motivations were first economic, then humanitarian. As a group that worked on the issue, we tried to relate the public policy to the economic interest of the corporation." Sallie Adams added:

> Essentially it was a case of the insurance industry and the public interest groups versus the manufacturers. The auto industry first developed the technology, but they felt that it was inconsistent to be for federal regulations mandating passive restraint and against it regarding pollution controls—which, of course, is really stupid.[8]

Congressman Bob Eckhardt, Democrat of Texas, led the fight. He explained the business politics of the situation this way:

> The insurance companies have had a continuing interest in auto safety. First, of course, in the short term, reducing the number and severity of accidents, injuries and resulting claims against insurance companies is obviously to their advantage. But what about the long term? Would not more accidents and higher payouts, inducing higher rates, ultimately benefit them? Not in this time of soaring insurance rates. The insurance companies believed that the rate structure had gotten to the point where further increases could no longer be passed through to policyholders without risking decreases in the amounts of insurance consumers would be willing to buy.
>
> The other major industry group in favor of the passive-restraint rule was, quite understandably, those who made them—air-bag manufacturers and researchers and the like. They included companies like Talley Industries, Thiokol, Minicars, Inc., Allied Chemical Corporation, and the Breed Corporation.
>
> Ranked on the other side of the issue with varying degrees of vehemence were the automobile companies. After all, they are a most significant sector of the business order which rankles at regulation almost as an article of faith. Even though the costs and risks auto makers would be directed to take were to be uniformly imposed, the companies were not equally able or willing to accept them.
>
> GM had the technology—had even marketed air bags for a short time. Ford was well on its way. Volvo had manufactured and sold a fleet of air-bag–equipped cars. Chrysler and AMC, on the other hand, would have to contract out to get the technology.
>
> Auto companies do not like to take risks with products they are not sure the

---

8 Ibid.

public will accept at the price, and there is a carry-over of this philosophy even to a situation where the product is mandated. Perhaps the load on total price will cut down on sales of automobiles generally. But GM's surveys, only recently released, showed that most consumers want—and would pay well for—air bags.

The public positions of the companies reflected their market positions. GM finally said, in essence, "Well, we don't think it's a great idea, but if you insist, we'll go along." Volvo and other foreign manufacturers have supported the air-bag concept all along, even, as in the case of Toyota, to the extent of putting air bags into small cars—a move which U.S. companies said was technically impossible. Chrysler has fought the concept to the last ditch.[9]

AIRLINE DEREGULATION

For years conservative and liberal economists had agreed that federal regulation of a workably competitive industry like air transportation led to a cartel-like structure that was inefficient and anticonsumer. First, President Ford and then President Carter pushed hard for legislation to reduce the authority of the Civil Aeronautics Board (CAB) to fix rates, permit entry, and set routes. Under the leadership of Sens. Edward M. Kennedy of Massachusetts and Howard W. Cannon of Nevada a deregulation bill was enacted in 1978 and signed into law.

The major group that lobbied in favor of the measure was the Ad Hoc Committee for Airline Regulatory Reform, an amalgam of consumer and business groups including Sears, Roebuck and Co., United Air Lines, Pan American World Airways, and the NAM. In a statement the Sears spokesman attributed his firm's actions to the "philosophy of competitive markets as being the best allocator of resources and the favorable effect of low transportation costs in keeping prices down. It's a question of leadership, since other firms fear the slings and arrows of unfavorable public reaction. . . . Sears would not lobby for an issue which was not in its economic self-interest."

Philip M. Knox, Jr., vice president of governmental affairs at Sears, while proud of his firm's work on this issue, adds that Sears rarely gets involved in politics because it has "no technical capacity to get into issues." Sears's rationale touches closely the explanation given for the NAM's participation by its lobbyist, Mary Jo Jacobi:

> Almost all business travel is by air. The staff goes for business reasons and it saves them money both as businessmen and consumers. . . . [And] the members [of NAM] are fed up with economic government regulation. They

9 Ibid.

feel that this will set a precedent for further deregulation.[10]

United, the largest United States airline, "felt that earnings were poor under CAB regulation, [and with] more freedom to adjust our own routes and fares, they would improve," according to company official Bob Williams. It took the firm 2 years to make its decision to break with the rest of the industry and support deregulation. As for the others, said Williams, "Fear of the unknown was and is the main factor behind airline opposition to government deregulation."

CARGO PREFERENCE

The American merchant marine has been in decline for decades, losing traffic to less costly foreign carriers. But because of its historic political power based on lavish campaign contributions, the merchant fleet has obtained hundreds of millions of dollars annually in direct and indirect federal subsidies. In 1977, though, its reach for cargo preference somewhat exceeded its grasp. Cargo preference would have required that 9.5 percent of all imported petroleum travel on American bottoms, a move that could have added $610 million annually in consumer prices, according to the Library of Congress. Consumers don't like added costs, and neither do the businesses which cannot always simply pass them on. So Common Cause, Nader's Congress Watch, the Chamber of Commerce of the United States, and oil companies all worked together against the labor-backed measure.

The interest of the oil firms was no mystery. As the director of federal affairs at Getty put it, "It was in our economic self-interest. . . . Switching to U.S. flag ships would cost us money." Robert Hawk of the Chamber of Commerce cited two reasons for his board's decision to work against this bill: "It tends to raise prices for the consumer and it is essentially a protectionist act which might engender protectionism in other areas—such as shoes and grain." The chamber sought to defeat cargo preference with some of the techniques used in anticonsumer battles. As Hawk described it, "The Chamber contacted members' offices, testified against the bill and met with Congressmen. The grassroot organization [member companies] wrote in to Congressmen. And we conducted an economic analysis of the state-by-state impact of the legislation on jobs and prices."[11] According to public-interest lobbyists working on the legislation, the latter approach proved to be extremely effective.

---

10 Ibid.

11 Ibid.

CONSUMER DISPUTE RESOLUTION

Another issue that attracted the attention and support of the chamber was Senate bill 957, cosponsored by Senators Kennedy and Wendell H. Ford of Kentucky. It provided for a $15 million Justice Department grant program to fund alternative ways of settling small economic and neighborhood disputes. The court system and its lawyers have become a luxury that few can afford, especially for small disputes in which the amount in question can be less than the likely attorney's fees.

Several congressional staff members attributed the Chamber of Commerce's strong support to its need to favor *some* piece of legislation labeled proconsumer, especially after its costly and successful campaign to defeat the CPA. Whatever the motivation, the chamber testified in favor of the concept and lobbied vigorously for the bill, but on one condition. It insisted on a provision that *required* grant recipients to permit business access to any dispute-resolution mechanism. Unfortunately, eighteen states, including Texas and New York, prohibited assignees or businesses generally from being plaintiffs in small-claims courts. These prohibitions were intended to solve the widespread problem of companies' using the courts as collection agencies and crowding out needy individuals. The chamber made a deal through its spokesman, Sen. James A. McClure of Idaho: it and he would not delay the bill to death at the end of the busy Ninety-Fifth Congress if the business-access rule was adopted. The Senate then capitulated. (The bill was passed by the Senate but not by the House.)

Ironies abounded. The chamber insisted on a provision that would create a federal string ("Business must have access") in a way that interfered with states' rights, since some states might have to change their laws in this area. But what happened to the chamber's usual philosophic aversion to the federal government's bossing the states? Despite its brinkmanship, which jeopardized the legislation, the chamber later took credit in press releases for the bill as its own, which was not true. On the basis of its price for supporting this bill, the chamber's handsome fifty-page booklet, *Model Consumer Justice Act . . . Up with Consumers,* should perhaps be retitled *The Business Dispute Resolution Act . . . Up the Consumer.*

CORPORATE BRIBERY

By 1978 more than 400 American companies had admitted to illegal or unethical payoffs abroad or at home; among them were more than one-third of *Fortune*'s 500 industrials. One would imagine that nonbribing companies would rise to criticize such contemptible behavior. Instead, as revelation followed revelation in the mid-1970s, most American business leaders either watched this scandal unfold silently or applied their imagination to excuse such practices ("Everyone does it"; "It's a way of life in such countries").

There was one exception. One chief executive officer played the role of the innocent announcing that the emperor had no clothes and publicly criticized such bribery. He was Bendix Corp.'s W. Michael Blumenthal, who in an interview later described what happened: "I insisted that the company pay not one penny in bribes. I was told that we couldn't do that—that we'd lose business. Well, we didn't. What did happen was that we attracted the best graduates from Harvard and Stanford, who had read about us. It helped morale at Bendix." Then, after pausing and smiling, he added, "And I became the Secretary of the Treasury."[12] Subsequently, on behalf of the Carter administration, Secretary Blumenthal supported a bill to make such payoffs a crime; it later became law.

Compare his response to that of another firm that similarly had taken a tough stance on bribery, Eli Lilly and Company. As one top official explained, "We really blew our chance. When there were some 100 companies bribing, including several drug companies, we weren't. We should have spoken out against the practice and distinguished ourselves. But we didn't."

CONCLUSIONS

Several patterns and conclusions emerge from this chronicle of proconsumer business activity.

First, companies may lobby for progressive causes to the extent that these promote, or at least are not inconsistent with, profits. With very few exceptions, companies will do good only if they can do well. Thus, the public and oil firms benefited from the defeat of cargo preference, the public and insurance companies were helped by passive-restraint systems, and the public and many businesses gained from airline deregulation and the resulting lower fares. The varying positions of energy firms in the 1978 Energy bill are also a case in point. "Virtually every member of the industry is calculating his cash flow, as one gas company executive put it yesterday, deciding whether his company has more to gain by passage or defeat of the bill."[13] This bottom-line analysis is not meant as criticism but as fact. As one comes across occasional corporate good works, it should not be forgotten that corporations are not eleemosynary institutions and cannot be expected to act in ways contrary to their dominant ethos, which is profits.

Second, there can also be the motivation, not inconsistent with the foregoing, to establish lowest-common-denominator standards to deter fraudulent

---

12 Personal communication to author at Aspen, Colorado.

13 *The Washington Post,* Sept. 13, 1978.

behavior. Since companies that defraud have a competitive advantage over firms that market honestly, the latter have an incentive to advocate minimal consumer standards. For example, Philip M. Knox, Jr., of Sears explained that the reason that his firm supported the Magnuson-Moss Warranty Act was "not so much because of the information it required we give consumers but because it prevented people who were competing with us from making false and misleading guarantees."[14]

Third, a handful of firms do stand out as being more publicly spirited than the average. Levi Strauss works diligently for consumer-advocacy offices, devotes an unusual amount of money to philanthropy, and seeks to help minority communities; Cummins Engine has committed itself institutionally in the same three areas; and J. C. Penney supports a major procedural reform, the public participation bill. One could argue that in-house people like Peter T. Jones or David Schoenfeld are largely responsible for such specific examples of benevolence. Their roles as catalysts may be important, but to credit them alone may be to confuse cause and effect. Jones would argue that the cause is a chief executive officer, such as Walter A. Haas, Jr., of Levi Strauss, J. Irwin Miller of Cummins Engine, or Donald V. Seibert of J. C. Penney, who wants his company to act more responsibly and who then retains people like Jones and Schoenfeld.

Fourth, peer business pressure makes it extremely difficult for even independent-minded executives or companies to break out of the pack. Business executives who share a common business milieu—who have attended the same business schools and frequent the same clubs, churches, and trade associations—are not likely to stick their necks out to ally themselves, even indirectly, with consumer advocates. J. C. Penney saw how difficult this course was. Many of the 100 companies supporting the CPA reported that other firms lobbied them hard to drop their support. When Atlantic Richfield Company (ARCO) came out against the oil-depletion allowance (though it did couple its opposition with decontrol of oil prices), ARCO vice president Ralph F. Cox reported, "Suppliers hated us for doing it and many wouldn't do business with us."[15]

Essentially, for companies to lobby for consumer causes is an applaudable though rare event. To urge companies to do more politically on behalf of good government is to risk naïveté or worse. For every J. Irwin Miller there are 100 Joseph Coorses. Representatives of the Chamber of Commerce of the United States are going around the country persuading companies to establish political action committees to promote a free enterprise economy, not to tighten enforcement of environmental protection.

---

14 Personal communication.

15 Personal communication.

We should, instead, look to a more modest set of goals for corporate responsibility. For example, the basic corporate social responsibility is to *obey the law*. According to white-collar law-enforcement statistics, this simple precept is too often observed in the breach. But legal costs and the public notoriety of Kepone for the Allied Chemical Corporation, Pinto gas tanks for Ford, Firestone 500s for Firestone, and foreign bribes for Lockheed Corp. are so great that many companies may see the light the more they feel the heat. An article in *Fortune* said that, as a result of the Kepone case, Allied "downgrades profitability as a measure of a manager's performance and gives much greater weight to his regard for social and environmental responsibilities."[16]

Companies should also support economic competition, which is consistent with the predominant corporate ideology of free enterprise, rather than surrender to the temptation to cartelize, monopolize, or price-fix or to run to the government for protectionist policies. As Walter Lippmann once put it, "Competition has survived only where men have been unable to abolish it."

Only when the precepts of lawfulness and competition are established can society reasonably expect corporations to support measures that *complement* the market on behalf of consumers. It should not be inevitable that modern business would simply repeat Alfred Sloan's conduct when he faced his great decision in the corporate-responsibility area. In the 1920s, his General Motors Corp. engineers had developed a shatterproof glass that, if installed, would save many lives and prevent many injuries. But since it would add slightly to price and since his competitors lacked the lifesaving technology, Sloan rejected it. Today it should not be impossible for companies to *go to the government* to urge minimum standards that would save lives and not competitively disadvantage any firm within the industry. While this is not impossible, it is not yet likely. Although numerous companies give money to local symphonic groups and charities, their benevolence rarely extends to the actual manufacture or service in which they daily engage. So corporate good works in the public policy arena remain an aspiration, not an expectation.

16 Marvin H. Zim, "Allied Chemical's $20-Million Ordeal with Kepone," Sept. 11, 1978, p. 91.

BUSINESS RESPONSIBILITY AND THE PUBLIC POLICY PROCESS

HENRY B. SCHACHT

Henry B. Schacht is chairman and chief executive officer of Cummins Engine Company, Inc., a major international manufacturer of diesel engines with headquarters in Columbus, Indiana. He attended Yale University and the Harvard Graduate School of Business Administration. Mr. Schacht has been with Cummins since 1964 and has served as its chief executive officer since 1969. He is also a trustee of the Conference Board, the Committee for Economic Development, the Urban Institute, and the Rockefeller Foundation and a member of the Council on Foreign Relations, the Trilateral Commission, the Management Executives' Society, and the Advisory Board of the Yale School of Organization and Management.

CHARLES W. POWERS

Charles W. Powers is vice president of public policy, Cummins Engine Company, Inc., and affiliate professor of social ethics, Christian Theological Seminary. He served as assistant professor of social ethics at Yale University from 1969 to 1971 and was associate professor of social ethics between 1971 and 1975. He is the author of Social Responsibility and Investments *(1971), the coauthor of* The Ethical Investor *(1972), and the editor of* People/Profits *(1972). He has written many articles on ethics and economic policy for both scholarly and trade publications.*

Mr. Powers is codirector of the Summer Institute on Ethics in the Management of Public and Private Institutions (Yale University), a member of the

The management of change is what corporate officials get paid for. Products, markets, employee expectations, material costs—all the factors which make up the internal operation of an enterprise—are constantly in flux. Effective managers are those who both see what is coming and keep their (and the company's) balance, reintegrating corporate plans and resources to seize new opportunities and cutting losses in areas where factors which make for profitability have disappeared. Be it a market shift, a supplier shortage, or a new advance by a competitor, all good managers have learned to be quick in response. It never occurs to us to question the legitimacy of these changes. We act, instinctively and immediately, to assure that when changes affect our operations, they do so in the most constructive way possible. This is the environment of the marketplace.

But we in private management have consistently responded differently and less effectively to other kinds of changes: the more encompassing claims by the communities in which we operate, rapid changes in the nature and scope of governmental restrictions on or expectations about our products and our production processes, and the higher decibel levels which emanate from a vast array of groups representing one or more interests which we are said to affect, usually adversely. Our reaction to the claims made at the interface where the company meets its external publics is very frequently one of surprise, frustration, and antagonism. And our actual responses, not surprisingly, are too often reactionary; that is, we tend to respond by trying either to deflect these claims or to confront them head on with jaws set. We simply do not manage our social and political environment as we do the environment of the marketplace. And the results of the encounters are persistently acidic and not very beneficial for either the company or the claimant.

RESPONSE TO SOCIAL AND POLITICAL CHANGE

For some time we have tried to figure out why business is so much less effective in managing the issues on its perimeters. We think that the reasons are to be found in three basic categories.

Diversity and Unpredictability

The first category is the very diversity and relative unpredictability of the social and political challenges which make their appearance at so many intersections of corporation and community. Our antennae are out for the first indications of a market shift, and the channels are well established to allow this information to travel quickly to the multiple places where the company must begin to take account of the implications of the changes. And the implications are usually definable. The adjustment process is rarely smooth, but it is efficient and seasoned.

25

But the political and social processes which give rise to a corporation's response to the broader environment are, or at least seem, less predictable. New governmental restrictions can seemingly appear at three or four points on the borders of a corporation with relatively little notice, or a community issue can erupt one day where things seemed placid the day before. There is an additional factor: changes brought about by political decisions are usually not evolutionary in the same way that market factors are. Either a regulation takes effect, or it does not; a court injunction, seemingly generated from almost anywhere, either catapults the decision into effect or stops it cold. To integrate the complexities of a production process and a marketing strategy in the midst of multiple changes such as these sometimes seems impossible. And thus the proponents or implementers of these changes appear almost perverse.

To the single-minded government agency or proponent of social change, corporate America's response must seem equally unpredictable and diverse. After concerted efforts to raise an issue or to evolve a regulatory approach, a court challenge or a last-minute effort to delay regulatory implementation or efforts to stall a reform initiative must appear to be unmitigated stubbornness born of a throwback mentality or selfish greed.

Inadequate Understanding

Second, much of the diversity-unpredictability problem, we are convinced, is the result of inadequate understanding on both sides of the public-corporate interface. There is usually truth in the protest that a public-interest advocate and a congressional staffer have never had to meet a payroll. The process of trying to create some semblance of coherent hours for a workforce and of trying to make decisions on expanding facilities while attempting to convince the investment community that the company can put together three good first quarters in a row is complex. The margins for error in this process do not easily accommodate a sudden massive investment to meet a new governmental test procedure or, alternatively, a decision to scrap the procedure.

On the other hand, rare is the corporate manager who understands the tedious back-and-forth compromises which constitute congressional committees' deliberations. Similarly misunderstood is the role of bureaucrats buffeted by the most recent interpretation of an agency's counsel, the decision on administrative procedure handed down yesterday by a circuit court, or the latest results of an agency's research group. Again, we do not usually appreciate the role of the public-interest advocate whose coalition is pulled apart by a personality conflict between two participating groups or by a professional association which suddenly backs out because its largest contributor has just gotten wind of the coalition's public position.

Our point here is that the processes of *integration* essential to corporate productivity and the processes of *social decision* inherent in the democratic process are each so different and so poorly understood by the people and institutions which stand on opposite sides of the corporate-public interface that conflict seems inevitable.

Legitimacy

Third, as a result of what we have described, the various actors in this environment tend to question the *legitimacy* of the opposite side. To be in dialogue or even in active contention with a worthy party or adversary is very different from being in combat with those whose very *raison d'être* is doubted. From the corporate side, we often question the right of activists to speak for their constituencies, and we question both the role and the intentions of bureaucrats. Legislative bodies are idly criticized as incompetent groups caught up in internal politics, unresponsive to their electors. From the public side, corporate management is seen as the unaccountable leadership of organizations whose very structure is at odds with democratic institutions.

These perceptions of double illegitimacy are the death knell to creativity in the management of complex interactions. With an unworthy adversary, one does not reach across to comprehend the other's mind-set except for tactical advantage. Every request for information is feared as a possible leverage point for intrusion. The channels for response become dominated by attitudes of defense, not cooperation.

SHIFT IN MIND-SET

Taken together, diversity and unpredictability, aggravated by a lack of mutual understanding which gives rise to a perception of illegitimacy, yield wooden, unimaginative, and aggressively risk-aversive management of the relationship of corporations and the broader environment. But for a market-oriented economic sector to survive in as complex a society as ours, the impasse has to be broken.

Public policy analysts, such as Charles L. Schultze in his book *The Public Use of Private Interest* (1977), have been offering constructive suggestions as to how the various publics, particularly government, can approach the area of social interaction differently. For our part, we would briefly like to describe the shift in mind-set which we believe will have to occur on the business side, a shift toward which we are struggling at Cummins.

There are, it seems to us, four basic premises on which a corporation's approach to the social and political environment should rest:

1. No corporation has an inherent right to exist. It wins its right by produc-

ing needed goods and services within the parameters set by law and acceptable conduct. In industry we have long accepted the fact that if a corporation cannot compete effectively in the marketplace, it will fail; we are less ready to accept the fact that the justification for our existence depends also on meeting the requirements set by the societies in which we operate.

2.   Within such a view, the corporation is seen as both dependent on and responsible to the full range of people whose lives it affects. A corporation is best pictured, then, as having a full gamut of stakeholders with each of whom a constructive relationship must be established or negotiated. No group of stakeholders has a total claim to what constitutes appropriate conduct of the corporation; but when the corporation's activities impinge, stakeholders should have avenues of access to set forth their claims and to say that they are being hurt. In turn, the corporation has a responsibility to respond appropriately and to ensure that at the very least its activities do not diminish the health and welfare of those it affects. Its failure to do so sets up a social dynamic in which everyone loses.

3.   One important aspect of this stakeholder responsibility is the recognition that no *product* has an inherent right to the marketplace. Customers (the better informed, the better) have much to say about this. But so also has the general public, especially as it expresses its will about the health, safety, and other environmental effects of the product.

4.   Each of these points has implications for the way in which corporations reach out to participate in social and political processes, especially the process of public policy formation. In pursuing its self-interest in these public contexts, a corporation should not advocate any policy or practice which, after subjecting the issue to as much objective analysis as the corporation can muster, it cannot justify as being in the public interest.

These premises by no means suggest that a corporation's response to every social initiative or to every public policy proposal will satisfy its proponents. What they do require is that a corporation will seek to comprehend every stakeholder protest and proposal arising out of a sincere expectation or fear of existing or potential harm. It will assess who has the authority and competence to determine the validity of the threat or the legitimacy of the expectation. It will assess its own activities in the light of this competent judgment. Then, and only then, will it respond.

It is at this point that the really hard work begins: the work of finding the optimal policy which meets the public need quickly and effectively and also takes account of how the patterns of redress, change, or additional effort will meet the rhythms of corporate technology development, human resources, and financial capability. The task of finding such a policy must be a cooperative venture between the corporation and those outside, whether community, government, or a narrower group. A sorting out of who has responsibility for the various parts of the task must occur. And the issue must be caught and addressed so early in the process that lines do not harden and protection of careers and reputations does not replace the focus on substantive problems.

CONSTRUCTIVE RESOLUTION OF ISSUES

We have been asked to describe several recent issues on which both Cummins and interested outside groups have each been able to reach across the gap and forestall the disintegration of trust and goodwill on which the constructive resolution of issues depends.

Community Relations

The first issue is a hometown one. Cummins's headquarters is in Columbus, Indiana, a city of about 30,000. With a workforce of 10,000 we are by far the largest employer in the area. Columbus is naturally intensely aware of our decisions, real and rumored. For several years it had been common knowledge that Cummins was in the early stages of planning a new headquarters building as part of a downtown revitalization effort. The plan had been delayed several times by other capital needs and by efforts to clarify the instructions to our architect. The city's leadership was naturally concerned to know the scope, nature, and likely completion date of the project. Would it be a Cummins facility only or part of a complex? Would the historic landmark in the middle of the site be preserved? Property values, plans of small business, public works projects, and the like would be directly affected. How great would the effects be?

In the summer of 1977, just as we began to clarify our thinking, community discussion began to increase. The people of Columbus knew that they had a stake in our decision and wanted to know what the decision was. A host of internal management issues remained to be resolved, but it became clear to us that community interest was likely to turn to speculation and suspicion. Rather than fend it off, we decided to call together a full spectrum of community leaders, not merely to tell them the unsettled state of our plans but conscientiously to ask their views on the role that a new office building could play in the community's evolution and on how that role could be enhanced. Representatives of our top management, along with our architect, listened for 3 days. The discussion was open and open-ended. We focused many of our own questions on those issues (almost all of which were yet to be decided) on which we perceived the community impact of our building would be greatest.

The sessions were extremely instructive. Many of our perceptions changed; the architect, Kevin Roche, incorporated a wide variety of the community's suggestions into his plans. The community gained confidence that it had been heard and that all appropriate information had been shared. Hence, the ensuing 8 months before we were ready to make a public announcement went smoothly. And when we presented our model publicly, it was greeted enthusiastically. Our needs and those of the community had been met. An issue which could have created the animosity almost endemic to the major initiatives of any large institution living in the midst of a relatively small population had been turned into a wellspring of trust on which we would draw for years to come.

Emissions Control

The second issue relates to our product, the diesel engine. Diesel exhaust contains gaseous emissions regulated under broad administrative authority granted by the Clean Air Act of 1970. But in 1975, when Congress began to consider amending the act, it decided to include in the statute itself much more specific instructions. The first version contained a series of provisions that we didn't begin to know how to meet. Worse, from our point of view, the proposed section seemed to have built in a collision course for government and industry. We did not question the legitimacy of strenuous legislation; we publicly stated that our product should meet governmentally established criteria of social responsibility as the condition for remaining in the market.

But we and others in the industry recognized that the appropriate goals of the legislation were certain to be undermined by both its form and its content. Rather than take our stand on that issue, however, we decided to try to figure out what legislation would get the job done. We wanted legislation that would create a competitive environment that would produce reduced emissions while satisfying the diversity of other social goals (fuel economy, inflation) which constitute the public interest in the manufacture and use of heavy-duty engines. After laborious effort, which drew heavily on both our technical and our human resources, we evolved such a strategy. We carefully worked through the specific issues of where government's responsibility lies in determining health threats and setting standards and of what incentives are most likely to bring forth the most effective corporate response. Only then did we go to Washington.

The doors of congressional offices, especially those which housed the more environmentally committed members, did not swing open on our arrival. But they opened a crack. When congressional people recognized that our approach was significantly different from the one which had inspired so much government-industry animosity since 1970, they took another look. Some congressional staff members who were attracted to our arguments began efforts to turn the strategy into legislative language. And when the issue finally came to a vote in committee, the approach, with relatively little emendation, was adopted unanimously. Two years later, it was law. Consistent and persistent efforts to explain the approach lay behind this decision. Trust levels did not rise easily, but they did rise. And the industry, Congress, and the Environmental Protection Agency (EPA) evolved an atmosphere of mutual respect which we hope will carry through to the actual regulation-setting process and stand the test of the many even more complex environmental issues involving heavy-duty engines which lie before us in the next years. But more important than the cooperation are the anticipated results: engines which most efficiently and cost-effectively do their societal work without threatening public health.

Employee Privacy

The third issue, employee privacy, is different in that it relates to the public's concern about how corporations respect the dignity of their own workers. Public concern about the privacy issue was first aroused by the proliferation of records, technological advances in record processing, and allegations about governmental invasions of privacy. By 1974 it became clear that public attention and governmental regulation would soon shift to the private sector's record-keeping practices. Governor Otis R. Bowen of Indiana, in response to several early legislative initiatives, formed a state commission on privacy, and I (Henry B. Schacht) agreed to chair the nongovernmental record-keeping subcommittee. For unrelated reasons coincident with the formation of the commission, Cummins decided to computerize its employee records. The two events were soon to be interrelated.

To sort through the issues, the commission's subcommittee sought out both representatives of diverse private-sector institutions to explain their record-keeping procedures and any or all individuals or their representatives who were likely to have experienced private-sector invasions of privacy. We found little actual abuse but enormous potential for abuse. At the same time, utilizing the data and principles gathered in these public sessions, our personnel, systems, and corporate-responsibility groups developed ways of modifying Cummins's evolving human-resources record system to avoid these privacy threats. In mid-course the Cummins manager handling this project made a presentation to the subcommittee, whose reactions provided an opportunity for further refinement.

The result is that at almost no additional cost Cummins has a record system which is likely to require little or no modification when legislation evolves in this area. We might note that both the subcommittee's report and the principles and methods we have utilized at Cummins have been picked up by the Privacy Protection Study Commission in Washington and by legislators attempting to devise legislation. We are hopeful that the legislation will require a lower business-sector investment, in part because of the relative simplicity, effectiveness, and efficiency of the system which evolved from these multiple interactions between the corporation and its social-political environment in Indiana. And most important, our employee stakeholders know this system and accept it, and their privacy is better protected because of its adoption.

These three examples are the ones whose processes we are trying to emulate and re-create in the increasing pace and widening scope of our interactions with the broader environment. We expect protest and political decision and regulatory requirements to keep coming and often to seem unwelcome and strange. But, if nothing else, the positive examples may keep us aware that it is at least possible for the present and potential claims of broader publics to be integrated into the kind of management with which we are most familiar. When corporations and the external constituencies can learn to live by and with the rhythms natural to each, not only will the crisis of institutional confidence ease, but the quality of life for each of us, manager, governmental official, and advocate—citizens all, will be significantly improved.

CORPORATE POLITICAL BEHAVIOR

HERBERT E. ALEXANDER

Herbert E. Alexander is professor of political science at the University of Southern California and director of the Citizens' Research Foundation. He received his B.S. degree from the University of North Carolina, his M.A. degree from the University of Connecticut, and his Ph.D. degree in political science from Yale University in 1958. He taught in the department of politics at Princeton University from 1956 to 1958 and subsequently was a visiting lecturer at Princeton (1965–1966), the University of Pennsylvania (1967–1968), and Yale (1977).

Dr. Alexander has written extensively on matters relating to money in politics. His book Financing the 1976 Election *was published in 1979 by Congressional Quarterly, Inc. He is also editor of a book,* Campaign Money: Reform and Reality in the States, *on the financing of the 1974 gubernatorial campaigns with an overview of how the campaign regulatory process worked in ten selected states, that was published in 1976 by the Free Press. He was special editor of the May 1976 issue of* The Annals *of the American Academy of Political and Social Science on election reform. He also is author of* Financing Politics: Money, Elections and Political Reform, *published in 1976 by Congressional Quarterly, Inc., of which he is preparing an updated second edition.*

For the past two decades, the Citizens' Research Foundation, located since 1978 at the University of Southern California in Los Angeles, has pioneered in the study of money in the political process. Through its research, studies, seminars, and publications, it serves as a nonpartisan observer and interpreter of trends in political finance. Its data collections and library are an information clearinghouse for scholars, the media, and policy makers.

Ever since the development in the late nineteenth century of the corporation as the dominant instrument for conducting business in the United States, Americans have been concerned about the role played by business executives and corporations in politics. This concern has been translated into legislative action prohibiting the use of corporate funds in political campaigns while permitting the establishment of corporate political action committees (PACs), as well as restricting the amount of individual and group contributions to candidates and mandating full disclosure, including the identification of the occupation and principal place of business of larger contributors. Despite the enactment between 1971 and 1976 of three reform laws to regulate political contributions and expenditures and to provide for some public financing of presidential campaigns, Americans are still uneasy about business influence in politics. In May 1977, for example, pollster Louis Harris reported that "most Americans are very wary of any kind of corporate-related contributions to political campaigns."[1]

In the past business executives and politicians alike were generally secretive about campaign contributions. Neither wanted to give the public the impression that senators, representatives, governors, mayors, or even Presidents could be influenced by those who gave financial support to their campaigns. Until the 1970s federal election laws were so vague and enforcement was so lax that there was usually little difficulty in hiding campaign contributions. Sometimes money was siphoned off from corporate funds and put into political campaigns. Occasionally, corporate executives were given bonuses with the explicit understanding that the aftertax balance would be contributed to campaign funds. Some few executives were assigned to work on campaigns while remaining on corporate payrolls. More often, slush funds were set up under various facades, and money was secretly dispensed from them, frequently in cash, to candidates. In general, the public did not know precisely what was going on, but the business executives and the politicians did, and neither side forgot when showdowns occurred on Capitol Hill or in executive departments and agencies.

WATERGATE REVELATIONS

It was not until the Watergate scandals, however, that Americans got something approaching a full view of the way in which many businesses went about financing political campaigns. A total of twenty-one corporations or their executives, or both, were indicted in 1973 and 1974 for illegally contributing corporate funds to political campaigns.[2] Most of the money went to the Nixon reelection campaign before the 1971 reform legislation

---

[1] Harris survey, *The Washington Post,* May 31, 1978.

[2] For an extensive discussion, see Herbert E. Alexander, *Financing the 1972 Election,* D. C. Heath and Company, Lexington, Mass., 1976, pp. 513–528, 708–710.

35

took effect in April 1972, but smaller contributions were made by some of these companies to Democratic candidates as well. The companies included such major corporations as American Airlines, Ashland Oil, Braniff Airways, Goodyear Tire & Rubber Company, Gulf Oil Corp., Minnesota Mining and Manufacturing Company, Northrop Corp., and Phillips Petroleum Co. For the most part, the companies or their executives pleaded guilty or *nolo contendere* and were fined. Several of the executives involved were forced by their companies to resign or to retire early, and some returned corporate money. The rest remained with their companies.

Most of the corporate executives who were solicited were approached by either Maurice Stans, who had resigned as Secretary of Commerce to head the Finance Committee to Re-elect the President, or Herbert Kalmbach, a California lawyer who was Nixon's personal counsel. According to the solicitors, it was never suggested to any corporate officer that an illegal contribution be made. The manner of solicitation was to ask a corporate official to "pass the hat" among executives and higher-level employees. A number of corporations fraudulently channeled corporate moneys on their own before delivering them or converted them into cash without any known participation in the process by Nixon campaign officials. The actions apparently were exclusively corporate actions. Some of the corporations were small, privately owned companies. Contributions of corporations involved in the indictments ranged from a few thousand dollars to $150,000.

To disguise, or "launder," the use of corporate funds as campaign contributions, the companies most frequently resorted to channeling the money through foreign operations and distributing it in cash. American Airlines ran its $55,000 contribution through the Swiss bank account of a Lebanese agent and charged it off as a "special commission" in connection with the sale of "used aircraft to Middle East Airlines." Minnesota Mining and Manufacturing, which gave the Nixon fund $30,000, laundered its money through a Swiss attorney who submitted false billings for his services. Goodyear Tire & Rubber used an account maintained in a Swiss bank for rebates received from foreign manufacturers buying Goodyear supplies. Braniff Airways made a bogus payment to an agent in Panama to arrange its $40,000 illegal contribution to the Nixon campaign. The $100,000 Gulf Oil contribution to the Nixon campaign was arranged through a Gulf subsidiary in the Bahamas and charged to the firm's "miscellaneous expense account." Ashland Oil used an oil-drilling subsidiary in Gabon to launder its $100,000 contribution. American Ship Building Co. and its chairman, George M. Steinbrenner III, admitted arranging various contributions through illegal schemes that included giving fictitious bonuses to loyal employees along with lists of committees to which they should make donations (the donations were smaller than the bonuses so that the bonus recipients' taxes would be covered). Both the company and its chairman were fined.

POLITICAL FUNDS

The revelations stemming from the Watergate scandals led to the discovery of long-standing secret political funds maintained by corporations and illegally financed with corporate funds. Among companies with such funds were Minnesota Mining, Gulf Oil, and Firestone Tire & Rubber Co. In a detailed accounting made in June 1978 to settle a civil suit filed by the Securities and Exchange Commission (SEC), Claude C. Wild, Jr., who was Gulf's Washington lobbyist from 1960 to 1973, said that he had available to dispense for political purposes "approximately $200,000 a year." Most of the money went to politicians from oil-producing states, and the recipients ranged from Lyndon B. Johnson, when he was a senator and Vice President, and Jimmy Carter, when he was governor of Georgia, to Judge Leander Perez, the political boss of Plaquemines Parish, Louisiana. Former Sen. Hugh Scott of Pennsylvania received $10,000 a year from 1964 to 1973. From 1970 until his retirement from the Senate in 1977 Scott was the Senate minority leader. Wild gave money to Washington politicians even though he often did not know how it was to be used. "Politicians have got all kinds of problems," Wild testified. "They've got deficits, they've got entertainment expenses, they've got cars to buy, kids to educate, fur coats to buy, mistresses, I suppose, to take care of, any number of things. When you make a transfer of money from one person to a politician or an agent, you are never really sure what it is for."[3] In Scott's case, its use never has been made entirely clear.

In at least one instance, some of the money earmarked by a corporation for political purposes never got to the politicians. In March 1978, Robert P. Beasley, who was Firestone's $200,000-a-year executive vice president for finance when he was forced to retire in 1976, pleaded guilty to charges that he had used for personal expenses money that was intended for political campaign contributions. He admitted using a "material portion" of $493,-000 in corporate funds for his own expenses from 1968 to 1972. Beasley, who was retired on a monthly pension of almost $10,000, was sentenced in June 1978 to 4 years in prison and fined $14,000.[4]

No one knows how widespread the corporate practices exposed by the Watergate investigations were, but the involvement of large companies and

[3] Stephen M. Aug, "Ex-Gulf Lobbyist Claude Wild Tells How He Spread Millions," *The Washington Star,* June 2, 1978.

[4] Arnold H. Lubasch, "Ex-Firestone Officer Admits Fraud," *The New York Times,* Mar. 1, 1978; "Ex Officer of Firestone Gets 4-Year Jail Term," *The New York Times,* June 1, 1978.

their top officers in the illegal use of corporate money for political contributions has unquestionably increased public suspicion of business involvement in politics and has made corporations hesitant about their role in political affairs. Reformers look on the Watergate revelations as the tip of an iceberg; spokesmen for business note that only a handful of the nation's corporations were involved in illegal domestic contributions.

Of course, most corporations behaved differently, and some turned down the Nixon campaign, just as they sometimes reject solicitations by others. The author knows of a major corporation whose president refused to make any contributions to the Nixon campaign. He took that position because (1) he knew that Nixon had already raised $20 million, which he thought was quite enough; (2) the request for a contribution came early in the spring of 1972, and he did not know who Nixon's opponent would be; (3) he did not consider anonymity important, even though it was permissible at the time, since he believed in disclosure; (4) he did not want to devote the staff time necessary to put together a large contribution by passing the hat for legal contributions; and (5) it never occurred to him to consider using corporate or illegal funds.

This analysis was rational, was marked by responsibility to stockholders, and was guided by ethical standards. Corporate behavior does not differ from any other form of human behavior if it is tempered by considerations of responsibility, legality, and morality. That some corporate managements succumbed to solicitations and adopted illegal means of giving while others did not reflects differences in both the individuals involved and the corporate structures. As will be seen, many companies have since devised corporate structures and procedures to overcome human failings. Many who refused to give in past years exhibited strong feelings and felt secure enough to decline. Many who yielded to solicitation by using corporate funds in violation of a long-standing law were insecure personally, or worried about what their competition was doing, or were concerned about possible governmental reprisals, or were ideologically motivated on an emotional rather than a rational basis.

Illegal or questionable corporate contributions also found their way to political funds and other sources in foreign countries, and a survey completed in 1978 by Charles E. Simon Co., a Washington research agency, showed that companies disguised illegal or improper payments (which the companies felt that they had to pay to get foreign business) in ways ranging from dummy invoices and inflated expense accounts to fictitious legal and consulting fees and phantom contributions to trade associations.[5] The Investor Responsibili-

---

[5] Judith Miller, "Study of Questionable Payments Accents Involvement of Officers," *The New York Times,* Feb. 15, 1978; Deborah Rankin, "Accounting Ruses Used in Disguising Dubious Payments," *The New York Times,* Feb. 27, 1978.

ty Research Center has reported numerous efforts by shareholders to get the annual meetings of corporations to adopt resolutions aimed at preventing further illegal or improper use of corporate funds for political purposes. Most of the resolutions have received insubstantial numbers of votes at the meetings, and none are known to have been approved by stockholders.[6] These resolutions have generally been opposed by management as unnecessary, but they have served to prod companies into adopting their own guidelines for political activity.

CODES OF ETHICS

In 1978 the Foundation of the Southwestern Graduate School of Banking, which is part of Southern Methodist University, reported the results of a survey of ethical-policy statements of corporations.[7] Of seventy-nine companies responding, only two said that they did not have a corporate code of ethics. The two, Crocker National Bank and Champion International Corporation, said that they believed there was no difference between corporate and personal ethics and no need for business codes of ethics because most people and corporations behaved properly.

Typical sections of business codes affecting politics prohibit slush funds and secret accounts and require clearance with the chief executive officer for the use of corporate funds for political purposes. (Although corporate funds may not be used in federal elections, twenty-one states permit their direct use in state and local elections, twenty-four prohibit direct corporate contributions, eight ban labor contributions, and five limit the amount of corporate, labor, or other group contributions. Those states which do not permit such groups to give directly do allow PAC activity on a voluntary basis.) The Allied Chemical Corporation's code, for example, states: "No numbered or secret bank account shall be maintained by or on behalf of the company, in the United States or in any other country, nor shall any other bank or other account be maintained which is not fully accounted for on the company's records and fully known and described to the company's auditors." The Coca-Cola Company's code declares: "No funds or assets of the company shall be used for political campaign contributions, even where permitted by law, without prior written approval of the general counsel of the Coca-Cola Company and prior written authorization of the chief operating officer."

---

6 "Corporate Involvement in U.S. Political Campaigns," Analysis C, Investor Responsibility Research Center, Washington, Feb. 23, 1976, pp. 1–4.

7 Working Paper for the Southwest Assembly on Corporate Ethics and Governance, June 9–11, 1978, prepared by the Foundation of the Southwestern Graduate School of Banking, Southern Methodist University, Dallas, Tex.

In commenting on the new corporate codes of ethics, Leonard Silk noted in *The New York Times:*

> The corporate reformation will be enduring only if statements of ethical standards are matched by the building of institutions and procedures within the corporation to insure that the standards are enforced. This will involve strengthening the independence and oversight powers of boards of directors and their audit committees. It will involve improving the flow of information to the board and up and down the organization. It will also require establishing oversight and review committees at different levels. Perhaps most important, it will mean supporting, encouraging and rewarding those individuals who express their own ethical values and who are willing to expose wrongdoing within the corporation, even when this is painful to the company's short-run financial interests.[8]

NEW CASES

One would have presumed that in light of the Watergate prosecutions most corporations and business executives would be extremely careful in the way in which they make campaign contributions, but a later generation of cases emerged. They were brought under the Federal Election Campaign Act[9] and were handled primarily by the newly created Federal Election Commission (FEC), which is charged with responsibility for civil violations of the act and thus shares election-law enforcement with the Department of Justice, whose jurisdiction extends to criminal violations. The FEC, unlike the Watergate Special Prosecutor, is an ongoing organization which will continue to investigate and prosecute violations of federal law, and it has a host of matters under review at all times. Many matters, including some alleged corporate violations, have been closed without further action, some have been settled with conciliation agreements, and others have resulted in findings of probable cause and decisions to prosecute.

Two matters which went the conciliation route in June 1978 involved the Committee for Jimmy Carter and the National Bank of Georgia. Carter's 1976 campaign committee arranged for his use of an airplane belonging to the National Bank of Georgia. The Bert Lance hearings revealed that the bank had never billed the committee for the flights and therefore had not

---

[8] Leonard Silk, "Economic Scene: Ethical Guides for Companies," *The New York Times,* June 15, 1978.

[9] Federal Election Campaign Act of 1971, 2 U.S.C., 431–454 (Supp. II, 1972; hereinafter cited as FECA); Federal Election Campaign Act Amendments of 1974, Pub. L. 93–443, 88 Stat. 1263 (codified in several titles of U.S.C.); Subtitle H, Internal Revenue Code of 1954, Int. Rev. Code of 1954, 9001–9042. "FECA" is used generally to describe the FECA of 1971 and its 1974, 1976, and 1979 amendments.

been paid until August 1977 (the matter was then under review), when a belated payment was made. The FEC found probable cause to believe that the flights constituted an in-kind contribution by the bank. The committee agreed to pay a fine of $1200, the approximate market value of the flights, and promised to avoid similar violations in the future. The bank, which had also arranged for flights by Democratic National Committee officials, agreed to pay a fine of $5000 and made a similar promise.[10]

Two other cases illustrate the range of matters handled recently by the FEC, from relatively minor, unintentional violations of the new and unsettled law to offenses of a much more serious nature. In the first of these, which was resolved through conciliation, the Okonite Company paid a small fine in a closely reasoned case decided on a narrow point of legal interpretation.[11] In the second, however, J. Ray McDermott & Co., the world's largest builder of offshore oil rigs, in February 1978 pleaded guilty to criminal charges of making two illegal campaign contributions to two members of Congress, one in 1974 and one in 1975, while Watergate-connected cases were in the news. The case, brought by the United States Attorney in New Orleans, also involved racketeering, bribery, and fraud charges, to which McDermott pleaded guilty. The company was fined $1 million on all charges.[12]

NEW LAWS

The rules and regulations involving corporate and union behavior in relation to political contributions and fund raising today are more precise than ever before. Paradoxically, they also sanction much greater freedom for both corporations and unions. The new laws and the regulations stemming from them evolved from legislation passed by Congress in 1971, 1974, and 1976 and from several key U.S. Supreme Court decisions during the 1970s. The laws and regulations are less ambiguous than the laws in effect prior to 1972.

The Federal Election Commission, a six-member bipartisan and independent agency, oversees the new election laws, issuing regulations and advisory

---

[10] Federal Election Commission, *In the Matter of Committee for Jimmy Carter,* June 21, 1978, *In the Matter of the National Bank of Georgia,* June 14, 1978, MUR 442 (1977), Conciliation Agreements.

[11] Federal Election Commission, *In the Matter of the Okonite Company,* General Counsel's Report, Dec. 17, 1976, MUR 200 (1976), MUR 213 (1976), p. 6; Conciliation Agreement, June 22, 1977, MUR 213 (1976), p. 3; "Corporation Fined for Funding Ad Praising Congressman in Campaign," *Campaign Practices Reports,* Aug. 22, 1977, p. 3.

[12] "McDermott Pleads Guilty to Fraud, Fined $1 Million," *The New York Times,* Feb. 23, 1978; "McDermott Staff Given Immunity," *The New York Times,* Feb. 24, 1978; "Legal Woes Beset McDermott on Merger's Eve," *The New York Times,* Feb. 27, 1978.

opinions that interpret them and publishing reports and analyses of political spending. All PACs must make detailed reports to the Commission.

The other major changes made by the legislation of the 1970s drastically limited individual and political committee contributions to presidential candidates and candidates for the Senate and the House of Representatives and spelled out specific rules under which PACs, relying only on voluntary contributions, could be operated by corporations, unions, and associations. Under the law an individual is limited to a $1000 contribution to a federal candidate in a campaign (primary or general election) and a total of $25,000 in political contributions relating to federal candidates during a calendar year. A PAC can contribute up to $5000 to a federal candidate in a single campaign, or a total of $10,000 in primary and general elections combined. No cash contributions in excess of $100 are allowed, and all contributions of more than $100 must be covered by a report providing the name, address, date, amount, occupation, and principal place of business, if any.

The legislation of the 1970s made no change in the long-standing but heretofore ill-enforced prohibitions against the use of corporate or union funds in federal elections. But one significant change was made: to permit use of the treasury funds of both corporations and unions to set up and administer a PAC and to solicit voluntary contributions to it. Regarding voluntary contributions, the law specifies that neither money nor anything of value may be secured by physical force, coercion, financial reprisal, or threats thereof; or as a condition of employment or membership in a union.

Company committees can seek contributions only from stockholders and executive and administrative personnel and their families. Labor union PACs can solicit contributions only from union members and their families. However, twice a year union and corporate PACs are permitted to seek contributions by mail only from all employees not otherwise available to them for solicitation. A trade association or its PAC can solicit contributions from stockholders and executive or administrative personnel or the association's member corporations if such solicitation is separately and specifically approved by the corporation, but a corporation cannot approve such solicitation by more than one trade association in any calendar year. The law also restricts the proliferation of membership organizations and corporate and union PACs. All PACs established by a company or an international union are treated as a single committee for contribution purposes. Most important, corporate, union, and association officials can determine how the money collected should be used within the limitations of the law. Some companies make certain, however, that their contributions are bipartisan. Others provide trustee arrangements whereby an employee can designate in confidence a candidate or party of his or her choice. The company conveniently offers payroll withholding of the amount and maintains the confidentiality of who gave how much to whom.

DEVELOPMENT OF PACS

For business executives, the potential of the PAC movement is the most important result of the reform legislation of the 1970s. By the autumn of 1978 a total of 821 corporate PACs were registered with the FEC. Registrations of trade associations, membership organizations, cooperatives, and corporations without public stock totaled 582. Some 281 labor union PACs were registered. The increase in corporate PACs has been dramatic, more than quintupling their number between 1974 and 1978.

In 1978 the PACs together raised $80.5 million and spent $77.8 million. Trade, membership, and health PACs led in direct contributions to federal candidates with $11.5 million. Labor PACs followed closely with $10.3 million, and corporate PACs contributed $9.8 million. More than 60 percent of corporate PAC money went to Republican candidates. In contrast, some 95 percent of labor PAC money went to Democrats. The two largest spenders among business association committees were the PACs of the National Association of Realtors, with $1.1 million contributed to federal candidates, and the National Automobile Dealers Association, with $975,675. Large contributors among corporate committees were those of the International Paper Co., with $173,056, and Standard Oil Co. (Indiana), with $154,800. Leading labor PACs were the United Automobile Workers, which contributed $964,465 to federal candidates, and the AFL-CIO's COPE, which gave $920,841.[13]

The number of corporate PACs is expected to continue to grow, a development that is filled with irony. Labor officials urged legislation beyond the rules for the establishment and operation of PACs, little realizing that it would become a cornerstone for political activity by business executives. A section of the law prohibited government contractors from making direct or indirect contributions. Because some labor unions had worker-training contracts, labor officials agreed with business lobbyists in 1974 to seek a relaxation and clarification of the law to permit government contractors to be treated in the same way as noncontracting corporations and unions. Thus the 1974 amendments permitted large defense and other contractors to use corporate funds for establishing and administering their PACs and for fundraising purposes, and many of the largest corporations in the United States have done so.

---

[13] Federal Election Commission, "FEC Releases Year-End 1978 Report on 1977–78 Financial Activity of Non-Party and Party Political Committees," press release, May 10, 1979.

Despite the restrictions in the 1976 amendments to the Federal Election Campaign Act and in the FEC's SUNPAC decision[14] implementing the corporate PAC aspects of the law, the corporate and trade association communities have demonstrated their ability to increase the number of PACs that they sponsor and the amounts that they raise and contribute to candidates. The Public Affairs Council, the National Association of Manufacturers, the Chamber of Commerce of the United States, the National Association of PACs, the Practising Law Institute, and others sponsor well-attended seminars on how to organize and administer PACs to make them effective. The business community watches over and lobbies regarding legislative activities that affect election law.

To some extent the PAC movement backfired on organizations such as Common Cause which had led the campaign for the enactment of the political reform legislation. The reformers had sought to reduce the influence of business, labor, and other organized groups in the electoral process, but the development of PACs as the principal vehicles for noncandidate political financing seems to be reinforcing the dominant roles in politics of organized economic interests. Partly as a result of the law, political fund-raising patterns are changing. To the extent that wealthy donors are now limited, focus is shifting to fund raisers who can organize and solicit interest groups. Thus, looking to the future, PACs and independent expenditures probably will become more important in the campaign process. The successful candidate increasingly will be the one who can predicate a campaign upon organized interest groups whose members can be mobilized as small contributors to the campaign, in addition to whatever help the groups' PACs may give. Corporations, trade associations, and unions have two inherent characteristics: large aggregates of people and internal means of communication, both of which are essential elements in effective solicitation. These are provided at no cost to the candidates and parties which benefit when contributions are made to them.

But there is still another twist to the PAC story. To the consternation of Republicans and conservative groups in general, considerable business PAC money has gone to liberal Democratic senators and representatives who are chairmen or members of key legislative committees and some of whom also receive funds from labor PACs. Corporate executives who are in charge of disbursing money from business PACs are practical, and they understand the power of committee chairmen and other members of Congress with seniority on important committees. They know the utility of access and goodwill derived at least in part from financial support. Critics say that some executives appear to be seeking to buy into the Democratic party, which controls both

---

14 Federal Election Commission, AOR 1975–23, published in *The Federal Register,* July 29, 1975 (40 F.R. 31879); revised in F.R. 75–32172, filed Dec. 2, 1975.

the White House and the Congress. This political pragmatism irritates Republican leaders and such business spokesmen as Fred Radewagen, director of governmental and political participation programs for the Chamber of Commerce of the United States, who say that business PACs should take more risks with their money. "They should contribute it," says Radewagen, "to worthy challengers who, given adequate financing, might be able to unseat nonbusiness-oriented incumbents in either primaries or general elections."[15] Such exhortations reflected reality when spoken in 1977 and early 1978 because Democrats led Republicans in receiving corporate PAC gifts at that time. Yet in both the 1976 and the 1978 elections Republicans received substantial contributions in the late general-election periods, and over the 2-year election cycles they received more money from business sources than did Democrats.

FUTURE TRENDS

Nothing is static in either business or politics, and there will continue to be pressures to change the law—to fine-tune it, if not to change it substantially. Common Cause and other reform groups will continue to press for public funding of congressional campaigns, but the defeat of such legislation in the Senate in 1977 and in the House of Representatives in 1978 and 1979 would seem to indicate that the extension of funding to congressional races is still remote despite President Carter's support of it. In addition, political reform movements tend to be cyclical. The current effort, which is a decade old, appears to be running out of momentum, and a backlash may well be in the making.

Further reforms, however, could stem from the growth of PACs. Edwin M. Epstein has posed a situation in which organized labor continues to contribute by way of its PACs and corporate and other business-related PACs match or exceed labor dollars. He says:

> [W]e may, arguably, be reaching a point where too much money is emanating from these sources. This would be particularly the case if their contributions proved to be redundant—supporting incumbents with little "risk capital" expended on challengers—thereby perpetuating the Congressional status quo.
>
> This projected avalanche of dollars is less a problem on the labor side given the realistic outer limits to union fund-raising capabilities[;] . . . such is not the case, however, on the business side. Arguably, among the greatest dangers facing the electoral system is the possibility that business firms may become too

---

15 John C. Perham, "Big Year for Company Political Action," *Dun's Review,* March 1978, pp. 100–105. See also *Congressional Quarterly;* "Big Business Remembers Democratic Candidates," *Christian Science Monitor,* May 5, 1978, p. 12; Walter Guzzardi, Jr., "Business Is Learning How to Win in Washington," *Fortune,* Mar. 27, 1978, pp. 52–58.

effective in their PAC formation and money-raising-dispensing activities. The possibility of 1500 PACs each contributing $75,000 ($112.5 million) to candidates is more than the electoral process can bear without at least the appearance if not the reality of contamination of the independence of the officials elected under it.[16]

Such developments may be well into the future. Rates of participation and amounts raised vary tremendously, some PACs producing few dollars and others relatively more. Results depend upon the degree of commitment of management, the extent of solicitation, the newness of the program, and the procedures used. Cynics say that those with higher returns must be exerting some pressure. But however much a single PAC raises, there is huge potential in the aggregate because most corporations have not yet established PACs. Their establishment could pose awesome problems if it occurs, given American attitudes towards so-called special-interest influence in the political process.

The growth of special-interest lobbying in Washington has already led to legislative efforts to require lobbyists to make more extensive reports on their activities. The lobbying law approved by Congress in 1946 required lobbyists to register only if their "principal purpose" was to try to influence legislation, and as a result few have registered or filed meaningful disclosures of their spending. Proposed legislation would strengthen the law and vest authority in the Comptroller General to administer and enforce it. Business groups have been opposed to the proposal, arguing that it would violate their constitutional rights to express their views. The American Civil Liberties Union also has opposed the legislation on First Amendment grounds. In 1978, at the request of Congress, the Internal Revenue Service reviewed its regulations involving the tax-exempt status of institutional advertising that some members of Congress consider to be grass-roots lobbying and thus not tax-deductible.[17]

Grass-roots lobbying by mail or by telephone networks has been used increasingly by both so-called special-interest and public-interest groups. It has become very sophisticated and at times is very effective. As restrictions on political campaign activity have been enacted and enforced, this weak link in the chain of influence in the decision-making process has been found and is being exploited.

Improved lobbying has resulted in part from the increased allocation of

---

16 Edwin M. Epstein, "The Rise of Political Action Committees," Colloquium Paper, Woodrow Wilson International Center for Scholars, Washington, June 15, 1978, pp. 86–88.

17 Steven V. Roberts, "Business Is Crying Havoc over New Lobbying Bill," *The New York Times,* May 7, 1978, p. 2F; Richard E. Cohen, "New Lobby Rules May Influence Grass-Roots Political Activity," *National Journal,* May 27, 1978, pp. 832–836; "The Swarming Lobbyists," *Time,* Aug. 7, 1978.

corporate resources to the public policy area. To replace the "bagmen" and the golf-playing lobbyists, some corporations now have policy-planning divisions staffed by people well trained to write position papers that decision makers should consider worth reading, to draft legislation, and to undertake future research into emerging issues. The posture is more issue-oriented than person-oriented and is an attempt to stake out positions that are defensible and public-spirited, not simply demands for more. Complementing a person-oriented PAC, a corporation thus seeks to relate its business concerns to the environment and society in which it operates.

There is danger, clearly, in our pluralistic society if groups are overly restricted in their political activity. The three most significant events of the last two decades—the civil rights movement, the Vietnam peace movement, and political reform—originated in the private sector, where the need for action was perceived and where the needed organization was accomplished to carry it out. Government reacted but did not initiate the activity, and government was part of the problem in each case. Hence, there is a strong case for the continued existence of interest groups, which are aggregations of like-minded people whose political power is enhanced by combining forces. Without groups, individuals in mass society are atomized and ineffectual. The First Amendment guarantees the right of association, and individuals take cues from groups with which they identify; the groups, in turn, are anxious to give them political guidance.

It is important, also, to retain some degree of private giving in the electoral system. For the citizen, the act of giving to the candidate or groups of his or her choice, even if only a small amount, instills a sense of participation in the political process. For the candidate, the need to meet with potential donors and solicit their contributions can provide a feedback on the concerns of the electorate that is both more immediate and more personal than that provided in many other campaign activities. This feedback tends to make candidates more attentive and government more responsive.

In this environment, the business community is learning political imperatives and the true meaning of competition in the political arena. At the same time that the business community seeks deregulation or lesser regulation in the economic sphere, it surely will pursue relaxation of government regulation of the political and electoral processes as well. But deregulation in the political sphere will come at a time when corporate political activity is increasing, triggering responses from labor, reformers, and others that may call for more, not less, government regulation of politics.

BUSINESS AND THE PRESS

MICHAEL C. JENSEN

*Michael C. Jensen has been economic affairs corre-
spondent for NBC News since mid-1978. He appears
regularly on the Nightly News with John Chancel-
lor, the Today Show, and Meet the Press. Before
joining NBC, Mr. Jensen was a financial reporter and
editor for* The New York Times *for 8½ years, and
before that he was an editor for the Boston Herald,
covering the business world. He has won numerous
awards for his investigative reporting of such matters as the Soviet grain deal, the energy crisis, the
inner workings of the International Telephone and
Telegraph Corporation, illegal contributions to
political campaigns by big business, and the financial
crisis of New York City.*

*A graduate of Harvard with a master's degree
from Boston University, Mr. Jensen has written for
such periodicals as the* Saturday Review, Harvard
Business Review, *and* Town and Country. *His first
book,* The Financiers *(1976), discussed the power of
investment bankers. He is working on a new book on
the tobacco industry.*

The newly elected board chairman of a large metal-fabricating company was giving one of his first press interviews since moving into his big new corner office. I had just asked him what, if anything, he would do differently from his predecessor (let's call him Fritz), who had retired a few months earlier. The answer: "The company will be run just as though Fritz was still sitting behind this desk. We have our policies, and they won't change." I scribbled his answer in my reporter's notebook.

At that moment one of the new chairman's top aides, looking perplexed, stepped into the office. "This situation has come up," he said, showing his boss some papers. "How do you want me to handle it?" The chairman took a fast look, then in a few words described what he wanted done. The aide looked at him questioningly. "You know," he said, pointing to one of the options he had presented, "Fritz usually did it this way." "Damn Fritz," said the new chairman. "I'm running this company now, and we'll do it my way."

The incident represents in unusually graphic fashion the difference between what business executives often tell the press and what they are really thinking or doing. The metals executive had blandly assured me that he would be following the policies of his predecessor. Then, apparently without considering or caring how the turnabout would look, he clearly indicated how hollow that statement had been.

What does this incident signify? A couple of things: first, my inquiry was naïve, and I try not to ask that sort of broad question anymore. More important, the response indicates a sort of mind-set that I have perceived on the part of business executives during interviews.

CORPORATE RESPONSES

On the basis of my years of reporting, I think it is fair to say that business executives seldom divulge to the media anything that doesn't suit their purposes. They usually evade tough questions or give bland answers. Many of them resent having to spend time giving interviews even when they acknowledge the necessity to do so. They often are scornful of the lack of knowledge of their companies and their industries that reporters display, usually with good cause. And they are hypersensitive to even the slightest criticism that finds its way into a published story about them or their companies.

Their attitude has not changed significantly during the time I have worked at the *Boston Herald* as a business reporter and as financial editor (in the early 1960s); as editor of a daily trade newspaper, *American Metal Market* (in the mid-1960s); for 8½ years as a business and financial reporter and sometime editor at *The New York Times;* and since 1978 as an economic affairs correspondent for NBC News. If anything, now in the post-Watergate era, when journalists are busily scurrying around the world investigating anything that seems even remotely scandalous, business executives' attitudes toward the press have become even more skeptical and hostile.

Clearly, some corporations and some executives are more receptive to the press than others. In that regard, I will discuss corporate responses ranging from cooperation to obfuscation to evasion to lying. First, however, I'd like to make some general observations about business executives and their relations with the press.

Increasingly, business reporting is being handled by journalists who apply the same standards that have traditionally characterized political reporting. Press releases are no longer being accepted at face value. Motives are being scrutinized. Performance is being weighed against both promises and the public interest as best it can be perceived. Contrary views are being sought. In short, a critical standard is being applied to business and financial reporting to a degree not often found in the past.

What does that mean to business executives? First, it is uncomfortable because it is new. For politicians, criticism is old-hat. From the time when they first run for office, they are criticized—by the opposing candidates, by the opposition party, by the press. Some of the criticism is fair, some unfair, some accurate, some inaccurate, but politicians learn to live with it. It becomes part of the game; they must respond to it.

But what about business executives? Many of them have never experienced public criticism. Stress the word "public." A chief executive who has reached the top of a large company obviously has survived a tough, competitive battle. But dealings with the press, for the most part, have been confined to relatively soft encounters with the trade press or the local media. The stories that have resulted have generally been flattering and often have been cleared, word for word, by the publications in advance.

Suddenly in a different position, the new chief executive of a major company is matching wits with reporters from the country's leading newspapers and newsmagazines for the first time. These reporters are not always better informed than their counterparts in the trade or local press, but they are usually feistier, more independent, more critical, and more willing to take the time to dig up negative facts as well as positive ones. The resulting articles and profiles often present a side of the executive and the company that both would prefer go unreported. Perhaps a new product line isn't making it, government pollution regulations are being violated, or executive perquisites are proliferating. Maybe the executive has a reputation as a martinet, has formed a profitable sideline company that has contracts with the corporation, or is using the company plane for personal trips with the family. That's all grist for the enterprising reporter.

Where does the reporter stop? That varies enormously according to persistence, judgments as to newsworthiness, and sometimes sense of good taste.

An example: several years ago, I was researching a major piece on a large advertising agency that was having serious earnings problems and was losing big accounts. I looked carefully into the background and operating style of the chief executive and came across a curious fact. At about the time when he entered the communications business he changed his name. Shedding a funny-sounding family name, he took a flashy show-business name. What to do? Clearly, this information would be interesting to readers. It had never been printed. It was true (the executive confirmed it during an interview). But was it relevant? Ultimately, I decided against using it. Although it would have been widely read and certainly gossiped about, it was not important to the story.

As it was, I already planned to call attention to the company's poor performance, but the chairman's name change was hardly important to the running of the company. If he had been a heavy drug user or an alcoholic, that would have been relevant. But I decided that disclosure of the name change would cause him and his family considerable anguish without advancing the story. So I didn't use it.

In other instances, however, I have used material that has been distressing to the executive in question. When I wrote about André Meyer of Lazard Frères & Co., for example, I mentioned that he had close links with the Kennedy family and was said to have drawn up Jacqueline Kennedy's marriage contract with Aristotle Onassis. I also told about the vitamin shots he took to bolster his health. That's not the sort of material that is ordinarily found in a business story, but it seemed relevant. Meyer's advanced age, in particular, and consequently his health were important factors in any assessment of his investment banking firm.

PREPARING FOR AN INTERVIEW

Over the years, I have observed an inverse relationship between the critical nature of the questions asked of a company and the company's willingness to provide answers. That's not surprising, but it's worth stating.

For example, if I want to know about a company's new products, its contributions to charities, or the outside directorships held by its president, all I have to do is call its public relations department. An inch-thick packet of material will be on my desk within hours. But if I want to know why the president has suddenly and unexpectedly resigned, why a seemingly profitable product has abruptly been withdrawn from the market, or why company executives have contributed so much to the campaign of a particular politician, the flow of information dries up.

That's why I have learned to go into interviews loaded for bear. Before I approach a company, I follow a predictable route. First comes a research phase. That consists of obtaining from the research library every story that has been written about the company and its officials in the *Times* or in other newspapers and magazines. If books have been written about the company recently, I read those too.

Next comes the preliminary reporting phase. In effect, I am working my way from the periphery toward the object of the story. I call securities analysts on Wall Street, former executives of the company, competitors, labor unions, and suppliers—anyone who knows about the company and will talk to me. Sometimes the discussions are off the record, sometimes they can be quoted (though not always for attribution), and sometimes they are fully on the record.

During this phase, I find out such things as the operating style of top executives: whether they are martinets or gentle prodders and how they get things done. I learn which products were disasters and how they got that way. I find out which Securities and Exchange Commission (SEC) actions were most painful and whether the company has been in serious trouble with the Federal Trade Commission (FTC). I check to see whether the company's profit margins are in line with those of the rest of the industry. In the meantime, I study the company's proxy statement, its annual report, and various SEC documents such as Form 8-K and Form 10-K. Sometimes I look at documents which specify how much of the company's stock its officers have bought and sold.

Drawing on this information, I decide what questions I want to ask during interviews with the company's executives. In some instances, I am looking for confirmation of material that I have dredged up elsewhere. Sometimes, I simply want to give individuals a chance to comment on allegations that have been made.

In most cases, failure to do that sort of homework results in bland, almost useless interviews. But even thorough research is no guarantee. Some time ago I interviewed J. Paul Austin of the Coca-Cola Company, a longtime friend of Jimmy Carter. I had done considerable research and asked Austin one question after another about his relationship with the President. Even faced with information about specific meetings with the President, he refused to respond. From my point of view, however, such an interview at least gives an executive a chance to set the record straight. I have learned to hold back on probing questions until an interview is almost over, because when the questions get tough, you can be sure that interview time will run out quickly.

Sometimes companies find it desirable to mislead journalists. One case in point: a few years ago, I learned that the International Telephone and Telegraph Corporation (ITT) was about to name a new president. Harold S. Geneen had been serving as both chairman and president but had been under pressure from Wall Street to name a successor. I called ITT and told a public relations official that I was writing a story, to appear the following morning in the *Times,* identifying the new president. At first the official denied any knowledge of such a development. He then said that he had in front of him the agenda for the directors' meeting the following day but that it included nothing about a new president. I said that we still were going to run the story. He then asked for a personal meeting. When I agreed, he rushed over to the *Times* and offered to give me an exclusive story about a pending divestiture if I would hold the story about the new president (which, as it turned out, was to be announced with great fanfare the following day, complete with press kits, biographies, and photographs). I said that I would be happy to accept the information about the divestiture and that we would run the two stories side by side. The public relations man left in a huff.

EFFECTIVE REPORTING AND CORPORATE PUBLIC RELATIONS

One of the keys to effective business reporting is access, and access to corporate executives depends mainly on two factors. First is the relative clout of the news organization that the reporter represents. When I was the editor of *American Metal Market,* a relatively small trade paper, it took me months to set up interviews with the heads of such powerful corporations as Bethlehem Steel Corp. From my desk at the National Broadcasting Company it takes only hours, sometimes minutes.

The second important factor is the relationship that a reporter has built up over the years with particular executives. Here are two extremes. During the early 1970s, I wrote story after story about ITT, which was then being buffeted by a series of scandals. During that period, Chairman Geneen never granted me an interview even though I made repeated requests. Word was passed to me that he believed he wouldn't get fair treatment. On the other side of the coin are executives like the late Edgar B. Speer, chairman of United States Steel Corp., and Irving Shapiro, head of E. I. du Pont de Nemours & Co. In most instances, all I had to do was pick up the telephone and talk to either of them in person. With Speer, that was because of the fact that we had had many interviews over the years. He apparently felt comfortable with the way his remarks to me appeared in the *Times.* As for Shapiro, he is one of the most articulate and accessible chief executives in the country. He is comfortable with the press and knows how to deal with it. Consequently, he does both his own company and big corporations in general a lot of good.

A word about how many reporters perceive themselves will probably help business executives to understand them better. Most seasoned journalists believe that they have an obligation to get at the truth. More than that, they think that they operate in the public interest, as a sort of surrogate. (Business executives do too, of course. Business is at the heart of our democratic-capitalistic system. It provides jobs, and it produces the goods and services that have made the United States economy the wonder of the twentieth century. As a journalist, I recognize that fact and want to preserve business's status.)

Many reporters subscribe to a credo that goes like this: "The role of a newspaper is to print the news and raise hell." This credo translates into printing the bad as well as the good: in business reporting, corporate problems as well as success stories.

But what happens to the flow of information when problems arise? Most companies withdraw into their shells, often offering a string of "No comments." In my opinion that's a mistake. Most responsible reporters feel an obligation to print both sides of a story. Even though companies complain that their side (when it's offered) is buried in the twelfth paragraph, at least it is printed. And it isn't always buried. The alternative for business executives is to remain silent and have their views go unreported.

Executives complain about the amount of publicity that Ralph Nader and other consumer advocates get. It's true that these advocates receive enormous amounts of publicity, probably inordinate amounts. But that's partly due to the fact that they have learned how to deal with the press. They usually provide credible information, and they are accessible.

Another important factor in business-media relations is the corporate public relations department. In a few companies, the top public relations official is a member of the policy-making team that runs the company. More often, he is a notch or two below that level but still has the power to deliver top executives when asked. At many companies, however, the public relations official is simply a minor functionary without the authority to speak for top executives or the ability to produce them.

Some of the best public relations officers, in my experience, are at big financial institutions like Citicorp and Merrill Lynch & Co. They know what they are talking about, and even when the stories involved are negative, they still produce an appropriate executive or comment quickly. I have found that some of the least responsive public relations officers are at the big automobile companies and the oil companies (Exxon Corporation is an exception). Even with huge public relations bureaucracies, these companies often take days to respond to simple inquiries. More often than not, their answer is that there is no answer.

ADVICE TO CORPORATIONS

Specifically, what does a journalist expect, or at least hope for, from a corporation? If 100 reporters were asked to provide a list, there would be 100 different answers. But here is what I would like corporations to do:

1. *Acknowledge that the mind-set of reporters is and should be different from that of business executives.* This advice seems so obvious that it almost shouldn't be stated. But time after time I have heard business executives ask, "Whose side are you on?" The answer is "Nobody's."

2. *Grant access to decision-making executives.* That's not as easy as it sounds. Executives are busy people, and they often are uneasy with the press. Many have been stung in the past. Some are wary of the "Mike Wallace treatment": a microphone stuck under the nose. Documents are suddenly produced. A "Do you mean to tell me . . .?" type of question follows. The concern of these executives is understandable, but there is no substitute for having the chief executive available for interviews. In most corporations the chief executive is the only one with both the authority and the information to answer sensitive questions. The success of such interviews presupposes that the reporter has done his or her homework and will not be wasting the president's time with elementary questions that could be answered by a lower-ranking official.

3. *Be candid or at least honest.* Clearly, a company is not going to bare its soul to every inquisitive reporter who comes along. The reporter must recognize that a corporation's officials are paid to earn a profit for their shareholders, not to offer details of their successes or failures to newspaper or television reporters. Still, it seems to me that there are times when candor can serve a useful purpose. In an open, democratic society, built on the public's right to know, corporations can hardly expect to be bastions of secrecy. And while no corporation can be expected to divulge its trade secrets, an open discussion with a well-informed reporter is not likely to hurt it. As for honesty, even a "No comment" is preferable to a lie. And as we have learned over the last few years, following hundreds of disclosures of corporate slush funds and illegal payoffs, corporations are capable of acting illegally and then lying about their actions. Cover-ups are not confined to the political arena.

4. *Avoid trying to buy the friendship of the press.* Times have changed. Most journalists today are relatively well paid, at least by former standards. Many not only don't want the bottle of scotch that companies send out at Christmas, they are offended by it. That's not universally true, of course. Many companies still have a list of reporters who walk around with their hands out, but most would admit that the list is shrinking. Increasingly,

reporters are looking for access and candor rather than a free lunch. So don't make the mistake of trying to buy their friendship.

5.   *Learn what motivates the press.* In 1978 the Ford Foundation sponsored a 3-day seminar at Princeton that was attended by more than a dozen of the nation's top business executives. At a horseshoe-shaped table, they debated with reporters, editors, and publishers of some of the country's leading newspapers, magazines, and television networks. Did they learn to love one another? Hardly. But they began to learn what makes the other side tick, and they aired some of their differences. That's important. Business executives spend years learning about marketing, finance, production, and research and development, but in an age in which relationships with the media are more important than ever little has been done to educate them in that area.

6.   *Treat reporters as professionals.* They may not know much about your business, but they know a lot about their own or they wouldn't be interviewing you. Don't write them off as fools because they don't understand the intricacies of corporate tax procedures or the Eurodollar market. Your patience in explaining such matters will work to your advantage when stories appear.

Having made these points, I admit that the advice is largely self-serving. Clearly, there are times when a corporation simply doesn't want to talk— when it is better served by keeping its corporate mouth shut and facing the consequences. There are also times when it finds itself dealing with uninformed reporters or, worse, with reporters whose biases are so strong that nothing that business executives say is likely to alter the preconceptions or misconceptions that the reporters bring to the story. Finally, some reporters combine an arrogance and an ignorance so powerful that they can only poison the atmosphere for other journalists.

ADVICE TO REPORTERS

Having offered advice to corporations, I'd like to do the same for business reporters or for generalists in the media who find themselves dealing with corporations.

1.   *Bone up on the subject.* Elementary advice? Of course it is, but we often fail to heed it. Naturally, research is not always possible. Not every paper is *The New York Times* or *The Wall Street Journal,* with a large staff of specialists and days, sometimes weeks, to work on a story. Too often an editor sends a reporter off to a corporation's suite with no more than a press release as background. And the reporter is expected to ask cogent, penetrating questions.

But usually there is time for the reporter to check the clipping files. And he or she can often make a phone call or two—to a securities analyst or the editor of a trade paper who follows the company or the industry closely. If there is time, the SEC public files can be checked. And the reporter can certainly read the company's proxy statement and, it is hoped, the footnotes of its annual report. When I started out as a business reporter nearly two decades ago, I didn't even know that the salaries and stock options of top corporate executives were routinely listed in proxy statements. It's all in knowing where to look.

2. *Don't go in with a chip on your shoulder.* Be prepared to listen to the company's side of the story. Ralph Nader and the Sierra Club aren't always right, and the company isn't always trying to pull the wool over your eyes. You earn your pay by trying to decide who is dissembling.

3. *In any event, give the company a chance to comment.* My rule is that the subjects of my stories should never be surprised by what they find when they pick up the paper or turn on the television set. They may be unhappy but not surprised. That's true because I have told them in advance what's coming and invited them to comment. Sometimes they do, and sometimes they don't. That's their choice, but at least they know what's coming.

4. *Don't be intimidated.* Big companies are usually well connected. Not only can they threaten to cut you off from future information, but they can try to damage your reputation as a journalist. They can write letters complaining about you to your editor and publisher. They can try to discredit your stories, especially if these are tough and critical. They can attempt to discover and harass your sources. They can issue press releases denouncing you.

Some reporters find all that hard to take. A few cave in and content themselves with writing pap. That doesn't serve anybody's purpose.

5. *Get it right. And if you don't, run a correction.* Again, both of these pieces of advice are so obvious that they should not have to be stated. But they do. Don't take chances with facts and people's reputations. If you have the goods, print the information, but do your job responsibly and carefully. If you get the story wrong and a company can demonstrate that you have, print a correction. It's the only way to keep your credibility. If this sort of thing happens often, find another occupation. You don't belong in journalism. But remember that everybody makes mistakes occasionally, and it's no sin to admit them.

FUTURE TRENDS

What of the future? Is there hope that the relationship between business and the media, now so stormy, will become more serene? Or are the two destined to remain combatants?

My view is that a rapprochement is still far away. On the media side, there is growing recognition that business and economics are important subjects and that they deserve comprehensive treatment. That means that money must be spent to hire competent reporters and editors and that specialists in those fields must be developed. It means that more space in newspapers and more air time in television broadcasting must be devoted to business.

On the business side, there is growing recognition of the power of the media and of the interest of the press in business and finance. But for the most part there is still no well-defined *modus operandi* for dealing with the press.

The relationship between the press and business has yet to pass through the sort of storm front that characterized the black movement in the 1960s and the women's movement in the 1970s. But there is a growing awareness in the media that big business is more than just an amalgam of products and annual reports. Increasingly, we perceive big business as one of the dominant factors in the quality of life in the United States—as a center of power, political, economic, and social. That means that the intensity and, it is hoped, the caliber of coverage will grow, probably in quantum leaps. Business should be preparing for that growth.

VOLUNTARY DISCLOSURE

An Idea Whose Time Has Come

A. W. CLAUSEN

A. W. Clausen is the president and chief executive officer of BankAmerica Corporation and its wholly owned subsidiary, the Bank of America, NT&SA. Headquartered in San Francisco, it is the world's largest privately owned financial institution. He was educated at Carthage College and the University of Minnesota Law School. Mr. Clausen has been associated with the Bank of America since 1949, having held positions in Los Angeles and at the world headquarters of the bank in San Francisco before his election as president in 1969.

Mr. Clausen is a director of SRI International, the U.S.-U.S.S.R. Trade and Economic Council, and the National Council for United States–China Trade. He serves as cochairman of the Japan-California Association and is also a member of the Business Council, the California Roundtable, and the California Bar Association.

Disclosure, in the context of corporate operations, has historically been a peripheral consideration to a company's basic business activities. First the company acted; then its actions were either disclosed or not disclosed. However, because of social, political, and economic trends, the last half of the twentieth century has brought a maturing concept of corporate social responsibility and a lengthening ledger of corporate accountability. Reports of attractive revenue and income trends no longer ensure that a corporation or an industry will be favorably evaluated by shareholders, government, or the public in general. There is intense new interest in corporate policies, practices, and actual performance both within and outside the context of profit making.

John deButts, chairman of the American Telephone & Telegraph Co., has said that business can best demonstrate its accountability "by adopting a sufficient openness to public inquiry—and a sufficient readiness to respond to public challenge—to make it clear that we recognize that what once we might have been disposed to call 'our' business is in fact the public's business and that the public, having a stake in our decisions, should have a voice in them as well."[1]

In short, public pressures to know more reflect the increased power and responsibilities of business. Corporate leaders can respond to these new pressures essentially in three ways:

● They can strongly resist these demands, fighting at every opportunity the inevitable proposals for either mandatory disclosure or substantive regulation.

● They can use delaying tactics, "leaning against the wind," in the hope of retarding the spread of disclosure requirements.

● They can respond to and even anticipate these pressures, moving ahead of, and possibly obviating the need for, mandatory reporting requirements with voluntary disclosure programs.

THE LOGIC OF VOLUNTARY DISCLOSURE

At BankAmerica Corporation we have opted for the third alternative, and I would like to expand on the conceptual framework for our position, in the belief that our deliberations and experience may help others to address this issue. Voluntary disclosure is difficult to discuss, both because it is a relatively new idea and because many business executives understandably associate the very word "disclosure" with regulatory interference and sometimes with ill-conceived compulsory disclosure requirements. But neither its novelty

---

[1] Address before the Union League of Philadelphia, *Management Journal,* Pacific Telephone & Telegraph Co., San Francisco, November 1976, p. 3.

nor the shadow of undue regulation should prevent voluntary disclosure from being carefully examined as a device which modern management can use in pursuit of an efficient corporate performance that is responsive and accountable in a manner consistent with the public interest. Within this context, the philosophical underpinnings for our position are deceptively simple.

Indeed, if the function of corporate management and governance is to achieve efficient operation in a responsive and accountable manner consistent with the public interest, then disclosure can be seen to have a substantive quality itself. For a company's actions simply cannot be judged "efficient," "responsive," "accountable," or "consistent with the public interest" unless sufficient information is available.

Viewed this way, disclosure becomes a formal corporate function, one which can, like other functions, be embodied in a policy, and that policy can be enunciated, implemented, monitored, evaluated, and reviewed. Such a policy can also be administered in coordination with other corporate objectives. The alternative form of disclosure is usually a series of improvised and often negative responses to external pressures.

While all companies have had to consider the general subject of disclosure and while many have agreed on informal or partial policies in this area, few have undertaken a comprehensive study or tried to articulate broad policy. Consequently, there has been little research or discussion concerning voluntary disclosure. Nevertheless, there are encouraging signs that, overall, the concept of voluntary corporate disclosure may be an idea whose time has come.

Certainly, the interest in corporate affairs on the part of the public and constituent groups cannot be ignored, nor, I think, do most corporate managers and board members believe that it should be ignored. There appears to be a growing recognition among business leaders that exercising corporate social responsibility is an effective and productive means of dealing with important problems. The antibusiness sentiment that flowered in the 1960s, particularly among this nation's youth, has made clear to many in the business community that the future of the private-enterprise system is assured only to the extent that the performance of business is judged favorably within the context of society as a whole.

The rationale for voluntary disclosure can be further delineated by examining three important ways in which it can help business earn the favorable judgment of our society: (1) by building and maintaining public support; (2) by focusing closer attention on internal methods and controls; and (3) by allowing the market system, upon which our capital economy is based, to function in a more efficient manner.

PUBLIC SUPPORT

In the long run, no company can thrive unless it has the understanding and trust of all those whose interests it serves: customers, investors, employees, and the public. A business is unlikely to secure and retain that trust if it treats its various constituencies as captive audiences which are entitled to very limited and slanted disclosure of information. If these constituencies believe that they lack necessary information to judge the adequacy of the company's performance by their standards and values, they will withdraw their support. Such a response was quite evident during the 1960s and early 1970s. Public confidence in the integrity of business underwent a massive erosion.

When we began drafting our voluntary disclosure code in 1976, we recognized that to reduce this skepticism and antagonism we and other enterprises had to initiate strong and specific measures to show clearly that we were serious about our integrity and about the way we employed it in our day-to-day business activities. I believed then, as I do today, that disclosure, by exposing a greater number of corporate activities to public examination, can enhance the climate for business and dispel public doubts and fears.

BENEFITS TO INTERNAL
OPERATIONS

The internal benefits of a disclosure code are numerous and important. First, the process of developing such a code demands that management explicitly determine where the corporation should be on the disclosure spectrum, from "None of your business" to "Everything you always wanted to know but were afraid to ask." Then management must address the question of what information an outsider needs for thorough understanding. It must also communicate with its various constituencies to determine what information they desire; if handled properly, this effort will initiate relationships which can provide essential information to management on a continuing basis. Another useful by-product is that some existing policies and practices which have not been evaluated for years are inevitably modernized. In our own case, the BankAmerica task force brought about a number of innovations. New information had to be released. Existing internal policies had to be articulated in different and more comprehensible ways. Among disclosure items specified in the code are, for example, the corporation's direct expenditures for all government relations programs and the criteria and procedures for selecting new members to the board of directors.

If the disclosure code is well conceived, it will provide additional benefits when it is in operation. No large organization can be sure that its system of delegating responsibility and authority will unfailingly produce action by its employees that is entirely consistent with its standards and objectives. Not even the soundest organizational structure, auditing procedures, and declarations of policy are entirely sufficient. Thorough disclosure brings more eyes to bear, internally and externally, on the same information, and the right questions are more likely to be raised. In addition, we believe that such disclosure can be a powerful deterrent to wrongdoing and can also bring timely attention to ineptitude.

In sum, a thorough system of disclosure exerts a favorable influence on corporate behavior.

DISCIPLINE OF THE MARKET VERSUS REGULATION

We also view voluntary disclosure as a reaffirmation of our belief that the best regulator of business is the marketplace. Logically, those who believe in the market system have an obligation to make it work.

Better disclosure practices can help to discourage misguided legislation and regulation by providing a positive response to genuine information needs before they are made the excuse for increased interference with business. Probably most important, strong commitments to disclosure in corporate governance not only can avert or temper restrictive regulation but can strengthen dependence on market mechanisms, rather than authoritarian controls, as the central means for the guidance of society.

The essence of a market system is its reliance on well-informed participants rather than centralized authority for allocative decisions. The best way to preserve that market system is to demonstrate that, given adequate distribution of information, the market system generally is far preferable to any system of regulation, direct or indirect.

As one who believes in the effectiveness of the free market system, I consider voluntary disclosure a much more desirable road to travel than disclosure that has been mandated by legislation or regulation because of public outcries. If the market economy is ever disregarded, we can be sure that our favorite villains—socialist economies and government regulators—won't be to blame. Business leaders themselves will be to blame for having lost touch with their *raison d'être:* meeting the needs of their constituencies.

HOW TO FORMULATE A DISCLOSURE PLAN

The decision to inaugurate a disciplined and systematized approach to voluntary disclosure leads to the next step: the formulation of such a system, or code, to guide disclosure practices and to inform the public of what is available. I cannot offer the contents of BankAmerica's voluntary disclosure code as a model to be followed by other corporations. Companies in different industries and even in various areas of banking and finance would be best served by codes uniquely suited to their own circumstances. In addition, the process of designing a code is a valuable exercise in itself. However, some discussion of our own methodology may be instructive.

The spectrum of corporate disclosure practice ranges between two extremes—from tight security to opening all corporate books for scrutiny. One extreme is merely a public relations exercise calculated to hide blemishes; the other involves an abdication of management responsibility for maintaining necessary privacy, confidentiality, and effective operations.

Our guiding principle in formulating BankAmerica's disclosure policy was that the corporation's various constituencies (customers, investors, employees, and anyone concerned with its activities) are entitled, within reasonable limits, to have available the information that *they* think *they* need to judge its activities by *their* standards.

Such a statement may not seem to be controversial, but it contains two ideas which represent departures from conventional corporate practice.

The first is the importance placed on what the constituencies want to know rather than on what the corporation wants to tell them. It is quite understandable that, focusing on the achievement of its objectives, a company tends to harness its communication efforts in pursuit of its own ends. But such an attitude invites violation of an elementary rule of communication: the need to put oneself in the audience's place, to understand its frame of reference and relate to its interests.

The second departure is in giving the constituencies' right to know prior recognition, in relation to limits, or constraints, on disclosure, some of which, of course, are necessary. In common practice, the burden is put on the audience to ask for information and to justify its request.

In our view, a voluntary disclosure code reverses this practice. The company's response is no longer "Why should we tell you that?" but a self-imposed obligation either to provide the information or to explain why not, by citing one of the recognized constraints, such as violation of the privacy of others.

We recognized that each of the constituencies (which can, of course, be further subdivided) has a set of expectations and standards for the sufficiency of information. These requirements are sometimes overlapping and sometimes mutually exclusive, even in conflict. But the goal in formulating our disclosure policy was, within limits, to give each constituency that information which it said it needed to judge the company's performance.

We also recognized that no disclosure policy would please everyone. But if the needs of major constituencies have been considered in the process of developing a disclosure policy, the final product will be useful and should be regarded as an important step forward.

DEFINING CONSTITUENCIES AND CONSTRAINTS

Within this framework, we focused first on defining constituencies and constraints. In this context, we defined constituencies as those groups with a reasonable interest in information about the corporation: shareholders, employees, customers, the investment community and security analysts, economists, legislators, regulatory bodies, and financial journalists.

Our study of disclosure as a management tool focused on how disclosure policies could contribute to the strengthening of the relationships between the corporation and its various constituencies. Existing disclosure practices, that is, the ways in which corporate information was made available to the various audiences, were analyzed to determine how each contributed to satisfying the constituencies' need to know and how each was limited by other corporate obligations. An understanding of the interrelationship of a company's obligations to its constituencies can help illuminate the confused debate over social responsibility, which tends to suggest that profit and social responsibility are incompatible whereas, in the long run, they are but separate phases of a basic requirement of responsiveness and accountability.

The legitimate limits, or constraints, on disclosure arise from the corporation's relationships with and varying responsibilities toward its constituencies. Its need for openness, for example, cannot infringe the rights to privacy of its customers or employees; its need to perform efficiently for investors, employees, and the public cannot be compromised by the disclosure of competitive information essential to its successful functioning. There are trade-offs in the area of disclosure which each corporation will assess in formulating its policies.

As might be expected, providing the necessary constraints on the corporation's disclosure policy was a crucial challenge in the formulation process. We wanted to provide the maximum amount of meaningful information without violating the privacy rights of customers and employees and without giving competitors costly advantages. Following extensive discussion and evaluation, the limitations of the disclosure code were spelled out as a set of five specific constraints:

1. *Privacy.* Since the disclosure must not violate the privacy rights of individuals or institutions, the corporation will not disclose information about individual customers or employees without their permission. The corpora-

tion will not provide aggregate data which might indirectly provide information that can be identified with a specific person or entity.

2.   *Confidentiality.* The corporation will not disclose information that, if published, might impair its own effectiveness or harm its competitive position. To preserve necessary candor in internal and external communications, the corporation reserves the right to decide the extent and form of its distribution of information.

3.   *Subjectivity.* The corporation cannot disclose speculative or judgmental material that might, especially out of context, induce unwarranted effects, such as speculation in publicly traded securities.

4.   *Proper presentation.* The corporation cannot disclose material in formats that invite misinterpretation due to oversimplification, presentation of irrelevant facts, or inadequate documentation.

5.   *Usefulness.* The corporation will disclose information only when usefulness justifies the expense of providing it. The corporation usually will decline to disclose specialized new information that involves extraordinary assembly costs.

The constraints were not intended to deter anyone from seeking information, merely to explain more clearly the necessary limits of the voluntary disclosure policy.

Another challenge was deciding on an appropriate format and content for a code. In our view, to be credible the disclosure code needed a degree of specificity, but too many specifics would make the document unwieldy and probably useless to many interested people. Another format consideration was organization of the code so that an intelligent, interested reader could understand both the philosophy of the corporation's disclosure policy and how to use the information within the code.

When the details of the code had been hammered out, the body of the BankAmerica document codified seventy separate categories of information regularly open to public gaze. These seventy categories represent only starting points, the items that the task force and its constituent consultants considered most material and relevant in judging corporate attitudes and performance.

EXPERIENCE WITH THE CODE

Upon publication of the disclosure code, BankAmerica assigned a full-time disclosure coordinator to supervise its administration. The coordinator, in addition to distributing more than 80,000 copies of the code to the public and the bank's constituencies, has acted as a sort of resource of last resort for people unable to obtain desired information through regular bank or corporate channels.

Our experience, virtually all of it positive and pleasing, has provided a few unexpected developments. For example, we have received surprisingly little new interest from consumer groups and less than expected interest from our own employees. Of course, as disclosure becomes a more generally accepted routine, with more information now integrated in our financial reports, proxy statements, branch-office lobby displays, and employee communications, there is less necessity to request supplemental disclosure.

Regardless of these indications of success, it is difficult to be assured that the form as well as the content of our reporting is always useful to the recipients. There are no established precedents for some categories of data. There are too many for others. BankAmerica's original voluntary disclosure code, published in 1976, was revised at the end of 1978 and now contains an improved index and additional pointers on locating desired data. Our code will probably never be totally satisfactory because it is aimed at a moving target: the information needs of the public and our various constituencies.

While I freely admit that voluntary disclosure is no panacea and that any disclosure code will be at best imperfect and subject to revision, I remain convinced that a steady flow of timely information permits healthy public judgments concerning not only how well a corporation does its job but whether it is doing the right job at all. In the final analysis, I believe that the future of the private-enterprise system is best assured by heeding the words of Sophocles: "The truth," he wrote, "is always the strongest argument."

CORPORATE POLITICAL RESPONSIBILITY

L. WILLIAM SEIDMAN

L. William Seidman is senior vice president and director of the Phelps Dodge Corporation, one of the world's leading producers of copper and other minerals. He was educated at Dartmouth College, Harvard Law School, and the University of Michigan. Mr. Seidman served as Assistant to the President (Gerald R. Ford) for Economic Affairs and was Executive Director of the Economic Policy Board between 1974 and 1977. Between 1969 and 1974 he was national managing partner of Seidman and Seidman, a firm of certified public accountants.

For most of United States corporate history, organized political activity by corporate management was considered to be unwise and perhaps unethical. Corporate management was to be nonpartisan and nonparticipatory. Since stockholders and employees were surely well represented in political parties and on all sides of any issues, management, as their elected representative, was to stay out of political controversy.

Unfortunately, some of those who refused to assume a neutral position became participants under the table rather than on top of it. Illegal political contributions were widespread. Too much corporate political activity was of an unauthorized, behind-the-scenes variety. When revealed, this activity created a popular perception of big business as politically organized and effective. In fact, political activity usually was limited to individual efforts. Relatively few corporate managements operated in the political arena in an organized and public way.

POLITICAL ACTIVITY
AS A SOCIAL DUTY

Today's political activism is changing the attitude of the business world. Corporate political activity is more than accepted: it is required. Corporate management's duty to be active politically is, and should be, a vital part of overall corporate social responsibility.

Much has been written about a corporation's social duty to be a good citizen. It has, for example, an obligation to support charitable causes and the arts, employ and promote the welfare of the handicapped and members of minority groups, educate the economically illiterate, protect the environment, improve community facilities, conserve energy, encourage employee safety, sell government bonds, protect endangered species, and perform other good works. These types of social duties are taken for granted as the obligation of corporate managers and directors. Also taken for granted by management and by most other observers is the sometimes nearly incidental responsibility to earn a fair return on equity investment, operate efficiently in allocating resources, pay living wages to employees, and produce goods useful to society.

The new social responsibility to be a good political participant and citizen is not yet fully defined. The law sets rules for the use of corporate funds for political contributions and for the establishment of political action committees (PACs) to give money to politicians. There are numerous admonitions concerning forbidden political action but relatively few recommendations for activity. Yet in this day of political activism, a primary duty of those responsible for a business is to assert political views in the most skillful and forceful way that the law allows.

Labor, environmentalist, socialist, welfarist, consumerist, and racial groups all compete for a place in the political decisions of a free society. Any

73

group which disdains to rise to the defense of its interests in the U.S. Congress, the statehouse, and the county building will soon lose each contest vitally affecting its future. Business interests are not different from other private-sector interests in this respect. They must fight the political battle or lose their economic position.

Today government is all-pervasive. It deals with so many facets of our life that regulatory overkill has become a leading political issue. No sector of society is so deeply involved in the new and difficult private-public interface as business and commerce. Government controls macroeconomic activity, levies taxes, limits profits, finances competitive enterprises abroad, sets standards of performance for safety, health, and energy utilization, regulates the prices of natural gas and petroleum, and in almost every way affects the profitability and viability of corporate America.

In fact, the growth of government involvement in business may some day eliminate the free enterprise market economy in the United States, not out of animosity but through ineptitude. Corporations have a primary responsibility to fight in the political wars to prevent this fate for United States business. They must fight by the rules, but with all the vigor they possess. No corporate managers today can responsibly discharge their duties without joining the political fight on the side of economic viability for corporate America, its employees, its customers, and its owners.

From time to time, the corporate world may disagree on what action is needed. (For example, many airline managements have fought deregulation, while most corporations fight for less regulation.) But the need is for action and involvement directed toward goals that each manager perceives as beneficial and essential to the corporation and the continuance of an economic system in which it can function.

It has been argued that this is a narrow, selfish point of view, with business seeking to benefit only those who profit from its enterprise. To the extent that labor, consumers, environmentalists, and welfare recipients battle for their economic interests, all are narrow partisans behaving in a comparable manner. This may or may not be true with respect to particular positions taken. But it is the genius of the American multiple-advocacy participatory political contest that even the losers know that they have had their chance to win in a contest of money, debate, wills, and rhetoric.

Corporate America has begun to respond to the necessity of being politically active. The Business Roundtable, the Chamber of Commerce of the United States, and the National Association of Manufacturers, once considered almost impotent, command increasing respect as their members increase their political activity.

BUILDING PUBLIC CREDIBILITY

As a creator of jobs and of capital return to investors, the corporation has a large constituency which can be organized successfully. The need to organize its resources to bring the full force of that group of supporters to its political aid is a key responsibility of management. But to be truly effective corporations must play by the new rules of the political game. Foremost is the need to build public credibility. In part because of an unfortunate record, the business community starts with its credibility at a low point. Full disclosure is what the game is all about. In the words of youth, "Let it all hang out." Corporate political activity implies the responsibility to make a significant improvement in the public's understanding of corporate activities.

All political activism in the United States today brings with it responsibility to keep citizens informed so that they can judge the objectives and motives of the advocates. Open contests of power must be fought in full view of the public. The public will make the ultimate decisions through its duly elected representatives in government.

The most recent development in American politics is the encouragement of political activism by all interest groups. Participants establish their credibility as part of their ammunition for successful action. Therefore, "sunshine" in the corporate world is fundamental to effective political activism. More and more, the credibility of an organization depends on its ability to explain its position to the public through the media—to allow the sun to shine on its activities.

Corporate decisions must be taken with public understanding in mind. A corporation must handle issues important to the public, such as permanently closing or moving a plant or determining a new plant location, in a way that helps to create understanding. Hidden boardroom actions must be brought into the sunlight to be understood by those affected by corporate activity.

Much experimentation is necessary to determine how the credibility of those making good business decisions can be improved. Perhaps public hearings and occasional open board sessions would be helpful. Some of the sunshine requirements affecting operation of the federal government might also be helpful, especially if instituted on a voluntary basis. The objective of such experiments would be to ensure a better chance for affected and interested persons to understand and, in certain cases, to participate in decisions.

The Securities and Exchange Commission (SEC) has moved to force corporations to disclose the perquisites of executives. It would have been more beneficial to industry's credibility if this action had been taken by industry itself rather than mandated by government. Such disclosure is the basis for political activity today; and corporate America must lose some privacy, as politicians have, as it becomes involved in their activity.

IMPORTANCE OF PLANNING

The determination of what political actions are necessary to improve the position of business is not always self-evident. A call to political action means that an important obligation of directors and management is to spend time in developing corporate political positions. Corporate determination of desired political results should be supported by a well-planned and articulate record. The positions adopted will not necessarily reflect the political views of the chief executive officer or the chairman of the board. Their views can be expressed in the ballot box and by their individual political activity. When there appears to be a real conflict between individual views and desirable corporate policy, the individual manager will normally allow the corporate view to prevail. If the issue is a matter of principle, the officer may resign to be free to pursue a personal viewpoint.

As in other corporate activities, an efficient, well-organized plan of action will most likely lead to the accomplishment of desired goals. Corporate planning for political action must command the attention of top management and the board of directors in the same way as strategic financial and product planning does. In many cases, profitability and the successful accomplishment of other goals will depend as much on the success of the political plan as on older, customary management activities.

CONCLUSIONS

In summary, corporation managers have a social duty to become politically active. They must determine and pursue political goals that will benefit their enterprise and the continued health of a market-oriented economic system. Establishing credibility with the public is essential to the success of their efforts. Such credibility will be enhanced by greater sunshine in corporate decision making.

Corporate political action programs should be determined and carried out with the authorization, care, and skill devoted to other major corporate activities. In pursuing the new corporate political activism, corporate managers can be secure in the knowledge that they are discharging their social duty and fulfilling a major corporate responsibility.

THE ETHICAL RESPONSIBILITIES OF MULTINATIONAL COMPANIES

TIMOTHY SMITH

Timothy Smith is the executive director of the Inter-faith Center on Corporate Responsibility (ICCR), a related movement of the National Council of Churches of Christ in the United States of America. The center provides research and coordinates action for some 15 Protestant denominations and 170 Roman Catholic orders and 12 dioceses active in bringing social concerns to corporate attention via dialogue with management, open letters, public hearings, legal action, stockholder resolutions, and the like.

Mr. Smith was educated at the Union Theological Seminary and the University of Toronto and currently resides in New York. He has been associated with ICCR in various capacities since 1972. He also serves on the boards of the American Committee on Africa, the Council on Economic Priorities, the Corporate Data Exchange, and the State Department Advisory Committee on International Investment, Technology, and Development.

The policies and practices of multinational (transnational) corporations are being scrutinized as never before. Newspaper headlines blare forth about bribes and political contributions at home and abroad. The United Nations Center on Transnational Corporations discusses codes of conduct for corporations. Churches, universities, foundations, trade unions, and other institutional investors debate the social responsibilities of the corporations in which they hold stock. Congressional committees sponsor hearings on the petroleum companies and the energy crisis and infant-formula companies with their overseas marketing practices. Such committees also propose legislation restricting further loans and investments in South Africa and setting limits on corporate advertising to children.

In growing numbers corporations are establishing public policy committees or publishing reports dealing with specific issues of social responsibility such as equal employment opportunity, South Africa, and the environmental impact of strip mining. Corporate legal departments find their purview expanded by lawsuits dealing with corporate abuses.

Perhaps this is partly the by-product of the post-Watergate mentality of many Americans. More important, there is a growing recognition that the power and influence of corporate America penetrate the lives of people globally as never before. This awareness is emerging in some relatively new quarters, the institutional church being one. For instance, the Interfaith Center on Corporate Responsibility now comprises 170 Roman Catholic orders, 12 dioceses, and 15 Protestant denominations. As investors and as churches concerned about the responsible use of corporate power, these agencies have employed a variety of novel approaches to corporations to press for greater accountability. Letters and meetings with management, attendance at shareholder meetings and the filing of shareholder resolutions, court suits, public education, testimony before the Congress and the United Nations, fact-finding trips overseas, research, and publication are all methods used by churches in their relatively new corporate-responsibility work. However, church concerns and actions are simply a mirror of expanding awareness and action in the society as a whole.

Corporations are being called to greater accountability: they are urged not simply to maximize profits regardless of the resultant impact on society but to integrate social costs into decision making. For some companies the demand that they march to a different drummer and forsake occasions for profit because of harmful results is unthinkable, and the reaction to the demand is hostility. For other corporations there is an emerging understanding that the social balance sheet also is important. The reaction to requests for changed policies and practices by these managers is often positive and creative. Both kinds of response are illustrated by the following examples.

ETHICAL QUESTIONS

For 5 years church stockholders urged Newmont Mining Corp. to improve wages and working conditions in Namibia (presently illegally occupied by South Africa). The management reacted initially by refusing to admit that there even was a problem, in spite of evidence of starvation wages and horrendous working conditions for thousands of African employees. Chairman Plato Malozemoff arrogantly defended Newmont's performance from criticism by the United Nations, churches, African leaders from Namibia, and investors like the Teachers Insurance and Annuity Association–College Retirement Equities Fund (TIAA-CREF), which finally sold its Newmont stock. Newmont made hundreds of millions of dollars from its Namibian investment, but the price in terms of damage to people's lives was extremely high. Newmont may have been shortsighted in straight business terms as well. It is possible that its history of poor labor relations and de facto support of South Africa's illegal occupation of Namibia will have created enough antagonism so that when Namibia becomes independent, Newmont may become the target of hostile expropriation.

Nestlé S.A., Switzerland's leading transnational corporation, has been the target of criticism by organizations concerned that the marketing and promotion practices of its baby-formula products in developing nations were contributing to the malnutrition and death of infants. A growing body of medical evidence from Third World countries has shown that Nestlé and other infant-formula companies such as Abbott Laboratories, Bristol-Myers Co., and American Home Products Corp. had been promoting their products to the public, even among poor mothers who lacked the income to buy enough formula for their children. Instead of nourishing children, formula overdiluted with contaminated water becomes a contributor to malnutrition and even death.

Nestlé's initial response was not to examine the merits of the issue itself but to take the offensive against its critics. In Switzerland Nestlé sued one organization and, at the same time, prepared an internal memorandum outlining the strategy that it felt should be followed to deal with the critics. Instead of understanding that criticism has creative potential, the memorandum recommended that Nestlé identify critics as part of a larger movement to undermine the free enterprise system. Further, when any abuses were discovered, Nestlé would say that these were isolated instances and not part of a pattern. This strategy led to almost-comic moments. In the spring of 1978, Sen. Edward M. Kennedy of Massachusetts sponsored hearings on the infant-formula issue. Among those testifying was the former head of Nestlé (Brazil), Mr. Balarin, who stated that he felt the churches pressing the issue in the United States were motivated not by humanitarian concerns but by a desire to undermine capitalism. This response brought laughter and angry rebukes by several senators. As the issue of baby-formula abuse grows in the United States and as a consumer boycott supported by a number of moderate organizations expands, Nestlé has begun to shift tactics and initiate a dialogue with critics. The Nestlé reaction is not atypical of the response of managers under criticism.

There are, however, numerous other companies that view the issue of corporate social responsibility not as a public relations problem but as an integral factor in their day-to-day business. Control Data Corporation, with headquarters in Minneapolis, is an excellent example. Control Data publishes reports on its social responsibilities just as it publishes regular financial figures. It has also published guidelines for responsible corporate behavior in a number of areas. For instance, it would not sell or lease a computer that would be used for the abridgment of human rights. This guideline has led Control Data to refuse business possibilities in South Africa when it has ascertained that its products would assist in repression rather than in humanization. When challenged by church investors regarding sales in South Africa, Control Data saw this challenge as an opportunity for dialogue and established a series of conversations with the churches on this and other corporate-responsibility issues.

Similarly, Abbott, which produces infant formula, initially responded in a quite different manner from that of Nestlé and negotiated with its critics. Both in substance (by an agreement to change certain policies and a decision to hire several persons to work on the issue) and in style (by an attempt at dialogue rather than confrontation) the responses of Abbott and Nestlé were as different as night and day. Similarly, Polaroid Corp. took its social responsibilities seriously and decided to withdraw from South Africa, even though it was still a positive profit center, when it discovered that its products were being used for repressive purposes there.

The issue is certainly not just one of style. Bank of America executives are willing to talk at length with church shareholders who urge a moratorium on future loans to South Africa. Yet they still defend their right to make loans to the apartheid government of South Africa itself, in a way that few other United States banks do any longer. While Bank of America tries to put "moral polish" on these loans by saying that they help the black population, in essence it has decided that the search for profit supersedes any social or moral responsibility which it may have. Fearful that a prohibition of loans to South Africa might leave it vulnerable to demands that it cut off other loans for social or political reasons, the bank fails to take even the first step. Thus it maintains its right to make loans that assist in the maintenance of white supremacy; in 1978 it had an exposure of approximately $200 million in South Africa.

In contrast, numerous other banks have taken contrary stands because of public and church shareholders' pressure. Chase Manhattan Bank, Chemical Bank, Irving Trust Co., and Mellon Bank have all prohibited loans to the South African government because of its apartheid practices. Chase maintains that it will not make loans which have a negative social impact. It has decided that loans to the South African government fall into this category.

Church shareholders have maintained that all United States banks must carefully evaluate the social impact of loans to South Africa even when those loans are profitable. They have called for the addition of social and ethical criteria to the list of lending factors. To many this attempt to change the standards of lending is unfair. Bank of America calls it "the politicization of the lending process."

From the churches' point of view, the politicization took place long ago. Loans to South Africa cannot be classed as apolitical or without political implications. Dollars which facilitate apartheid's racial exploitation have clear ethical and political connotations. Thus Bank of America and other banks have been asked to follow a higher standard of behavior in their lending policies than simply to lend where a loan is safe and profitable.

How does one explain this difference in corporate reaction in terms of style and substance? Is it simply the character of top management? Is it a different set of rules or expectations that managers are required to meet? Or is the difference simply a facade, a public relations style that obscures the real corporate personality?

Certainly the difference of mentality in top management must be considered. William C. Norris, chairman of Control Data, has a deep personal commitment to his company's acting in a socially responsible manner. In contrast, Newmont's Malozemoff seems untouched by the issue of Newmont's labor record in Namibia. However, much more than personal leadership is required if a corporation is being asked to integrate social costs into its business decisions. Control Data clearly expects different standards from executives than does Newmont. Newmont's record on many levels would not be acceptable at Control Data. The people who are congratulated for bringing in sizable profits at Newmont would probably be fired at Control Data.

It seems clear to me that the fairest way to let employees know what a company expects of them is to outline policy clearly in a corporate code of conduct and indicate that social performance will be a factor in determining raises and promotions. For example, a number of companies have sent to South Africa managing directors who know full well that their contribution to the companies will also be measured on the basis of positive changes in wages and labor policy for blacks. That is a clearly expressed expectation, not simply a result of the personal views of a particular manager.

Whether these expectations are formalized in a code of conduct or outlined in a series of carefully constructed guidelines, the limits and expectations are clarified. Executives know that they will be dismissed for making a bribe or political contribution overseas and that they will be rewarded for bettering a record of equal employment opportunity in the United States. It is important to press for such codes so that expectations do not fluctuate with changes in top management.

FUTURE ISSUES

What are the corporate-responsibility issues of the future that will concern both United States businesses and the public? The list is growing, as is the seriousness with which the public regards the issues. While it is difficult to look into a crystal ball, from the point of view of church investors who have been actively involved in encouraging social responsibility on behalf of corporations for more than a decade, the future agenda will likely include the following:

1. *Domestic equality issues.* The issue of equal employment opportunity, aimed at an end to discrimination for women and minority groups, is central. In addition, corporations like J. P. Stevens & Co. with extremely questionable labor practices will be the focus of a coalition of trade unions, churches, and others. The power of union investment funds will be felt as never before on labor questions. Billions of dollars of state and municipal government investment funds will be used as leverage on numerous issues. Thus a whole new set of checks and balances on corporate power will emerge.

2. *Urban issues.* Bank and insurance redlining will receive tremendous attention as people in the cities fight to regain economic vitality in their neighborhoods. Insurance companies such as Hartford Fire Insurance Co., Aetna Life & Casualty, and Connecticut General Insurance Corp. will all face pressure not to desert the cities by cutting back on home insurance. In addition, corporate flight from communities like Youngstown, Ohio, a phenomenon which causes massive unemployment, will be fought.

3. *Issues of transnational corporations.* The role of transnational corporations undoubtedly will come under increasing scrutiny by Third World governments, the United Nations, and many organizations within the United States. In the foreseeable future the issue of bank loans and investment in apartheid South Africa will be hotly debated. Dozens of universities have been involved in serious studies of their responsibility as investors. It is likely that additional banks will adopt policies prohibiting loans to the South African government and that corporations will place a moratorium on expansion plans. Some will even withdraw from South Africa, while others will work

vigorously to minimize the effect of apartheid in the workplace in order to offset the chorus of criticism in the United States.

Other issues such as the morality of loans to repressive governments like the present government of Chile, bribes and political contributions, the contribution (or noncontribution) of transnational corporations to social and economic development overseas, and the sale overseas of products that are banned in the United States, are on the agenda.

4.   *Issues of agribusiness, nutrition, and hunger.* The impact of agribusiness companies on world hunger will be discussed even more extensively. Domestic concerns such as the advertising of junk foods to small children, land use, and the small family farm will be balanced by international questions such as cash cropping, wages and working conditions for employees of agribusiness companies, and the creation of counterproductive consumption patterns by Third World nations. It is also likely that in the 1980s there will be an upsurge of pressure on baby-formula companies to change their marketing and promotion practices.

5.   *Issues of stock ownership.* Through the competent work of the Corporate Data Exchange, based in New York, and the office of the late Sen. Lee Metcalf, information about who owns and votes stock in United States corporations is emerging. The concentration of voting power is already a controversial item for debate. That debate will widen, and banks will be pressed to pass voting rights on to the beneficial owners of stock rather than to bank trust departments.

6.   *Military issues.* The sales of military equipment to repressive governments will certainly be on the corporate-responsibility agenda. In addition, pressure to have companies develop plans for the conversion of production to civilian purposes will grow. Rockwell International Corp. stockholders voted in 1977 on a resolution asking for a summary of the corporate conversion plan in case development of the B-1 bomber was canceled. Management had not prepared any such contingency plan, and many workers were laid off when development of the bomber was in fact canceled. Many employees who participate in stock-ownership plans will vote for such contingency planning as an exercise in enlightened self-interest.

7.   *Energy issues.* Many energy issues have already emerged. The controversy about nuclear power is sweeping the country, as is the debate on whether the United States should follow hard or soft energy paths. Corporate influence on government policy will increasingly be criticized.

8.   *Environmental issues.* The effect of corporate policies and practices on the environment will continue to be examined.

9.   *Health and safety issues.* The media are making regular reports about industrial carcinogens to the public, adding to the reports of brown-lung

disease in textile mills and black-lung disease in mines. Here again the power of trade union investment funds may be mustered to protect workers.

ROLE OF LABOR

In a fascinating book entitled *The North Will Rise Again* (1978), Randy Barber and Jeremy Rifkin remind us of the mammoth wealth of trade union pension funds. The size of public pension funds is also huge. The opportunities for creative action as labor or public employees discover ways to apply a new set of checks and balances on corporations are considerable.

In some ways trade unions are only now beginning to discover the "power of the portfolio." The J. P. Stevens corporate campaign, led by the Amalgamated Clothing and Textile Workers Union (ACTWU), exhibits many novel ways to challenge this particular corporate giant. For instance, the union has challenged any board interlocks between J. P. Stevens and other corporations. Manufacturers Hanover Trust Co., a bank with hundreds of millions of dollars in union accounts, faced union-sponsored shareholder resolutions, threats of withdrawal of union accounts, and a public relations controversy because Stevens's chairman, James D. Finley, sat on its board. Representatives of dozens of trade unions with stock or banking relationships with Manufacturers Hanover attended the 1977 stockholders' meeting to challenge the Finley candidacy. Within a year Finley had resigned from the board of the bank. Soon after, David W. Mitchell, chairman of Avon Products, was forced to resign from the Stevens board.

The pressure to cut these board interlocks was applied not only by the ACTWU but by numerous unions that discovered their stock portfolios could be real instruments for pressure. In an even more dramatic move, the ACTWU announced the candidacy of two persons for the board of the New York Life Insurance Co. to challenge Finley's seat on that board and Chairman R. Manning Brown, Jr.'s position on the Stevens board. Since New York Life is a mutual insurance company, the law allows candidates to be nominated to its board for a vote by policyholders. With approximately 6 million policyholders, however, the expense of polling all of them would have been enormous. Faced with this dilemma Brown and Finley resigned from each other's boards.

The lessons derived from this development are much broader than the J. P. Stevens campaign. Unions and public pension funds are reexamining their portfolios and the use of them. Public pension funds are being urged to choose alternative investments such as housing or credit unions rather than solely blue chips.

In all these areas and many more the United States government will also be asked to intervene, but the petitions for changed policies will definitely be aimed at the management, boards of directors, and shareholders of the corporations themselves. In short, it seems likely that the movement for greater social responsibility by corporations will grow by leaps and bounds. Top executives will hear questions and requests with which they have not been trained to deal. It is important that the imagination and hard work shown by United States companies in their production of goods and services be harnessed to deal creatively with the challenge to be socially responsible.

Part 2

THE SOCIAL DIMENSIONS OF CORPORATE CONDUCT

Promoting Employment Opportunities for Women and Minorities; Corporate Philanthropy

Throughout the 1960s the most pressing social issue confronting business was the deterioration of the nation's urban areas. Much of the initial revival of interest in the concept of social responsibility on the part of the business community revolved around such issues as the lack of black employment, the need to create job opportunities for unskilled youth, and the dearth of corporate investment in inner-city areas. Although public interest in these issues has waned, the problems themselves remain even more pressing than when they dominated the nation's headlines. A number of corporations continue to be actively involved in finding ways of using their particular skills and resources to reduce the gap between those who have shared in the affluence of the economy since 1960 and those who remain outside the mainstream of the American economic fabric.

In his essay, "Affirmative Action and the Urban Crisis," Milton Moskowitz, a longtime observer of the impact of corporate policies on minorities, surveys the different ways in which corporations are currently responding to a variety of social issues. While Moskowitz is disappointed with the overall effect of corporate decisions on the status of women and minorities, he is impressed by the extraordinary changes that have taken place within the

87

business world in the 1970s. He reports that a number of corporations, including American Telephone & Telegraph Co., General Motors Corp., and General Electric Co., have managed to increase substantially their recruitment of members of minority groups, while others such as Control Data Corporation, Ralston Purina Co., Hallmark Cards, Ford Motor Co., Clorox Co., and Federated Department Stores have demonstrated their willingness to use their resources to help revitalize urban areas. He concludes, "Companies are doing things today that they never dreamed of doing a decade ago, and every opinion poll shows that the public expects them to continue to be sensitive to social needs."

One of the most ambitious corporate efforts to combine long-term growth with a commitment to increasing economic and educational opportunities for inner-city residents has been undertaken by Control Data. In his essay, "Business Opportunities in Addressing Societal Problems," William C. Norris describes in detail Control Data's three-pronged strategy. It includes the location of plants in depressed inner-city communities, the design of a computer-based education program aimed at improving educational skills, and a program to facilitate small-business formation and operation in inner cities through business and technology centers. Norris argues that business must take the initiative in planning and managing the implementation of programs designed to meet society's current needs but cautions that "a major barrier to the widespread adoption of a strategy of seeking business opportunities from meeting major social needs is the relentless pressure by the investment community for short-term earnings improvement."

The Equitable Life Assurance Society of the United States has also made a serious commitment to address social problems in this area. Its efforts include the creation of a minority-enterprise small-business investment company (MESBIC) to provide capital for minority enterprises, a purchasing program designed to promote the economic development of firms controlled by members of minority groups, women, and handicapped individuals, an affirmative-action policy with respect to minority-owned banks, and a decision to allocate a minimum of 10 percent of its total advertising budget to minority-owned media. Equitable's president, Coy G. Eklund, notes that each of these policies reflects his belief that the "highest purpose of business is [not] to maximize profits" but to conduct itself in accordance with the "social values established by society." Eklund argues that "social irresponsibility is about as unacceptable as financial irresponsibility."

Under the leadership of its president, Robert C. Holland, the Committee for Economic Development (CED) has embarked on a major effort to explore ways in which the private sector can help increase employment opportunities for disadvantaged segments of the labor force. After publishing a widely circulated report describing sixty of the most successful training and job programs in which the private sector had participated, CED concluded that greater cooperation between the private and public sectors was critical if unemployment was to be further reduced. Holland reports that he is pleased with the Carter administration's responsiveness to the committee's recommendation that the role of the private sector in hiring and training the hard-core unemployed be expanded. He suggests that corporations are increasingly "recognizing that hiring the hard-to-employ is not merely good social policy but good business as well."

Levi Strauss & Co. is a corporation with a long commitment to promoting employment opportunities for minorities. In his essay, "Corporate Social Responsibility: A New Term for an Old Concept with New Significance," Walter A. Haas, Jr., discusses his company's pioneering efforts to improve the economic position of minorities, some of which have been more successful than others. He also describes Levi Strauss's community-based program of corporate philanthropy. Haas suggests that Levi Strauss's persistent effort to demonstrate its concern for the people whose lives the company affects is a reflection of the personal philosophy of the individuals who have managed the company since its founding in the 1850s. While recognizing that corporate social involvement can be adequately justified in terms of the "long-term economic self-interest" of a corporation, Haas argues that the fundamental motivation for Levi Strauss management is that this is "the right thing to do." Haas concludes that business has the potential as well as the responsibility to play a more innovative role in responding to the changing needs of society.

Dayton Hudson Corporation is another company with a long tradition of corporate citizenship. Its program of philanthropy dates back to 1917; its policy of donating 5 percent of its pretax earnings to worthwhile projects in the communities where it has facilities is now 3½ decades old. In his description of Dayton Hudson's approach to corporate philanthropy, the company's chairman, William A. Andres, notes that "business [is] an insufficiently tapped resource for solving the complex social problems which government alone cannot handle." Andres argues that corporate programs of corporate social responsibility cannot be afterthoughts. If business is to respond adequately to the public's increasing expectations, a sense of social concern must become "a fully integral, fully committed, fully professional part of the corporation's operations."

AFFIRMATIVE ACTION AND THE URBAN CRISIS

MILTON MOSKOWITZ

Milton Moskowitz writes a three-times-a-week busi-ness column that is distributed nationally by the Los Angeles Times Syndicate. It is currently appearing in twenty-five daily newspapers.

Mr. Moskowitz has followed "social responsibility and business" since 1968, when he founded the newsletter Business & Society, *which he wrote for 6 years. He is senior editor of the quarterly periodical* Business and Society Review. *He has contributed to numerous newspapers and magazines, including* The New York Times, California Living, California To-morrow, New West, *and* The Nation.

In 1978 the following developments took place:

- Firestone Tire & Rubber Co. recalled 10 million radial tires (Firestone 500s), offering to replace them free of charge with its new 721 radial tires. The recall came after much prodding from the National Highway Traffic Safety Administration (NHTSA), which said that Firestone 500s were implicated in highway mishaps that had caused at least forty-one deaths and sixty-five injuries.

- American Airlines announced that it would move its corporate headquarters (and 1300 jobs) from New York to the Dallas–Fort Worth Regional Airport. New York City officials denounced the airline as a "traitor." And one company, Warner Communications, issued orders to its 6000 employees that they were no longer to fly via American.

- The Consolidation Coal Company division of Continental Oil Co. (now Conoco, Inc.) agreed to pay $370,000 to women who had had difficulty in getting jobs as miners. Its agreement with the U.S. Department of Labor also pledged the company to fill 20 percent of its miner trainee slots with women.

- Barbara J. Stuhler, professor and associate dean of community relations and extension services at the University of Minnesota, was elected a director of the Northwestern National Bank of Minneapolis, the largest commercial bank in Minnesota and the eighteenth largest in the United States.

- International Telephone and Telegraph Corporation (ITT) drew the wrath of the Securities and Exchange Commission (SEC), which asked a court to fine the conglomerate $100,000 a day until it released documents relating to dubious payments made by ITT in a number of countries. (ITT had been under a court order to release the documents since 1976.) In addition to the fine, the SEC asked that ITT be required to place on its board of directors new members "who [had] not had prior affiliation, association or financial dealings with ITT."

- The U.S. Supreme Court, following its decision in the Bakke case, agreed to review a lower-court ruling upholding a reverse-discrimination complaint brought by Brian F. Weber against his employer, Kaiser Aluminum & Chemical Corp. Weber charged that he was refused admission to a training program even though he had greater seniority than two blacks who were accepted.

These developments, each in its own way, illuminated the state of corporate responsibility as the decade neared its end.

The Firestone recall testified to the regulatory power that can now be brought to bear against corporations. Daniel Bell, leading American sociologist, has pointed out that in the mid-1960s the automobile industry was completely unregulated. Today it's subject to cumbersome regulations because it failed to heed the early warning signs. "When Ralph Nader began to issue warnings of the hazards of car construction, he was ignored, and worse, later spied on, forcing General Motors to make a public apology," Bell recalls.[1] It's a lesson that Firestone and some other companies still haven't learned. The head of the NHTSA, which initiated the Firestone recall, is Joan B. Claybrook, a former top aide to Ralph Nader.

The controversy in which American Airlines found itself as a result of a decision that it said was made for business reasons reflected the widespread feeling that corporations have a responsibility to the communities in which they operate. It's a feeling that surfaced strongly in the 1960s, when inner cities became the province of the poor and the nonwhite, leading to riots, elections of black mayors, and fire bombings of buildings. In 1967 the life insurance industry made a $1 billion commitment to use its resources to reverse urban decay. This urban investment program marked the start of the modern corporate social responsibility movement. But corporate desertion of cities, especially New York, continued. In 1970 New York was the headquarters city for 33 of the top 100 industrial corporations in the nation. By 1978 only 17 of the top 100 made their headquarters in New York, and at least 1 of these, Union Carbide Corp., was to move to Danbury, Connecticut, in 1981 to occupy a building that would cost $100 million to construct.

The $370,000 paid by Consolidation Coal to women who had wanted to be miners was one of a long series of back-pay awards made by companies to settle complaints of race, sex, and age discrimination. One of the largest was the $38 million settlement made by American Telephone & Telegraph Co., the nation's largest employer, in 1973. A 1978 settlement covering women and minority workers cost the General Electric Co. $32 million.

The election of Barbara Stuhler as a bank director in Minneapolis was in keeping with one of the clearest trends to emerge from corporate-responsibility programs: the broadening of the membership of boards of directors. In the late 1960s there were virtually no blacks on corporate boards; a decade later more than 100 companies had black directors. Whereas there had been virtually no women on boards unless they were related to the owners or top managers, more than 300 women now hold seats on major corporate boards.

The SEC's complaint against ITT fit a design that was woven in the 1970s: disclosures by company after company of bribes, rebates, and other questionable payments in connection with sales activities, primarily overseas. The disclosures were fallouts from Watergate, and they had much to do with the declining confidence in business shown by the public. They revealed, as in the ITT case, a crazy-quilt pattern of accounting legerdemain that had been

---

[1] Address given at the First National Conference on Business Ethics, Bentley College, Waltham, Mass., Mar. 11 and 12, 1977.

used to conceal these practices from shareholders, directors, most employees, and the independent accountants engaged to audit the books.

Kaiser Aluminum & Chemical Corp. v. Weber, the "blue-collar Bakke case," challenged the legality of affirmative-action programs mounted by corporations to strengthen minority representation in their employee ranks. These programs were established largely as a result of government regulations or pressure. Here, in the Weber case, was a backlash that threatened to undermine what progress had been made in the past decade. In 1979, however, the Supreme Court ruled against Weber.

EXTENT OF PROGRESS

How much progress had been made is a matter of serious debate. Election of blacks and women to corporate boards must certainly be regarded as a positive step. It's too easy and too cynical to sneer at this phenomenon as tokenism. Having Vernon E. Jordan, president of the National Urban League, sitting on the boards of the American Express Co., Bankers Trust Company, Celanese Corp., J. C. Penney Company, and Xerox Corp. is to place there a link between corporate power and powerless blacks. To grasp the change in thinking that the presence of Jordan and other blacks on boards of directors represents, one only has to imagine the reaction that any of these corporations would have had in 1965 to the suggestion that the head of the Urban League belonged on its board. We have come some distance when this kind of representation for minority groups and women is accepted by many large corporations as a matter of course.

There's also no gainsaying that blacks and women have broken down many discriminatory barriers in employment. Offices are no longer a sea of white faces. The number of blacks employed by large corporations has increased sharply, and the job horizons for women have widened considerably.

However, any look at the American corporation, whether in the form of a rigorous study or simply as an informal inspection, will reveal the residues of institutional racism and sexism. Equal employment was mandated by two acts of the 1960s: Title VII of the Civil Rights Act of 1964, which barred discrimination by companies engaged in interstate commerce; and Executive Order No. 11246 of 1965, which barred discrimination by federal contractors. The problem is, of course, that discrimination antedated these statutes by many years. And corporations, like people, are victims of their legacies. Deeply embedded structural practices are not easily uprooted. As a result, the progress that has been made serves to point up the gaps that remain. It's undeniable that the higher one looks in a company, the more the ranks are dominated by white males. In 1978 *Fortune* published the findings of a systematic survey of 1300 companies. The proxy statements issued by these firms disclosed the compensation of 6400 officers and directors (the law requires these statements to disclose the names and salaries of the three highest officers and of any director earning more than $40,000). Of these 6400 management persons, only 10, or a "measly 0.16 percent," as *Fortune* put it, were women. And only 3 of these women had worked their way up without family connections.[2]

The picture is just as devastating for members of minority groups. In 1977 the U.S. Equal Employment Opportunity Commission (EEOC) published a study, *Black Experiences versus Black Expectations,* reporting on the penetration that blacks had made in corporate employment between 1969 and 1974. The study was based on an analysis of the EEO-1 reports that companies are required to file with the federal government. Black representation in six selected job categories was as shown in the accompanying table in the two years. This table indicates that in 1969, when blacks accounted for 10.2 percent of the population, they held only 2.1 percent of the professional jobs in corporate America and only 1.5 percent of the management positions.

Job categories	Percent of total	
	1969	1974
Officials and managers	1.5	2.9
Professional	2.1	3.1
Technicians	5.6	7.3
Sales workers	4.0	5.5
Office and clerical	6.1	8.8
Craft workers	5.0	7.0

Dr. Melvin Humphrey, who conducted this study as director of research for the EEOC, characterized the progress between 1969 and 1974 as minuscule, pointing out that at this rate "it will be sometime in the 21st century before the employment gaps will close and blacks achieve fair-share levels of employment in all six of the selected job categories."[3] Indeed, in the top category, officials and managers, blacks would not achieve parity with whites until the year 2017.

The extent to which discrimination against members of minority groups and women was a routine, everyday, unquestioned practice in the business world is generally not appreciated by today's corporate managers. Carey McWilliams, longtime editor of *The Nation,* recalled for a San Francisco audience how it was in the California aircraft industry in the early 1940s.

---

2 Wyndham Robertson, "The Top Women in Big Business," *Fortune,* July 17, 1978, pp. 58–64.

3 Melvin Humphrey, *Black Experiences versus Black Expectations,* Equal Employment Opportunity Commission Research Report No. 53, 1977, p. 41.

Two of the largest companies, Lockheed Corp. and Consolidated Vultee Aircraft, hired only whites and had no compunction about stating publicly that this was their policy. American Telephone & Telegraph has made what could properly be called gigantic strides. Between 1965 and 1970 it increased its nonwhite employment by 152 percent, and it increased it by another 23 percent between 1972 and 1978. Members of minority groups now account for about 12 percent of its workforce. But how much the company had to make up for is clear from the figures cited in an EEOC complaint filed in 1970: in 1940, when the company employed 316,000 persons, members of minority groups represented 0.7 percent of that total. One of the great training grounds at General Motors Corp. is its degree-granting college, the General Motors Institute. As recently as 1970 only 1.6 percent of institute students were from minority groups; today minority representation is 16 percent. (The GM experience parallels that of other institutions. In 1970 the National Guard was 1 percent black; today it's 16 percent black.) As for women, the story is different. They were hired, but only for very specific low-level jobs. If banks and insurance companies had followed anything close to an up-from-the-ranks promotion policy, many of them would be headed today by female chief executive officers. As it is, very few women hold top-management slots in these financial institutions.

It's clear, then, that the racist and sexist policies of *yesterday* explain the discriminatory patterns that obtain *today*. American companies are in the position of playing catch-up, a game plan that makes not surprising such actions as *Kaiser Aluminum & Chemical Corp. v. Weber.*

URBAN COMMITMENT

One litmus test of corporate social involvement is the degree of commitment to urban-core centers. It's a test that New York officials believe American Airlines failed. But it's not always easy to sort out all the factors in these decisions and translate them into "good guy" and "bad guy" ratings. There was a feeling abroad in the late 1960s that American corporations could help to save the cities by staying there, putting up new plants there, rehabilitating homes and neighborhoods there, and shoring up community organizations. It is this feeling that undergirded the insurance industry's urban investment program and the urban coalitions established in cities across the country. Corporate participation was a key element in these efforts.

To be sure, there was a certain amount of public relations commotion connected with those programs. Business leaders, reacting to urban riots, needed to stand up and be counted. They were also responding to pressures from Washington. Michael Harrington, who reminded everyone that poverty was still with us, described the period as follows:

In the Sixties, when Kennedy-Johnson liberalism was on the ascendant, the companies followed in the steps of their liberal critics in government. There was much talk of the social responsibility of business, of a partnership between the public and private sector. . . . *Fortune* magazine was a cheering section for this movement, documenting how do-gooding could be profitable.

Do-gooding did not turn out to be profitable. Many of the programs launched under the banner of corporate social responsibility proved to be disasters. White families continued to desert the central cities. So did corporations. Very few manufacturing plants were established in the inner cities. Reflecting on that period 10 years later, James L. Ferguson, chairman and chief executive officer of General Foods Corp., said:

A lot of businessmen suddenly discovered the notion of "corporate social responsibility." And they didn't put any limits on it. . . . A lot of things were done and said in those days that seem a little silly by hindsight. I would add that terms like "corporate social responsibility" came into disrepute in some quarters as a result.

Ferguson's ultimate moral:

No matter how you slice it, a business enterprise is neither an arm of the government nor an eleemosynary institution.[4]

That's traditional business dogma, the old-time free enterprise religion that corporate leaders are comfortable with because it gives them a rationale for steering clear of serious social involvement. In the same vein were the responses made by some business executives to a letter they received in late 1977 from the House Committee on Banking, Finance and Urban Affairs. The letter solicited their views on the problems of the central cities. Here are five typical replies:

Marvin G. Mitchell, chairman and president of Chicago Bridge & Iron Co.:

We suspect that unemployment in central cities is part of a larger problem. That larger problem is a very sluggish economy, resulting in a slowing in investment . . . on the part of U.S. corporations, brought about in part by a lack of confidence in solutions proposed by the government. We respectfully submit that the Congress might well be advised to work on the larger problem first.[5]

Edmund B. Fitzgerald, chairman of Cutler-Hammer, Inc.:

Business tends to view coercive social legislation as harassment. Coopera-

---

4 Address given at conference sponsored by the Conference Board, Apr. 12, 1978.
5 Ibid.

tion, thus, is minimal. . . . On the other hand, tax incentives to business to achieve social goals can unleash on a problem the diverse creativity of the multifaceted competitive enterprise system.[6]

Thomas F. Russell, chairman of Federal-Mogul:

We have one manufacturing plant and 42 warehouses located in central city locations. They employ 523 out of our 10,540 U.S. employees. We have no plans to expand or contract these operations other than what is required to serve our customers. . . . We have no job training activities specifically directed at the unemployed in the central cities. . . . In general, the cost of doing business is higher in central cities than in less populated areas. . . . We find that local governments of large cities do not appear to want manufacturing jobs. . . . Extremely liberal welfare and unemployment benefits encourage people to avoid work. . . .[7]

John Latona, special counsel of Houdaille Industries:

Four of our twenty divisions are located in central city locations. . . . We have no present plans to expand these facilities. . . . Environmental and OSHA requirements have the potential to shut down two of the four plants. We assume they will not, but much struggling with red tape is involved. In states like New York and Ohio, state and local taxes and labor policies are an additional burden. It is doubtful if any program could induce us to go into an area that did not make basic business sense in the first place.[8]

John W. Hanley, chairman and president of Monsanto Company:

It seems to me that any massive new infusion of Federal aid might well sidetrack municipal administrators from their primary task of adjusting to a shrinking population and a contracting economy. . . . I am all for incentives—if they are the right kind. But, regrettably, we have seen numerous examples of Government incentives that give individuals and companies an excuse for doing what is harmful to the community over the long run. Successive increases in the minimum wage have hastened the demise of low-skilled jobs. Mounting welfare benefits have given inner city residents an incentive for not seeking work[;] . . . the most helpful thing the Federal Government can do for the cities is to avoid actions that interfere with their financial health and impede their natural rejuvenation. . . .[9]

The message from this quarter of the business community is clear. There's antipathy toward government aid to the cities or to the poor. This is by no

---

6 Ibid.

7 Ibid.

8 Ibid.

9 Ibid.

means a new message. It's a replay of business reaction to the New Deal programs of the 1930s.

If we have learned anything from the movement to involve business in social concerns, it's this: not every company is the same as the next one. Kellogg Co. might fulminate against government efforts to curtail its advertising to children, but Quaker Oats Co. will admit candidly that the TV programs beamed to children are a disgrace. Members of minority groups and women who are interested in a retail career would appear to have a much better chance with Sears, Roebuck and Co. and J. C. Penney than with K Mart Corp. The Bank of America departs from industry custom by refusing to allow its officers to sit on the boards of other companies. Levi Strauss & Co. is able to find room on its board for two minority directors, but Gulf & Western Industries can't (or won't) locate one. General Electric does such an assiduous job of recruiting that it comes away with the lion's share of black engineering graduates. Standard Oil Co. (Indiana) stands far above most companies in the nation in terms of purchases from minority suppliers. A 1973 study by the Council on Economic Priorities showed that Armco Inc. and Inland Steel Co. were the steel producers least likely to pollute air and water while National Steel Corp. and Republic Steel Corp. were the most likely. Cummins Engine Company and Dayton Hudson Corporation give 5 percent of pretax profits to charity, the maximum deduction allowed by the Internal Revenue Service; most large corporations give 1 percent.

In the area of corporate commitment to the central cities, there are a number of examples worthy of special attention. Control Data Corporation, which is one of the few companies to have succeeded in establishing new facilities in central cities, formed a new for-profit company, City Venture Corp., in 1978. City Venture will plan and manage programs designed to improve conditions in economically depressed inner-city areas. This is a throwback to a concept talked about in the 1960s: private-enterprise solutions to social problems. In St. Louis, the Ralston Purina Co. decided a decade ago to keep its headquarters in the central city and has served as the official developer of a 130-acre (52.6-hectare) renewal project adjacent to its offices. Hallmark Cards Incorporated has spearheaded an even more impressive redevelopment, Crown Center in Kansas City, Missouri. Many people thought downtown Detroit could not be saved, but blue-chip industrial and financial corporations, led by the Ford Motor Co., have begun to turn the tide with Renaissance Center, a $350 million hotel-office-retailing complex. Henry Ford II showed that he meant business when he ordered the relocation of the Ford Division from suburban Dearborn to Renaissance Center. Redevelopment is also going forward in downtown Oakland, across the bay from San Francisco. One of the prime movers has been the Clorox Co., which was founded in Oakland in 1913. In 1976 Clorox moved its corporate headquarters into the heart of the downtown urban-renewal area. The company has also provided the leadership for the Oakland Council for Economic Development. Oakland's plans for a 30-acre (12.1-hectare) City Center, consisting of stores, office buildings, restaurants, theaters, and a hotel tower, received a major shot in the arm in 1978 when Federated Department Stores agreed to anchor a shopping mall with a Bullock's branch. The Federated decision unlocked a $13.8 million federal grant. Ralph Lazarus, chairman of Federated, the nation's largest department store group, said pointedly that the decision to go into Oakland "gives us a chance to reaffirm our very strong commitment to America's downtowns."[10] Finally, it should be noted that redevelopment does not always require the bulldozer. *Business and Preservation,* a book published in 1978 by the New York research organization INFORM, presented seventy-one case histories of corporate efforts to preserve old buildings and neighborhoods.

In the preface to *Business and Preservation,* Roger G. Kennedy, vice president of the Ford Foundation, observed: "This book could not have been written ten years ago, and it would not have been written five years ago."[11] Much the same could be said about the corporate-responsibility programs that are in place today in American business. Companies are doing things today that they never dreamed of doing a decade ago, and every opinion poll shows that the public expects them to continue to be sensitive to social needs. That expectation is unlikely to change.

---

[10] Statement issued by Federated Department Stores in 1978.

[11] Raynor Warner et al., *Business and Preservation: A Survey of Business Conservation of Buildings and Neighborhoods,* INFORM, New York, 1978.

BUSINESS OPPORTUNITIES IN ADDRESSING SOCIETAL PROBLEMS

WILLIAM C. NORRIS

William C. Norris, chairman and chief executive officer of Control Data Corporation since he founded the company in 1957, is a pioneer in the development of computer technology. He is a graduate of the University of Nebraska. Since 1957 Control Data has become a leader in world markets through the application of computer technology and has grown rapidly to revenues of more than $2.7 billion and assets of $5 billion. Today it is the leading company in electronic data services.

Mr. Norris is a member of the Massachusetts Institute of Technology Corporation Visiting Committee for Sponsored Research and serves on the evaluation panel of the National Academy of Sciences for the Institute for Computer Sciences and Technology. He also is on the Advisory Committee to the White House Conference on Balanced National Growth and Economic Development and the Commerce Technical Advisory Board. In addition, he is a trustee of A.T. International, a member and trustee of the Urban Institute, and a director of the National Rural Development and Finance Corporation.

The term "corporate social responsibility" denotes vastly more today than when it first appeared a decade ago. From a few small efforts to "do good," it has come to mean, in an increasing number of companies, serious and substantial projects aimed at meeting some of society's pressing needs. Business has for too long been living in the past, preoccupied with doing things in the traditional way. Meanwhile, the world has changed. The problems and needs of United States industrial society today are different from those of the nineteenth century or the first half of the twentieth.

This difference is reflected in the growing controversy between the *social* responsibility of business and the *profit* responsibility of business. Business needs to be reminded that the fundamental reason for its existence is to deliver the goods and services and jobs that society needs. In our system profits are essential to the continuation of business, but society may decide that the business system itself, as we know it, is not essential unless it becomes more responsive to society's real needs.

While business has been mainly ignoring the major problems of society, the government has demonstrated its inability to cope successfully with them alone, and they are growing to disastrous proportions. The list of needs is long. It includes more and cheaper energy; the rebuilding of cities; environmental protection; lower food costs; more easily available and less costly health care; lower-cost, more readily available, and higher-quality education; better availability of technology; and, most important of all, a greater number of jobs, especially skilled jobs.

Solutions are critical to our future, and they are interrelated. For example, vast numbers of new jobs will come from the development and production of new energy sources and from programs for energy conservation, environmental protection, and city building and rebuilding.

What is required is a fundamental change in which business takes the initiative and provides the leadership for planning and managing the implementation of programs meeting these needs, in cooperation with government, labor unions, universities, churches, and all other leading segments of society. The major problems of our society are massive, and massive resources are required for their solution. The best approach is to view them with the strategy in mind that they can be profitable business opportunities with an appropriate sharing of cost between business and government. If the resources for solving particular problems are beyond those of a single company, as most are, they should be pooled through cooperative projects or joint-venture companies.

Control Data Corporation adopted this strategy a dozen years ago. It has been pursued vigorously and has proved sound. Although we undertake some social projects just because they are the right thing to do, we view the major unmet needs of society as opportunities to pursue profitable business. Control Data has established a number of programs to implement this strategy.

105

INNER-CITY PLANTS

Control Data has successfully located four new plants in depressed inner-city communities, and a fifth plant is under construction. When the fifth plant is completed, total employment in these plants will reach 1600 persons.

By whatever criteria are used to measure these plants—tenure, absentee-ism, profitability—they are equal to or better than our conventional operations. At the same time, we are serving the interests of each community and providing a path for disadvantaged persons to enter the mainstream of industry.

Northside Plant

Planning for the first inner-city plant began in 1967 during a time of rioting in Minneapolis. A site in a black poverty area on the troubled north side of the city was selected, and the plant opened in January 1968.

We are careful to observe a number of rules that bear heavily on the success of an inner-city plant:

1. Opening and operating such a plant is not philanthropy but a business venture that will return an attractive profit.

2. The start-up cost is to be viewed just as business views research and development for a new product.

3. There is a total commitment to success that is widely visible inside and outside the company. To help assure this commitment, the plant must be new and must use the most advanced facilities, and it must also make an important product so that the company is as dependent on the plant's success as are the people working there.

4. The community has an equal contribution to make to the plant's business in the form of knowledge about the community, its people's problems, and potential solutions. Community leaders commit themselves to help assure success, and there are clearly established links between them and the company.

5. Unusual problems must be solved promptly, not kicked around. There were plenty of unusual problems in starting the first plant. I will briefly describe some of the problems which are also typical of those encountered with the other inner-city plants.

One problem was the need for employees to obtain credit. We solved that by providing loans from our Commercial Credit Co. subsidiary. Another was the lack of adequate day care for children, which resulted in absenteeism by mothers who needed to work. With the help of the community, a day-care center was established. We found, too, that Monday morning's production would suffer because part of the workforce had landed in jail over the weekend. The solution to that problem was twofold: we established a procedure whereby one of our young lawyers made a trip to the city jail early Monday morning with a book of bail bonds to get people back to work; the other action was to provide more extensive counseling and legal help to solve personal problems and accommodate workers to the requirements of full-time employment.

To bring the Northside plant up to the efficiency level of other plants cost $2.5 million, of which the government paid $1 million. The $1.5 million that Control Data paid was regarded as the equivalent of research and development for a product. Considering that we now have an efficient production operation, with average tenure of employees at more than 5 years, and considering what we have learned, the payoff is a handsome one, comparable to the payoff from R&D.

Northside Child Development Center

When the Northside plant began operation, there were no child-care facilities in the neighborhood, but many of the residents, employees and potential employees, were female heads of households with young children. Clearly, child care had to be provided if the most urgent employment needs in that neighborhood were to be served. So we enlisted the support of the community and got a day-care center started in a vacant 80-year-old school building.

In 1976 the day-care center was moved into a new building specifically designed as a center for child development. It was built with 90 percent private funds and loans from local firms.

The center provides care for more than 130 children aged from 6 weeks to 13 years. Trained personnel conduct a carefully designed program for enriched child development. The program encompasses personal management and social development, physical development, arts and crafts, sciences, and black history and awareness. It is an A1 + center which I unabashedly proclaim as the finest, bar none.

Part-Time Job Opportunities

We also learned that there were many job seekers who could not meet full-time work-hour requirements. These included female heads of households with school-age children as well as high school, vocational school, and college students in need of income to help them stay in school or to supplement family income.

To address that problem, early in 1970 we opened a plant employing part-time workers in the middle of the depressed Selby area of St. Paul. The operation was started in an abandoned bowling alley, and in 1974 a new facility was opened to accommodate growth. This was the first new industrial facility to be built on a mile-long stretch of Selby's dilapidated commercial strip since a trolley-car powerhouse had been erected in 1889.

The Selby plant's employment level is now at 230 persons. The first shift is mostly made up of mothers of school-age children; the second shift, primarily of high school and college students.

Near the Selby operation is our newest and largest inner-city plant, housing Control Data's worldwide distribution center. The fourth inner-city operation is the Capital plant in Washington, D.C. These two plants function similarly to Northside and Selby.

EDUCATION

Basic to jobs are education and training. Control Data's largest program addresses the worldwide need for better, more readily available, and lower-cost education.

The only practical way to make major progress in solving this massive and urgent problem is through the use of technology such as television, audio-video tapes, and telephone, cable, and satellite transmission coordinated in a network learning system with computer-based education. Control Data has been engaged in developing such a system, called PLATO computer-based education, since 1961. We see PLATO computer-based education as ultimately becoming the largest segment of our business.

The PLATO system provides a broad and flexible range of courses and lessons stored in a central computer. This material is accessible by a student through a televisionlike terminal, operated by the student at his or her own pace via a typewriterlike keyboard and a touch-sensitive screen.

The system utilizes many features that facilitate rapid, personalized learning in a self-paced, easy-to-use manner. Students communicate with computer-stored instructional materials via the PLATO terminal. These materials are displayed in the form of numbers, text, drawings, and animated graphics. Each individual receives continuous personal attention and immediate feedback through step-by-step lessons. The system can also accommodate a number of persons at the same time, each with varied knowledge levels or even each studying different subject matter.

The PLATO method of learning has proved to be extremely successful in a wide variety of subjects, ranging from adult remedial education in basic reading, language, and mathematics skills to complex postgraduate courses. Learners have total control over their rate of study and can privately repeat tests or parts of tests as many times as necessary to achieve full understanding of the subject matter. The PLATO system has infinite patience and a virtually inexhaustible memory, and it gives students immediate feedback, encouragement, and support.

Our multifaceted education program includes the sale of complete computer-based–education systems and the offering of education and training through our learning centers and vocational training schools. There are nineteen vocational training schools called Control Data Institutes in the United States and fifteen in other countries. The curriculum consists of PLATO computer-based–education training courses for entry-level positions in computer operation, maintenance, and programming. Currently, approximately 7000 students are graduated annually.

Fair Break

One application of the computer-based–education program is called Fair Break, aptly named because it prepares and assists young disadvantaged persons to get and keep jobs and makes more jobs available to them. Twenty PLATO Fair Break centers are now operating and delivering innovative training in basic skills, job readiness, life management, and job-seeking skills. The young people, who work part time, not only receive an income but are helped to identify any problems which should be resolved before they seek employment in the community. The program is delivered in cooperation with public schools with financial backing from Comprehensive Employment and Training Act (CETA) funds.

Basic-Skills Learning System

Our basic-skills learning system is worthy of special mention. This program, which Control Data has been codeveloping for several years in cooperation with leading educators, is designed to help underachieving students advance from third-grade to eighth-grade equivalency in reading, language, and mathematics skills. Some impressive results have been reported. In one study in Baltimore, 24 functionally illiterate adults advanced almost one full grade level in reading after only 22 hours of instruction, of which 15 hours were spent on PLATO. In mathematics, 49 students tested advanced an average of 1.2 grade levels after only 30 hours of instruction, of which 20 hours were spent on PLATO. With another group of 200 students in Florida, an average advance of one grade level was achieved after only 14 hours of terminal time on PLATO.

We've taken the PLATO system to the heart of the inner city and into four prison systems in two states and proved that it works. With the basic-skills learning system, we've taught functionally illiterate people how to read and write in these toughest of all environments.

Rosebud

An effort that will ultimately find important application in inner cities and in poverty-stricken rural areas is our program to improve Indian health care on the Rosebud Indian Reservation in South Dakota. Control Data has worked with tribal leaders to apply computer technology and managerial resources to improve the delivery of health care dramatically. Previously, one small hospital was responsible for the care of 8500 native Americans. Those who required care had to travel up to 130 miles (209 kilometers) to get it, and the number of professional staff was woefully inadequate to the task. Significant improvements have been evident since Control Data's medical van began traveling in the reservation and providing care to 900 residents per month. In addition, four clinics have been established, and Indian paramedics have been trained. All this was accomplished with a front-end investment from Control Data's funds for corporate social responsibility.

Even though substantial improvement has been made at Rosebud, there is still urgent need for further improvement and an even greater need at most other reservations, where health care is not only poor but shamefully poor.

The next phase of the program is to teach self health care to avoid illness through the use of PLATO computer-based education. This is a gargantuan task, but it is the only possible way to bring about the needed improvement in Indian health.

Control Data is committed to a large-scale effort to help make the necessary changes in health care through training, not only for American Indians but for all. And we have the dedication and can marshal the resources of other companies and the government ultimately to achieve that goal.

TRANSFER OF TECHNOLOGY AND AID TO SMALL BUSINESS

The development of solutions to society's problems is handicapped when proven technology is not replicated. This has certainly been the case in urban efforts. The successful problem-solving technologies of one city or one neighborhood may never be applied in another setting. Control Data's TECHNOTEC service addresses this problem. It is a worldwide computer-based communications system for collecting and helping to transfer technology. Although all types of technology are stored in the data base, priority is placed on solar energy, agriculture, food processing, and urban technology. In agriculture emphasis is placed on technology for small family farms, including urban farming, and small-scale food processing, because we believe that they offer the best means in the future to reduce food costs and increase production.

A host of new technologies, such as lower-cost energy sources and lower-cost and energy-efficient construction are required for better inner-city living. Many already exist and are being stored in TECHNOTEC. Easier access to needed technologies will be especially helpful to small enterprises, which will play an important role in rebuilding neighborhoods and commercial centers and in providing many other services. Participation in small enterprises gives control to residents of the inner city and provides them with the long-absent economic opportunity and incentives for success. And a revitalization process that is founded on diverse profitable enterprises instead of depending upon a host of public programs will be a principal means of rebuilding a community. From within the community can become self-sufficient and responsive to changing needs.

Business and Technology Centers

Because of the importance of small business in creating and maintaining a solid base for urban revitalization, a new program of Control Data focuses on facilitating small-business formation and operation in inner cities through business and technology centers. A business and technology center is a business engaged in providing various combinations of consulting, shared facilities, and services for facilitating the successful start-up and growth of small businesses.

A building or a cluster of buildings containing flexible laboratory and office space is subdivided and leased to small businesses. Within the buildings are centrally shared facilities and services, including a library, a model shop, drafting, accounting, purchasing, and legal services, and a complete range of computer services, including technology-locating and transfer services and computer-based education.

Economies of scale will make it possible to provide occupants with needed facilities and services of much higher quality at a considerably lower cost than each one would be capable of procuring alone. Benefits will also be obtained from the enhanced environment for peer interchange. It is intended that computer-based education will provide not only a wide range of courses, including management training, accounting, and compliance with Federal Trade Commission (FTC) regulations, but also enhanced collaboration and technology interchange with universities and government laboratories.

A roster of professional consultants, including members of university faculties, will be maintained. There will be an important element of social service, in that the professional consultants, both from business and from academia, will provide a certain percentage of time free of charge in helping would-be entrepreneurs to prepare plans.

Community Cooperation Office

Obviously, a business and technology center needs a high degree of community support to be successful. As with inner-city plants, Control Data will not undertake a center without a commitment for full support by the community and an organized way of providing it. Support includes an appropriate piece of land at a reasonable price, CETA funds for training, and seed money for new companies.

It is my belief that the most effective manner for a community to provide seed money is through the type of organization that Control Data and others have established in Minnesota. We call it the Minnesota Cooperation Office for Small Business. It is a nonprofit corporation that is supported by private contributions. Members of the board of directors are leaders from all the major sectors of society: business, labor, church, government, academia, nonprofit organizations, etc. The small permanent staff is supplemented with volunteers having the professional expertise that is required in the many different fields in which the small businesses will be engaged.

The *modus operandi* is simple. An investor has an idea for a new product or service and wants to start a company to develop and market it. Financial backing from the usual sources is not available; venture capitalists are usually not interested in unproven ideas. The community cooperation office provides assistance. A volunteer team of experts is assembled from local businesses and universities to review the idea and, if it is sound, to help in the preparation of a business plan and in the prompt completion of the many other steps required in setting up a business. Since there is substantial risk, the initial capital is spread among a number of investors, including all types of businesses, banks, insurance companies, larger industrial companies, and venture capitalists, plus labor unions, religious organizations, and local civic and government units.

CONCLUSION

A major barrier to the widespread adoption of a strategy of seeking business opportunities from meeting major social needs is the relentless pressure exerted by the investment community for short-term earnings improvement. For some reason many companies conduct their businesses as though they believed that financial institutions were their only constituency. In fact, of course, these institutions are only one part of their constituency. Financial institutions may influence the price of a company's stock in the short term, but since they themselves frequently recognize no constituency of their own, they can exert only limited influence over the long term.

In our society individuals have the franchise to maintain or change systems. Our experience indicates that the majority of individual shareholders will accept, indeed support, the concept of allocating substantial corporate resources to longer-term payout programs that address major social needs as business opportunities. What is required is that they be offered that alternative by aggressive, forward-looking, and socially responsible corporate managements.

See essays "Corporate Governance," by Donald E. Schwartz, and "Affirmative Action and the Urban Crisis," by Milton Moskowitz, for additional data on Control Data Corporation programs.

CORPORATE RESPONSIBILITY AND MINORITY ECONOMIC DEVELOPMENT

COY G. EKLUND

Coy G. Eklund is president and chief executive officer of the Equitable Life Assurance Society of the United States, which is headquartered in New York. A graduate of Michigan State University, he began his insurance career with the Equitable as an agent in 1938. He entered the Army in 1942 and saw World War II service in Europe.

After the war, Mr. Eklund rejoined the Equitable and, in 1947, was appointed agency manager to start a new agency in Detroit, which in 12 years he made the second-largest agency of the company. He was elected vice president in 1959, agency vice president in 1961, and senior vice president in 1964. Named to the board of directors in 1965, he was elected executive vice president in 1969, president in 1973, and chief executive officer on April 1, 1975.

Mr. Eklund is a director of the Bendix Corp., the Burroughs Corporation, the Salk Institute for Biological Studies, and Grand Central Art Galleries. He also serves on the boards of Americans for Indian Opportunity and the Women's Action Alliance and is chairman of the National Urban League.

In recent years, it has become clear that the public expects corporate executives to be more explicit about what we do and to assume an increasingly participative role in society. While some may still believe that business should not be bothered with social concerns, most of us hold the opposite opinion. Certainly we must assiduously live up to the fiduciary responsibilities incumbent upon us by virtue of the fact that we are responsible for the stewardship of our stockholders' or members' interests first and foremost, but within that fixed restraint we have a sure responsibility to participate in imaginative and reasonable ways in the total community of which we are a part. We believe that the inescapable burden of business freedom is social responsibility. For us today, social irresponsibility is about as unacceptable as financial irresponsibility.

IMPORTANCE OF SOCIAL RESPONSIBILITY

I should frankly admit that I am the traditionally conservative businessman with a fixed allegiance to the profit-motive system. I hold the firm conviction that the profit-motivated private-enterprise system is the goose that lays the golden egg. But I don't believe that the highest purpose of business is to maximize profits. The uppermost objective of any business is to stay in business. Survival comes ahead of everything else. In the future, it will require more than first-rate profits for any business to survive: responsible social conduct has become a sine qua non. Long-term survival of the corporate world depends on meeting the expectations of social consensus. We must continue to hold the confidence of the people of the United States and validate to their satisfaction the social legitimacy of the private-enterprise system. Nothing less than corporate survival is at stake.

Society granted our corporate charter—our licensed privilege to exist as a corporate enterprise. Clearly this is a privilege subject to whatever requirements society decides to impose. We will continue in business only as long as we reasonably meet those requirements. They constitute a condition of survival.

In originally creating the corporation, the people intended it to fulfill certain of their purposes and to perform in ways beneficial to society. They certainly did not bring forth the corporation so that it could behave in ways detrimental to their interests or in ways that would jeopardize their well-being.

Today our chartered mandate calls not only for goods and services of usefulness but, just as insistently, for corporate conduct that accords with the social values established by society. Moreover, the rules of conduct will be subject to continuing revision as new issues emerge and broad social consensus evolves. Always it will be the people who define what constitutes acceptable social behavior on the part of the corporation.

Business people have always been sensitive to social consensus in the marketplace. They have passionately catered to it, meeting needs, tastes, and preferences to win customers' favor. Satisfying customers has always been the key to success, the sure way to build a lasting business. The marketplace also has always supplied a discipline. It has been ever ready to sound the death knell for any business that fails to achieve customer satisfaction. That discipline continues to operate.

Today business is dealing with still another marketplace, one that is much larger and more sophisticated and looks not only at the performance value of the product but at the performance value of the producer of the product as well. The performance of the corporation must be not only legal but ethical, fair, open, and considerate; it must accord with the total well-being requirements set by society.

The insistent call upon corporate enterprise is to behave in ways that will preserve the integrity of the economic, social, political, and ecological systems deemed essential to the betterment of life and even to the continued existence of life. In short, we are called upon to behave with social responsibility, which in a nutshell means "coming right with people." Social responsibility calls for thoughtful inclusion of people considerations in every decision and every action; it means applying the simple standards of honesty, decency, and fairness in all we do.

THE SOCIAL RESPONSIBILITY REVIEW PROCESS AT THE EQUITABLE

At the Equitable, we are working to see that a sense of social accountability pervades the total management process and that it is institutionalized as an integral part of our corporate value system. The Social Performance Committee of our board of directors monitors and reviews our total business conduct, manifesting the board's concern for these matters. We also have an Office of Corporate Social Responsibility to advise, counsel, and assist top management in staying abreast of the broad spectrum of social concerns. That office formulates and proposes plans and policies and is responsible for the periodic evaluation of social performance. However, achieving desired social performance is a functional responsibility placed squarely on the shoulders of line managers accountable for each major component of our business—accountable for social performance just as they are for financial performance and for goal achievement in general.

Periodically, top management meets for a thorough review of progress in achieving the social performance goals established each year. Fundamental to each review session is a comprehensive report that presents data on a wide range of social performance indicators. The reports extend from affirmative-action statistics to customer-satisfaction indices, to details on corporate contributions, and to quantification of newly approved social-priority investments. The Office of Social Responsibility reviews and analyzes the data and adds to the report its own evaluation of the Equitable's social performance for the period.

Each section of the report is analyzed and commented on by the responsible senior officer at review sessions, which all top officers attend. Weak spots are targeted for action. The review sessions often involve sharp questioning and engender wholesome discussion. Following the management review session, the same material is presented to the Social Performance Committee of the board, where it receives a careful overview and evaluation with top management.

Our social performance review system is by no means as nearly comprehensive or as precise as we want it someday to be, but we believe that it is a highly valuable means of focusing our attention as an organization on the vital matters involved.

AID TO MINORITY ENTREPRENEURIAL DEVELOPMENT

Partly as the result of our formal review process, we regularly identify aspects of our business in which there is further opportunity to make a contribution to the total well-being of society. For example, we believe that we can have a favorable effect on the economic development of minority groups. We believe that one of the most vital ways of improving the general welfare of the minority community is through the development of profitable business enterprises owned and managed by members of minority groups. We have identified a number of ways in which we can support such entrepreneurial development.

Affirmative Financing

One important way to support entrepreneurial development is to provide the foundation capital that the owner of a minority business needs to obtain additional financing from banks and other conventional financial institutions. This is accomplished through Equico-Capital Corporation, our wholly owned minority-enterprise small-business investment company (MESBIC) subsidiary. Equico-Capital Corporation is the largest privately owned MESBIC in existence.

In cooperation with other financial institutions, Equico-Capital seeks to finance businesses that have promising growth and profit potential and are large enough to support a strong management team. While its maximum investment in any one company is $300,000, its participation with other financial institutions has enabled one minority-owned company to raise as much as $6 million. Since 1974 Equico-Capital has steadily increased the size and scope of its operations, and it is now able to consider investment opportunities in most cities in the United States.

Affirmative Purchasing

As a large business enterprise, the Equitable purchases everything from paper clips to electronic computers. Since it is our policy to promote the economic development of firms controlled by members of minority groups, women, and handicapped individuals, we have established a purchasing program designed to increase the volume of purchases from firms in which such people have a majority interest. All our purchases of supplies and services are included for consideration under this program.

While each line organization is made accountable for carrying out this policy, personnel with purchasing responsibilities are charged specifically with seeking out these firms, increasing purchases from them in accordance with this policy, keeping a record of all such purchases, and reporting them to an appropriate senior executive officer for our periodic social performance review.

Affirmative Banking

For several reasons, the Equitable is obliged to maintain banking relationships throughout the nation. It is our policy to adopt an affirmative-action attitude with respect to selected minority-owned banks. In developing such relationships, fair and consistent criteria are carefully considered:

1.   The bank must be at least 51 percent minority-owned and -controlled, be operated for the primary benefit of the minority community, have a majority of minority employees including officers, and be officially designated as a minority bank by the U.S. Department of Commerce.

2.   It must be a sound bank in all financial respects, with appropriate facilities, including branch locations, which meet our requirements.

Once a minority bank has been selected in accordance with these criteria, the account then established will be actively used; it will not be a dormant, nonworking account. The treasurer's department will initiate an affirmative effort with the bank to create this activity.

All bank relationships are, of course, monitored in accordance with the

Equitable's established procedures, which recognize the imperative responsibility for safeguarding and productively employing all company assets.

Affirmative Advertising

The Equitable allocates annually not less than 10 percent of its total national advertising budget to minority-owned media. Priority consideration is given to black-owned media.

SUMMARY

Through affirmative financing, purchasing, banking, and advertising programs, we endeavor to contribute to minority entrepreneurial development in various ways. These and other business-conduct activities are tied together by the social performance review process, which is the key to marshaling the diverse forces of our large organization to the achievement of our corporate goals.

We are pleased, but certainly not satisfied, with what we are accomplishing. As we continue always toward bettering the bottom line, we will determinedly continue to emphasize coming right with people. We will strive always to contribute significantly to the preservation of the whole and wholesome society upon which corporate survival ultimately depends.

JOBS FOR THE HARD-TO-EMPLOY

ROBERT C. HOLLAND

Dr. Holland is president of the Committee for Economic Development (CED), an independent, nonpartisan, nonprofit research and educational organization composed of approximately 200 trustees who develop specific recommendations for business and public policy. Most of these trustees are board chairmen, presidents of major corporations, or presidents of universities.

Before joining CED, Dr. Holland served as a member of the Board of Governors of the Federal Reserve System (1973–1976). He attended the University of Pennsylvania and was awarded a B.S. degree in finance in 1948, an M.A. degree in 1949, and a Ph.D. degree in economics in 1959. From 1961 to 1973 he held various research and administrative staff positions at the Board of Governors of the Federal Reserve System, culminating in service as Executive Director (1971–1973), Secretary of the Board (1968–1971), and Secretary of the Federal Open Market Committee (1966–1973).

Dr. Holland is a member of the Council on Foreign Relations, the Business and Labor Economic Policy Council of the United Nations Association of the United States of America, the Wharton School Board of Overseers and the Wharton School Finance Department Advisory Committee, the Lutheran Resources Commission Advisory Committee, the Comptroller General's Consultant Panel, and the Lutheran Church in America Board of Pensions.

Jobs are the lifeblood of a productive economy. Achieving high employment with stable, noninflationary economic growth has been a major goal of national policy in the United States for three decades.

The most socially beneficial acts that a corporation can perform are to provide jobs, incomes, products, and services that meet the needs and desires of the people. A national organization of business leaders and educators, the Committee for Economic Development (CED), has been deeply committed to the goal of high employment without inflation since its formation in 1942.

COSTS OF UNEMPLOYMENT

Why have business leaders made high employment a priority? Clearly this is a matter of enlightened self-interest. High and persistent unemployment erodes the efficiency and flexibility of the economy. The jobless do not contribute to the nation's output; rather they must be supported by the rest of society.

There is another dimension to the costs of unemployment: the human dimension. For many, joblessness means hardship and deprivation in terms of forgone income, lost skills, lack of self-respect, and general physical and emotional debilitation.

The nation must also cope with the costs imposed by higher levels of crime, illness, alcoholism, family breakup, child abuse, and other social burdens and disorders brought on by unemployment. It must pay the price in higher budgets and higher taxes and in a deterioration in the quality of life. The sum total of all these costs of unemployment is formidable indeed, both for businesses and for the country as a whole. Thus it should be no surprise that enlightened business executives want to reduce these costs through more efficient and effective programs.

CED has consistently supported the view that the single most effective means of reducing unemployment is a strong economy. It has long advocated policies that aim at steady and vigorous economic growth to achieve high employment, and it has consistently rejected prescriptions for using massive unemployment or chronic stagnation as a means of combating inflation.

Still, there are large groups of people who want to work but cannot find jobs even in the best of economic times. These so-called structurally unemployed may be undereducated, unskilled, or inexperienced, too young or too old, or unable to work full time. They may be subject to discrimination or to restrictive labor practices, or they may lack the basic work disciplines and abilities to acquire a steady job and keep it.

CED PROJECT

CED recognized that the attack on unemployment could not be fully effective unless it was in good part aimed directly at those groups that were consistently left out of the mainstream of the labor force. Hence, a project was undertaken to examine the problem of jobs for the hard-to-employ and to recommend solutions.

Work on that project began in 1975, when there was serious concern among CED's trustees over the general high level of unemployment and, particularly, over the extraordinarily high jobless rates among numerous disadvantaged segments of the labor force: members of racial minorities, oldsters, the physically handicapped, and especially young people without prior work experience whose entire careers were being blighted before they began. At that point, however, many of the business trustees seriously questioned whether much of that labor force could be absorbed directly into private employment. There were feelings that regular personnel practices could not handle such people and doubts that extraordinary corporate expenditures to train and orient such would-be employees would be fruitful or could be justified to shareholders. Many government officials and academic experts shared these doubts, and numerous disappointing experiences seemed to corroborate such attitudes. The view was prevalent that training and initially employing these individuals was primarily a job for government.

As the study progressed and insights were shared, it became clearer that government training and public-service employment had great drawbacks, too. Government-run training programs often did not develop skills that matched emerging job opportunities. Public-service jobs were typically dead-end, and by their nature they helped to sag the interest and initiative of those employed. Furthermore, providing government jobs boosted the federal budget and its deficit.

Recognizing that four-fifths of the labor force is privately employed, CED searched carefully for better ways to utilize the private sector, which clearly could offer the best opportunities for job dignity, permanence, and advancement. It began to learn of first one and then another instance in which a private job program of some sort had been devised in some city, plant, or branch office and was working successfully. Sometimes only a few workers were involved. Sometimes the program was just a local manager's good idea. Sometimes local public and private officials had worked out a program in partnership. Often partial and temporary government financial assistance was involved, usually through subsidies for on-the-job training. A nationwide survey of CED firms was taken, and dozens of such cases turned up. Correspondence and follow-up field investigations convinced CED that many of these programs were workable and could be replicated in at least some other areas. These practical demonstrations of what could be accomplished became the key part of a comprehensive policy statement, *Jobs for the Hard-to-Employ: New Directions for Public-Private Partnership,* published by CED in January 1978. An accompanying volume spotlighted sixty of the most successful private and public-private training and job programs.[1]

The central message of the CED policy statement is that a stronger public-private partnership needs to be developed to increase training and job opportunities in the private sector and to speed the transition of the hard-to-employ from government income support and subsidized public or private jobs to permanent private employment. CED trustees have come to believe that while not all unfortunate persons can become employable, most of them can. Making that distinction is a key to wise public policy.

CED's agenda for action has strong policy implications for business and government. The report recommends:

1.   New and expanded use on a nationwide basis of private-sector programs that already work effectively and creation of a clearinghouse for disseminating information about successful and innovative programs

2.   Stronger organizational mechanisms to mobilize private-sector involvement, including much wider use of

a.   Direct government employment contracts with private nonprofit organizations created by consortia of business firms

b.   Other types of intermediary organizations that can help business handle job development, training, and placement activities

c.   Jobs corporations to provide training and jobs for the hardest-to-employ

d.   Cooperative community efforts, involving businesses, nonprofit organizations, unions, schools, and governments, to increase training and job opportunities

3.   Increased incentives and reduced disincentives for private employment of the hard-to-employ, including additional experimentation with categorical tax credits, with stipends for trainees and apprentices, and with selective exemptions from the minimum wage and higher ceilings on social security earnings

4.   Improved approaches to the problems of particular groups among the hard-to-employ, including

a.   Increased stress on business involvement in skill training and upgrading of the disadvantaged

b.   Improved transition from school to work for youths as well as for other age groups, including increased use of apprenticeship and cooperative education programs

---

[1] *Training and Jobs Programs in Action: Case Studies in Private-Sector Initiatives for the Hard-to-Employ,* Committee for Economic Development, in cooperation with Work in America Institute, New York, 1978.

c.   More productive use of older workers, including steps to smooth the transition from regular work to retirement

d.   Increased and wider use of alternative work patterns to make more employment available to the young, the old, and other workers who cannot conform to a full-time work schedule

5.   Greater business use of alternatives to outright layoffs in recessions, including skill upgrading and work sharing

6.   Improved management and closer integration of government programs that facilitate the employment of the hard-to-employ, particularly the U.S. Employment Service and the Comprehensive Employment and Training Act (CETA) programs

This agenda for action is neither impractical nor visionary. Corporations large and small, nonprofit organizations, and governments throughout the country are currently conducting many such programs, as CED's case studies have demonstrated. These and other successful programs that have subsequently been uncovered are serving as models for further action and innovation by business and for stronger cooperation among business, government, and the community.

RESULTS

At the federal level, the results have been heartening. The Carter administration, at the urging of CED and other business organizations, has given renewed emphasis to the role of the private sector in hiring and training the hard-core unemployed. The new Title VII of CETA provides encouragement and financial support for local private-industry councils (a type of intermediary organization recommended in the CED report) that can undertake to develop and operate jobs programs in cities with a high proportion of the chronically unemployed. The National Alliance of Business is reorganizing to provide impetus and support for these programs.

The challenge is to promote a broader understanding of successful approaches among those who have a stake in the plight of the jobless and are in a position to take corrective action. At local policy forums conducted by CED and others across the nation, leaders from all major community segments are meeting to exchange views on mechanisms that work and ways in which these can be applied to the problems of specific cities. As a result of such discussions, new local programs are being examined, tested, and introduced more frequently, with greater vigor, and with stronger hope for success.

But these locally held discussions are also uncovering tough problems. For example, preparing the worker for the workplace is only one side of a dilemma that also demands a commitment on the part of the employer to prepare the workplace for the worker. The school-to-work transition requires a much more intensive effort to match education to the reality of the jobs market. And, in developing a career ladder, a much greater corporate commitment is needed to promote and upgrade personnel in entry-level positions.

The problem is both huge and complex, and progress can only be gradual. But the national atmosphere for finding solutions has substantially improved because genuine progress has been made. The success of numerous private-sector and public-private partnership ventures has finally begun to relieve the gloom that had settled over the future of millions of hard-to-employ Americans.

More than ever, American corporations are recognizing that hiring the hard-to-employ is not merely good social policy but good business as well. In case after case, hiring practices adopted out of a sense of social responsibility or in response to government prodding have produced favorable financial returns along with enormous human and community benefits.

CORPORATE SOCIAL RESPONSIBILITY

A New Term for an Old Concept with New Significance

WALTER A. HAAS, JR.

Walter A. Haas, Jr., is the chairman of the board and director of Levi Strauss & Co., a major international manufacturer of jeans and other clothing items, headquartered in San Francisco. He also serves as a director of the Bank of America and BankAmerica Corporation and of Ual, Inc., and United Air Lines, vice president of the Levi Strauss Foundation, trustee of the Ford Foundation and of the Committee for Economic Development, director of the National Urban League, and member of the SRI International Advisory Council.

    Mr. Haas was educated at the University of California at Berkeley and at the Harvard Graduate School of Business Administration.

The new term "corporate social responsibility" refers to a relatively old concept that is being expanded to address an increasing number of societal demands on business. These demands reflect a widely held belief that business lacks a significant concern for how its decisions and operations affect society. The general yet comprehensive nature of the term makes definition difficult. Nevertheless, at Levi Strauss & Co. we believe in the comprehensiveness of the concept, and we wish a concern for society to permeate every level of our company and to become a part of the day-to-day decision-making process.

Leaving aside the definitional problem, most contemporary observers of corporate behavior begin by positing three basic rationales for the acceptance of an expanded role for business in society. These are:

● A moral obligation, usually stated as "the right thing to do"

● A self-interest concept, usually stated as "a long-term economic self-interest of a corporation"

● A sociopolitical rationale, usually stated as "a necessity to preserve the private sector"

A MORAL OBLIGATION

We believe that all three rationales present compelling arguments for the acceptance of this new role, but for Levi Strauss & Co. our strongest motivation is the moral obligation. Simply stated, we believe that this is the right thing to do. This obligation has been reinforced over the years by a family tradition reaching as far back as Levi Strauss himself. As early as 1850 Strauss established the goals of our company: a quality product, the best possible working conditions for our employees, and community service. Today he would be called socially responsible. Then he was simply called a good man.

Corporate executives develop an idea of what they want their company to be. If this conception remains constant over long periods of time and is institutionalized, it becomes, in effect, a personality characteristic of the corporation. Levi Strauss & Co.'s commitment to a genuine concern for people is a character trait of our corporation which is worthy of being maintained. Our primary concern in this regard is to demonstrate in every aspect of our business and in our dealings with the public that we are a corporation that cares about people. By example and encouragement, our top management has attempted to make the work environment a place where a genuine concern for people could manifest itself. As the leadership of the corporation changes, we've tried to ensure that this concept of what the company should be is maintained.

Part of the challenge revolves around current business operations that give rise to the phenomenon of the "transitory manager." Transitory managers affect the ability to maintain a corporate personality because their present work is not likely to be their lifelong environment. Thus, they lack a vested interest in identifying with or perpetuating a particular corporate trait which they do not believe has broad acceptance or has a significant impact on their careers. Their primary concerns and goals are short-term: daily, weekly, and monthly bottom-line figures. Contemplating sociological and political implications of contemporary social problems and how these will manifest themselves 15 to 20 years down the road is an alien process for most and is considered irrelevant by some. Encouraging this concern and providing an environment which allows this process to develop is the greatest challenge of top management. At Levi Strauss & Co. we pride ourselves on our ability to attract and retain managers who can grow with our "personality" and our business practices.

LONG-TERM SELF-INTEREST AND MAINTENANCE OF THE PRIVATE SECTOR

Being sensitive to the needs and demands of society and joining in cooperative efforts to help meet those needs is in our long-term economic self-interest. If more companies had anticipated the change in societal values from a desire for greater quantity and diversity of material goods to a concern for the environment and the quality of life, many current environmental regulations might have been avoided. At Levi Strauss & Co., our early commitment to quality produced a consumer loyalty to our product that has certainly been in our long-term economic self-interest.

There are, of course, other reasons why addressing social problems is intimately related to our self-interest. The most important is the improvement in a community's general climate. A community with a wide range of opportunities and services such as good educational, recreational, and cultural activities, a comprehensive health system, social services that care for those in need, and an accessible and fair justice system provides a quality of life we all seek. The cycle is reinforcing: people want to live in a good community and work for a good company, and a company wants to locate in a good community and needs good people.

It is important to remember that the role of business in society has been granted through the consent of the governed. Neither the free enterprise system nor the corporation was legitimized by the Constitution. American political institutions and their response to society's goals will determine the future course of American business. Government regulation of the private sector and curbs on business's independence of action have not occurred in a linear progression upward over the years. Instead, packages of legislation have been passed at periodic intervals and have usually been spurred or accompanied by a general perception, valid or not, of widespread abuses on the part of business. Thus, the degree to which business maintains its present level of independence rests on a willingness to monitor itself and on an ability to discern and react to new societal demands.

When Levi Strauss & Co. started a plant in Vallejo, California, two of the first operators hired were blacks. That meant that new employees coming into the plant saw that that was the way it was. Shortly after that an operator who came from the South complained to me about our policy. I said, "Look, I'm sorry, but that's the way it is. And if you leave, we'll be sorry." She didn't leave.

Then we took a bigger step in the South. Frankly, we didn't have the courage to take it as soon as we had wanted. We just didn't know whether it was right to impose our views. This sounds like medieval times now, but you must put yourself back to that period. We didn't know then whether it was proper to force our views on some of those small Southern towns. But we decided to, and Paul Glasgow, who was then in charge of operations, was quite in tune with this decision.

In Blackstone, Virginia, we weren't attracting enough people to our plant for one reason or another. Paul came to us and said, "I think the time is right to integrate that plant." So we said, "Good. We're with you." He went down and spoke with the powers that be. Blackstone was a small Southern town. He came back and said that they wanted a wall to divide the plant into black and white sections. We said, "No, we're not going to." Then they asked us to paint a dividing line. Again we refused. Then they wanted separate drinking fountains and separate rest rooms. We refused, and they didn't like our refusal. But they swallowed it, and our payroll continued and we expanded.

Of course, when we went into communities in the South, affirmative-action programs were not required by law and weren't even so identified, but we were a relatively important employer in all those communities. These developments go back 25 years now. In the end, the economic clout of a potential payroll of several hundred employees overcame any local objections to integration. I think we changed attitudes in many communities.

A lot of my business friends complain that they have trouble with their employees and the unions. Why do we take on this additional burden? "Why bother?" they ask. I guess we do because we believe in it.

We do these things because they seem morally right, and they usually turn out to be good business too. In the Blackstone case we kept a plant going. By having an integrated policy we had a much greater labor pool to draw from, which in a labor-intensive industry is important. But our policy didn't start that way. We just had a conviction that integration was right.

One of our first attempts to aid the disadvantaged was a plan to help small retail businesses. We had six small retailers in the general San Francisco Bay area to whom we gave technical assistance. But, you know, it's very difficult for a small business to succeed anywhere today regardless of whether it's minority-owned or not. If small businesses don't have management capability and if they're located in a poor area, they have a hard time getting credit, a hard time getting insurance, and a hard time getting delivery. I'm sorry to say that after several years and a lot of help from others, all six retailers failed.

Next we tried contracting with a manufacturing firm in Oakland named Ghettoes Incorporated. It sounded like an ideal situation: we would provide the technical know-how, and we would buy the firm's products. We loaned it sewing machines and an experienced full-time manager, but that firm eventually failed too.

Then we decided that we'd try giving steady employment to a group of disadvantaged people. We made a study to find an area that had the lowest economic level in the country. I think Greene County, Alabama, came out as the third or fourth poorest county in the United States; it was almost entirely black. We thought that by opening a plant there we could provide jobs and improve the whole community by giving people buying power. For a lot of reasons the venture didn't work out as we had hoped. But we felt a responsibility to the people, and thanks to our community affairs department we were able to help organize a group of local black businessmen who took over the operation; so it's still in existence. We found technical assistance for the group and helped it get government contracts. And then we sold it all the equipment in the plant for $100.

I really don't know of any other corporation that would have stayed with this program as we did. I think a lot of people feel as the economist Milton Friedman does: the only responsibility that a corporation has is to make money. I disagree with them completely.

PROGRAM INNOVATIONS

Levi Strauss & Co. has developed several innovative programs which we believe are investments in the future. The most innovative of these programs and the one of which we are proudest is our Community Involvement Team (CIT) program. It is difficult to discuss the teams of this program as if they were distant dots or lines on an organization chart. Knowing these people and their work creates a personal bond.

Community involvement teams are groups of employees who combine volunteer time and company time to solve local community social problems. They are located wherever we have plants and distribution centers throughout the United States and in twelve locations in our international group. Their goal is identification and evaluation of and direct involvement with possible solutions to community problems.

Interestingly, the initial program was never written up as a proposal with rationales, goals, and budgets seeking management's approval. It began because two of our managers noticed the beginnings of a problem which some would later identify as alienation. Paul Glasgow was concerned that the rapid growth of our company was producing a we-they dichotomy between the home office and the field. At the local level, plant managers were becoming isolated, with less and less time for personal contact with their employees. New production schedules and pressures left them less time for community activities. Their "hands on" knowledge of the social problems affecting their communities, and therefore their own employees, was dropping rapidly. Paul felt that a mechanism could be devised to increase personal contact between management and workers as well as contact between the workforce in general and the community.

Bud Johns, on the other hand, was concerned with the increasing inability of individuals to have a meaningful impact on the problems which directly affected their lives. He was interested in finding a mechanism that would give individuals some clout—a way to affect their environment materially. Bud and Paul together formed the first CITs and chipped in from their department budgets to get them started. The concept really began to gain momentum when, a year later, we made Tom Harris and the newly established community affairs department responsible for the teams. Members of each team were encouraged to become involved in their community, to make contact with the administrators of nonprofit agencies, to attend city council meetings and get to know their representatives, and to gain a working knowledge of the distribution of resources in their community. Individuals who had never had an opportunity to make a significant impact on their community, and in many cases had never met a local mayor, found themselves standing up at community meetings and pledging that if the town would grade the road, they would build the ball field, and that if the local theater group would perform at an orphans' home, they would buy the props. The pride and sense of achievement derived from such encounters carry over into the work environment in an increased sense of self-worth. To say it is fun to watch these teams is an understatement: it's inspiring.

This program began a decade and sixty-two community involvement teams ago. Under the guidance of the community affairs department, the program has been institutionalized and has expanded to become a major community service program in all our plant communities. The cost is very modest, and even if it were substantially larger, we would continue our efforts. Why is the program such a success? The reasons are many and were not immediately clear. Over the years, however, general trends have pointed to unique results which we did not expect or even consider when we began our program.

Although it was not our original intent to design a program to raise employee morale, the program has important implications for research involving worker participation and job satisfaction as well as for the broader issues of isolation and alienation. The diversity of the communities where these teams are located makes the consistency of our observations significant. Participation literature, for example, argues that job interest, commitment, and satisfaction are all heightened by the introduction of various forms of participation. The assumption is often made, however, that participation in some way must be directly connected to the work environment to have an impact on employee morale. Our observations tend to argue that the environment within which that participation occurs is less important than previously supposed. The focus of our program is not directly related to the work environment, but it does provide a participatory vehicle which demonstrates that they, our employees, are worthy of being consulted and that they are intelligent individuals whose opinions are important ingredients in the decision-making process. Indeed, we continually strive to make it known to employees that their opinions and suggestions are a crucial and integral part of decision making.

Our experiences and observations had significant implications on whether or not the expansion of our CIT program to the international group would be a success. When we first decided to introduce the concept to the international division, there were those who felt that we were exporting uniquely American values. The comment was made that "volunteerism" and "activeness" were distinctly American phenomena. On the contrary, we have found that our international CITs, albeit very new, are proving to be just as active and successful as our domestic teams. We agree with recent statements made by social scientists that activeness and involvement may be very general and basic characteristics of people everywhere.

The essential criteria for spawning this activeness seem clear. They are (1) an organized unit, i.e., a community involvement team encouraged to lever other community support and participation for projects that it selects; and (2) a physical and financial resource base, i.e., the company, which can be called upon to ensure that projects have a reasonable potential for success. The structure is a mix of centralized and decentralized management. Local control over seed budgets and selection of key problem areas ensures that exigencies peculiar to the particular locale receive priority and are filtered into the decision-making process of the entire company. Support by the centralized community affairs department staff ensures guidance and direction for major new programs and thrusts.

Leaving a major part of the responsibility for determining the direction of philanthropic activities to the local unit has proved beneficial. In many cases, the local team has discovered trends in community needs before they have been recognized as general problems deserving national attention. For example, our CIT teams began to notice the expanding needs of the elderly several years ago. They had identified the expansion of this age group and the strain that it was placing on local agencies before it became a significant national issue. The same was true of family violence. Our teams were involved with battered children and battered wives before there was significant national exposure. They are, in effect, lightning rods, or early warning devices for future problems. Although any one team's individual project may appear modest, the totality of all the teams' activeness creates a mosaic of problem solving that deals with many aspects of major community social problems. The issues of the needs of the elderly and family violence both are now major areas of focus for the Levi Strauss Foundation staff.

Another unique by-product has been a decline in managerial isolation. Managers who take active roles with CITs report better communications and morale with and among their employees. Additionally, a partial reintegration into community life may also be occurring. Because we encourage the solicitation of communitywide support, managers are in closer contact with local officials and other community organizations. When we first began to form CITs, many managers and employees were unable to discuss the problems affecting their communities beyond a generalized recognition of national issues such as inflation and unemployment. Now many can relate to the magnitude and uniqueness of their own community problems and have a general knowledge of how resources are allocated toward their solution. This increased awareness is significant since many can now identify more readily with the problems of local agency administrators and local political units. Thus, the almost-automatic negative reaction to government programs in the social welfare area and, perhaps, to government in general begins to diminish with a mutual understanding of each other's problems. This is a positive step toward making business and government partners instead of adversaries.

LIMITATIONS AND CONCLUSIONS

Discussing the limitations of corporate responses to the concept of corporate social responsibility is difficult, if not impossible, in the absence of a consensually accepted definition. If, however, we use "fairness" as a general guideline, we are limited only by prevailing ethical values within the population. Here, too, business can have a leadership role, especially internally, in the type of ethical work environment that it provides for its employees.

In terms of community service, corporations are limited by training, by staff, and by resources. Our most important contribution, requiring the overwhelming majority of our personnel and resources, is the providing of jobs and the production of products. Business executives are not equipped either by education or by background for an easy transition to the service sector. For this reason programs should be developed to help facilitate this area of corporate-public cooperation. As with our primary responsibilities, our new social responsibilities require that a material commitment to professional staff and professional programs be made. In the final analysis, however, the extensiveness of any business's effort must be related to the size and nature of its enterprise.

But to dwell on our limitations is to overlook our potentials. One such potential is to share information more openly with both the public and one's own employees. Levi Strauss & Co. publishes on a regular basis financial information on the Levi Strauss Foundation and on company contributions. We have issued a Worldwide Code of Business Ethics and stressed our commitment to social responsibility in our stock prospectus.

There are numerous other areas, and perhaps the limitations referred to above are only the limits of our imagination. The individual talents subsumed in any given corporation have yet to be tapped. The search for viable ways in which to make those talents accessible to society should and must continue. Government and business must cease being adversaries in the face of social dilemmas and become partners in cooperative solutions. Zealots of philosophical laissez faire economics must become the converts of social realities and social responsibility. If nations, governments, institutions, and individuals are prone to act only in the context of narrowly drawn definitions of self-interest, then the onrushing complexities of global resource scarcity, overpopulation, and environmental degradation will bury the worst and devour the best. Let us hope that the separation and alienation we have known over the last two decades will give rise to a new era when individuals, business, government, and developed and underdeveloped countries will come together to address their need for one other and the common needs of this planet. In this latter regard, we are limited only by our willingness to try, to risk, and to make mistakes.

CREATIVE CORPORATE PHILANTHROPY

WILLIAM A. ANDRES

William A. Andres is chairman and chief executive officer of Dayton Hudson Corporation, a diversified retail company operating nationally through department stores, low-margin stores, specialty stores, and a chain of soft-lines stores and headquartered in Minneapolis. Mr. Andres began his retail career in 1949 after receiving his master's degree in retailing from the University of Pittsburgh.

He joined Dayton's department store as a merchandise trainee in 1958. After serving as department manager, divisional merchandise manager, vice president for home furnishings, and senior vice president for operations, he was elected chairman of Dayton's in 1968. He was named senior vice president of Dayton Hudson Corporation in 1968, executive vice president for retail operations in August 1971, and president in November 1974. Since September 1976, he has been chief executive officer. He was elected chairman in December 1977.

Mr. Andres is a director of the First Bank System Inc., the International Multifoods Corp., and the St. Paul Companies, Inc. He serves on the boards of United Way of the Minneapolis area and the Guthrie Theater.

At Dayton Hudson Corporation, we believe that business exists for one purpose only: to serve society. Profit is our reward for serving society well. Indeed, profit is both the means and the measure of that service, but it is not the end.

From its inception, the Dayton Hudson business strategy has recognized the centrality of service. Our corporate statement of philosophy identifies the four major publics that we serve: our customers, our employees, our shareholders, and the communities in which we do business. We find no conflict in serving all four constituencies because their interests are mutually entwined. The common denominator in serving all is maximum long-range profit, without which we could serve none well.

Most assuredly, our philosophy is based on enlightened self-interest. Business must serve society because society holds the franchise on the free enterprise system, which permits our very existence. As long as society believes that business serves it well, the franchise remains secure. But should the American people become thoroughly dissatisfied with business, perceiving they are not well served, the franchise is in danger and the system in jeopardy.

While we make no claim that the free enterprise system is in imminent danger, evidence of public dissatisfaction with business mounts in many forms: adverse legislation, stringent regulation, pressure groups. Left unchecked, this mounting public pressure will punish business severely, denying us the maximum long-range profits which are the means of our service and our survival. Eventually, this trend could alter the free enterprise system or replace it with another, regardless of its merits.

Granted, public mistrust is in no way confined to the private sector. The public sector has come under fire as well. Both business and government have been shaken by local, national, and international scandal. Public confidence in these two major institutions of our free society is at an all-time low.

While neither sector has consistently fulfilled its basic obligations to serve the changing needs of society, there appears to be a marked difference in the public's complaints against them. According to one analysis by Yankelovich, Skelly and White, the public and its leaders are cynical about the *competence* of government, but they question the *priorities* of business. According to Yankelovich, what is emerging is a "new agenda" for business responsibility, with items which the public views as its "entitlements."[1] The public has changed the rules and is demanding a different kind of business institution, one devoted to the public interest.

Dayton Hudson views this new agenda as a challenge to corporate America to accept full partnership with government as a dominant force in society

---

[1] "Public Policy Pressures," Fifth Annual Study, prepared by Yankelovich, Skelly and White, July 1977, p. 25.

today. We think it foolish for these two major forces in American life to be adversaries when the public is challenging both equally.

We see business as an insufficiently tapped resource for solving the complex social problems which government alone cannot handle. Not only does business have resources, it has talent and a reputation for efficiency and effectiveness. The public apparently respects that performance and is challenging business to participate in the achievement of national goals. At Dayton Hudson, we believe that to ignore the public's challenge is perilous to the future of all; to accept it, a great opportunity.

DEVELOPMENT OF THE DAYTON HUDSON PROGRAM

What distinguishes Dayton Hudson is that our corporate forefathers understood the necessity and recognized the benefits of this public-private partnership long before society began articulating its expectations so clearly. Almost from the beginning, Dayton Hudson management recognized the subtle but important difference that the business of business is serving society, not just making money. For our corporation, social responsibility begins with the way in which we do business: clean stores, courteous employees, quality merchandise with "satisfaction guaranteed," and full and honest disclosure with suppliers, stockholders, and consumers alike. The concept is strengthened with community involvement of Dayton Hudson and its people at every level.

Over the years, this philosophy of service has been translated into a sound business strategy with impressive results. Dayton Hudson Corporation now ranks as the seventh largest nonfood retailer in the nation, with more than $3 billion in annual sales. Throughout this growth, our concept of corporate citizenship has extended to contributing an amount equal to 5 percent of federally taxable income to worthwhile projects that we feel will enhance the quality of life in the communities where we operate, making them better places in which to live, to work, and to do business.

In 1980 our community giving program reached more than $10 million, marking the sixty-third consecutive year in which the corporation and its predecessor independent companies conducted a systematic program of charitable giving and the thirty-fifth in which that giving reached the 5 percent level.

Inherent in Dayton Hudson's decision to serve communities is our recognition that external factors affect profits just as surely as do internal factors. Crime rates, housing conditions, the quality of education, and the availability of cultural resources all influence business success just as much as do merchandising and management practices.

Moreover, we know from experience that corporate citizenship can impact these factors—positively, if the commitment and contributions are there; negatively, if not. No business, whether it is a local, regional, or national corporation, can avoid citizenship in the communities where it operates.

For maximum impact, our giving efforts are focused in terms of both geography and program. Although national in scope, our corporation is made up of individual operating companies with strong local identities; thus it makes good sense for us to focus on funding creative, innovative efforts and organizations in the local communities that contribute to Dayton Hudson profits.

In our view, it also makes good sense to focus our funding emphasis rather than have it diffused. Traditionally, our funding has stressed social-action programs and the arts, because we feel that both are vital to the well-being of our communities—social-action programs because the most significant dimension of a livable urban community is its social health and the arts because a rich cultural environment has a humanizing influence critical to a high quality of life for all the citizens of a community.

Although these areas receive primary emphasis, with approximately 40 percent of total contributions to each, other needs are met as well. About 20 percent of corporate contributions support such general efforts as educational, medical, environmental and community development projects. Gifts and grants from Dayton Hudson and its operating companies underwrite such diverse projects as:

● A 5-year action plan to revitalize an inner-city neighborhood in Minneapolis

● Needed transportation for Chicanos in the Phoenix area so that they can better utilize community facilities for the aging and those providing education, health care, and job counseling

● The most complete exhibition ever held of the paper cutouts of the French artist Henri Matisse, at the Detroit Institute of Arts

● A challenge grant to the Allied Arts Foundation of Oklahoma City, which served as an incentive to complete its fund drive in a single month

Dayton Hudson contributions have maximum impact not only because they are focused but because they are leveraged as well. They are leveraged, first, with the time and talent of Dayton Hudson people in community service; and, second, with the contributions of other corporations, particularly in our headquarters state of Minnesota, where some forty-five companies contribute at the full 5 percent level.

For us, serving the communities in which we operate is neither an afterthought nor an appendage to some other program. Dayton Hudson's program of social responsibility is a fully integral, fully committed, fully professional part of the corporation's operations.

Our comprehensive program took shape in incremental steps throughout our corporate history. What began as a private sense of social obligation by the company's founder was first formalized into a foundation in 1917. The 5 percent policy was initiated in 1946 and expanded into a comprehensive environmental development department in 1965. At the time when the company went public in 1967, the policy was reconfirmed as a sound business proposition and an integral part of the corporate philosophy. Since that time, we have been fine-tuning the instrument with such additions as the social responsibility committee of the board of directors, created in 1973; and an alliance with other corporations in the Minnesota Business Partnership, formalized in 1977.

DIMENSIONS OF THE DAYTON HUDSON PROGRAM

Ours is not a perfect model, nor is it necessarily appropriate for every corporation. But we know that it works: social involvement is an excellent business practice that enhances the profitability of our company. Why it works so well has been the subject of analysis over the years, both internally and externally. Our own appraisal identifies several innovative dimensions that we feel have helped make the Dayton Hudson corporate citizenship program the nationally recognized leader it is today.

The *commitment* at the board of directors level is the cornerstone of our success. It is a commitment to more than philosophy; it is a commitment to action. Without it, neither the size nor the quality of our environmental development program would be possible. Our 5 percent policy is reexamined annually when the board of directors approves the corporate gift to the foundation. Without board commitment to the concept, the policy might never have been resoundingly reaffirmed following the business downturn of 1974.

The *professionalism* of the Dayton Hudson approach is another distinguishing factor. Our environmental development department is held to the same standards as any profit center within the corporation, with specific goals, objectives, and appraisal review. The giving program is staffed by professionals whose credentials as philanthropic experts and whose performance criteria compare favorably with those of any line or staff executive in the business.

The *structure* of our contribution program is uniquely designed to make it responsive to management, yet independent of its whims. Not only is it managed by professionals, the program is coordinated by an internal Dayton

Hudson Foundation board of trustees concerned with philosophy and program effectiveness. Grant applications, depending on their size, are approved by the trustees, a trustee contributions committee, the foundation chairman, or its president. The process is monitored by the social responsibility committee, which reviews results and recommends to the board the amount of the annual corporate gift to the foundation.

The *emphasis* given the corporate citizenship concept within the Dayton Hudson Corporation is another important factor. The chief executive officer of each operating company must report regularly to the social responsibility committee of the board of directors on what steps have been taken to improve business environment, including affirmative action and equal employment opportunity, as well as local operating-company community giving, which is matched by the foundation. Those efforts determine approximately 5 percent of each chief executive's performance appraisal.

The *scope* of our public-affairs program facilitates a partnership with government that results in corporate contributions being leveraged with public funds in some cases. We have long made it a practice to lobby in the public interest: funding for the arts, for public housing, and other government commitments essential to the health and growth of urban communities. Our legislative program is openly executed and scrupulously bipartisan; it has earned Dayton Hudson the respect of both major political parties.

The sum of these dimensions is a program which has helped Minnesota set a standard for corporate citizenship, good government, and quality of life that is known throughout the country. *Time* magazine called Minnesota "A State that Works,"[2] and *Fortune* magazine, in an article on Minneapolis, stressed the character of Dayton Hudson's headquarters city in these words:

> In a magic sort of way, the city has taken on a cloak of glamour as the place where a lot of things are going right. . . . Corporate executives devote an astonishing amount of their time and money to good works and civic affairs. . . . Their business leaders have set a standard of corporate citizenship that, if widely copied, would profoundly alter the shape of American philanthropy, culture, and cities—all for the better.[3]

A CHALLENGE TO ALL COMPANIES

The New York Times has called Dayton Hudson Corporation "one of the

---

2 "Minnesota: A State That Works," cover story, *Time,* Aug. 13, 1973, pp. 24, 25.

3 Gurney Breckenfeld, "How Minneapolis Fends Off the Urban Crisis," *Fortune,* January 1976, p. 132.

top 15 corporate philanthropists in the country,"[4] even though some 200 corporations are larger in terms of revenue. While the statistic speaks well of us, it reflects poorly on the corporate sector as a whole.

The national average for corporate charity is typically below 1 percent instead of the 5 percent allowed by the government as a tax deduction. In 1970, when the President's Commission on Private Philanthropy and Public Needs (Filer Commission) studied corporate giving, only 20 percent of the nation's 1,700,000 corporations reported any charitable contributions at all, and only 6 percent made contributions of more than $500.[5] There are few indications that those figures have changed significantly.

Though we recognize that charitable giving is only one measure of corporate conscience, we think that it is perhaps the best measure of concern for the whole of society. We think business performance in this regard has been unimpressive and inadequate. Further, we think that the 5 percent policy is a national bargain. For corporate America to bypass such an opportunity defies logic, given its traditional criticism of government waste and mismanagement.

A group of national business executives, meeting in Minnesota, was once chided about this inconsistency by the late President Lyndon B. Johnson, who said, "In spite of the fact that your federal government has seen fit to allow a charitable deduction of five percent of your profits, the record is quite clear that you business leaders still feel the federal government can spend this money more wisely than you can."[6]

Were all companies to donate their full 5 percent, according to *The New York Times* almost $9 billion would be generated to help address this nation's contemporary social agenda instead of the current $1.5 billion.[7]

Were all to answer the challenge, corporations could compete not just in goods and services but in public services as well, each selecting the fields most appropriate to its expertise and the needs of its constituencies.

Were all to seize the opportunity, each company's annual public-service report would become as critical to its stature as its annual financial report.

Were all to base their business strategy on a philosophy of serving society, defining their own constituencies and implementing a comprehensive program that included 5 percent contributions, then this nation could embark on a truly golden age of achievement.

---

[4] Ann Crittenden, "Philanthropy, the Business of the Not-So-Idle Rich," *The New York Times,* July 23, 1978.

[5] *Giving in America: Toward a Stronger Voluntary Sector,* 1975.

[6] Comment made on Industry Day, Mayo Foundation House, Rochester, Minn., Nov. 19, 1970; recorded by Wayne E. Thompson, now senior vice president, Dayton Hudson Corporation.

[7] Ann Crittenden, op. cit.

Were all to recognize the business sense of such a concerted effort nation-wide, the financial security of the United States would be enhanced and the future of the free enterprise system would be secured as well.

Part 3

THE PHYSICAL DIMENSIONS OF CORPORATE CONDUCT

Environmental and Consumer Protection and Occupational Health and Safety

The essays selected for Part 3 focus primarily on the impact of corporate policies on the physical well-being of consumers, employees, and the public. Whether or not there has been an actual deterioration in the quality of corporate performance in these areas in recent years, public expectations of corporate conduct have certainly increased markedly. Thanks to the passage of federal regulations establishing uniform standards of environmental and consumer protection and occupational health and safety, corporations are now required to consider carefully the social impact of their daily business decisions.

Yet, for a variety of reasons, the social performance of corporations continues to differ markedly from company to company. One of the most respected and most influential of the public research organizations, the Council on Economic Priorities, was established for the purpose of measuring and reporting these differences. In her essay, the council's founder and executive director, Alice Tepper Marlin, summarizes the results of the organization's extensive research into the social behavior of corporations in the last decade. She ranks the pollution-control performance of firms in four industries: paper and pulp, steel, oil refining, and power generation. Strikingly, the council's

151

studies reveal that the firms with the best pollution-control records also tend to be the most profitable. Marlin notes that while most executives regard the consideration of social factors as a threat to profits, "the more innovative, top-performing executive will see these social 'constraints' as challenging opportunities and will think beyond government and act to serve the public by resolving basic human problems while reaping consistently good returns."

INFORM, another research-oriented public-interest organization based in New York, has adopted an approach similar to that of the Council on Economic Priorities. In her essay, INFORM's founder and executive director, Joanna Underwood, analyzes the consumer-sales and land-use practices of large-scale residential development companies and the occupational safety and health conditions of copper mines. She finds considerable variation in corporate performance and concludes that companies hurt themselves economically when they are unwilling to engage in two-way communication with the many publics affected by their operations.

Sandra L. Willett makes a similar plea to business executives in her essay, "A Consumer Agenda for Corporate Leadership." The executive vice president of the National Consumers League, Willett urges corporations to cooperate more closely with the organized consumer movement. She argues that this will both improve the public image of business and increase the public's satisfaction with the products produced by corporations.

The final two contributions in this section come from chief executive officers whose companies have been particularly responsive to changing public expectations in these areas of environmental protection and occupational health and safety. Paul F. Oreffice of the Dow Chemical Company describes his company's extensive and highly organized efforts to protect the quality of the air and water in the area adjacent to Dow's chemical plants. He traces Dow's historic sensitivity to environmental issues to two factors, one social and the other geographic. First, the location of the company's headquarters in the small town of Midland, Michigan, meant that the company's executives and employees would personally bear the consequences of the company's environmental policies. Secondly, Midland is located at the confluence of three small rivers, each large enough to be used to float logs (upon which the company was initially dependent) but too small to absorb chemical pollutants.

In the final essay in this section, Irving S. Shapiro describes E. I. du Pont de Nemours & Co.'s efforts to avoid exposing its workers to hazardous substances. Drawing on Du Pont's long history of interest in occupational health and safety, Shapiro concludes that "an emphasis on safety-conscious management, medical surveillance, and toxicological research, combined with a prime directive to make only those products which can be manufactured, transported, consumed, and disposed of safely, can make a difference." While recognizing that government has a critical and legitimate role to play in establishing uniform safety standards, he contends that corporations themselves have a responsibility to consider both the potential risks and the benefits of the products they produce.

CORPORATE SOCIAL PERFORMANCE

A Comparative Perspective

ALICE TEPPER MARLIN

Alice Tepper Marlin is the founder and executive director of the Council on Economic Priorities. The goal of the council, which has been called by Business Week *"the Dun and Bradstreet of Social Responsibility," has been defined as making social responsibility an additional standard by which corporate practices are evaluated and exposed to the investing and general public. The council has researched and published more than seventy studies and reports on corporate social performance and has established a reputation as an unbiased authority in this area.*

Alice Tepper Marlin was graduated from Wellesley College and worked as a Wall Street securities analyst. She has served as Woodrow Wilson Foundation senior visiting fellow (1974–1977), adjunct professor at Rutgers University School of Business and Administrative Sciences (1974, 1975), a member of the faculty of Antioch College (1970), and a member of the IMP faculty of the Graduate School of Business (1972). She has testified as an expert witness before congressional committees, has served as an adviser on government committees, has lectured widely, holds local elective office, and has served as a board member of many prestigious local and national organizations. She is a member of the United States Association for the Club of Rome and of the Women's Forum.

The reasons for superior social and ethical corporate activities and their impact on profitability are difficult to ascertain. Fortunately, there have been business leaders who have shown a high degree of social responsibility. There is considerable evidence that it is possible to behave responsibly and be a good business manager at the same time. For example, in a survey of the paper industry the firms that showed the best pollution-control records were also the most profitable. But historically the link between responsibility and profitability is not yet sufficiently universal to obviate government intervention.

Few would argue that government intervention is desirable for its own sake. It is needed because business has not been more independently responsible. There is a school of economic thought (e.g., Milton Friedman in *Capitalism and Freedom,* 1962) which argues that it is government's job to regulate and that business should wait for government to set the rules. This approach ignores the rapidly changing social and environmental conditions of the marketplace. Any firm operating today in strict accordance with that directive puts itself at a distinct competitive disadvantage.

A long-term profit-maximization strategy would take into account the results of a firm's social performance, including the likelihood of government corrective regulation. I can therefore suggest that in the short term business executives need social-impact indicators against which they can evaluate and augment profits.

Business today and in the foreseeable future seeks to maximize profits on investment subject to a social-impact constraint. In practice, social factors often appear as conflicting objectives to most executives. The passive executive will at best adhere to the letter of the law. The more innovative, top-performing executive will see these social "constraints" as challenging opportunities and will think beyond government and act to serve the public by resolving basic human problems while reaping consistently good returns.

THE ROOTS OF SOCIAL ACCOUNTABILITY

Pressure to make corporations accountable for socially responsible performance is not altogether a new phenomenon. It should not be seen solely within a context of the dramatic social changes of the 1960s and 1970s. In this century the social pressures of an earlier progressive era brought about the abolition of child labor and won legal status for organized labor. They resulted in early and important pure food and drug legislation, the Fair Labor Standards Act, the setting of minimum wages, and many other social improvements. These measures were first perceived by business as threatening the very existence of private enterprise in the United States. Indeed, they seemed to threaten the very foundation of the United States itself. Time has,

157

of course, proved these dire predictions false. The extra costs imposed by these regulations are now accepted as routine costs of doing business.

Since the late 1960s it has been largely through the efforts of organized public-interest groups, with the added threat of government intervention, that a recognizable social responsiveness has entered the boardrooms and executive suites of most major corporations. Increasingly, external pressures have combined with evolving internal sensitivity to create a corporate environment more responsive to social change and more open to an acceptance of its probable long-range contribution to profitability.

MEASURING CORPORATE SOCIAL PERFORMANCE

Decisions made in pursuit of immediate economic gains—profits for companies, jobs and business for communities—no doubt once were made with the expectation of negligible negative consequences. However, time and experience have proved that the costs to society (externalities) of short-term profit maximization can be heavy. Long-range profitability, which takes some of these costs into account, requires a very different approach. Management must deal with numerous analytic uncertainties. New concepts of social performance greatly complicate the analytic problem. How do we specify and quantify costs and benefits of actions so that we can make intelligent choices and reasonable allocations of both human and material resources?

POLLUTION-CONTROL RANKINGS

For roughly a decade, the Council on Economic Priorities (CEP) has been assessing the social performance of corporations, ranking them on a comparative basis. Our standard has been the best performance among industry leaders as well as legal requirements. In CEP's 1973 study of pollution in the steel industry,[1] for example, it became clear that the industry lagged far behind legal requirements and available technology (the state of the art) in its efforts to control pollution from its mills. The study covered forty-seven major steelmaking plants operated by the seven largest steel companies and analyzed mill-by-mill data on the kind and the amount of air and water pollutants discharged. Finally, it rated the companies on the effectiveness of their cleanup efforts. The seven companies were compared by the council on more than a score of specific pollutants. On particulate emissions, for instance, the companies were rated on pounds of particulates released for each ton of steel produced; the survey showed Armco Inc. to be the best at about

---

[1] James S. Cannon, *Environmental Steel,* Council on Economic Priorities, New York, 1973.

4 pounds (1.8 kilograms) and National Steel Corp. the worst at nearly 22 pounds (10 kilograms), or *five times* as much. Figure 1 shows the relative performance of all seven firms.

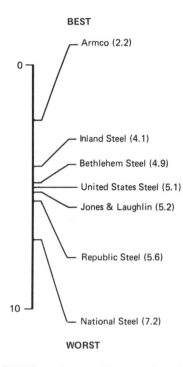

FIGURE 1   Iron and steel industry pollution-control performance: the top seven firms ranked from best to worst.

In its 1977 update of the study on the steel industry,[2] the council found that since 1972 only Armco had made across-the-board progress in controlling air and water pollution. The study again rated the companies' forty-seven basic mills individually on their performance in controlling the seven basic steelmaking air and water pollutants and compared the 1976 data with those of the 1972 study. While all the companies had made progress in controlling at least one of the seven air and water pollutants, only Armco had scored improvements in each of the seven areas.

When CEP does an update, such as this one for the steel industry, there have been few cases of plants having closed over the time period because of

[2] James S. Cannon and Frederick S. Armentrout, *Environmental Steel/Update,* Council on Economic Priorities, New York, 1977.

the cost of meeting government regulations, nor have there been large job losses. In fact, the threat of plant closings and job losses has been vastly exaggerated in the industries that CEP has studied. Actual closings and job losses have invariably been a small percentage of any industry's predictions.

In 1975 CEP studied pollution in the petroleum-refining industry.[3] Sixty-one refineries operated by the Atlantic Richfield Company (ARCO), Exxon Corporation, Gulf Oil Corp., Mobil Corporation, Shell Oil Company, Standard Oil Co. of California, Standard Oil Co. (Indiana; Amoco Oil Co.), and Texaco Inc. were surveyed, and the success of each refinery in controlling emissions of nine major pollutants into air and water were evaluated. The air pollutants surveyed were sulfur oxides, carbon monoxide, hydrocarbons, and particulates, while the water pollutants under consideration were biochemical oxygen demand, chemical oxygen demand, oil and grease, phenols, and ammonia. Atlantic Richfield had the best overall pollution-control performance and, along with Standard Oil of California, the best air-pollution–control record. Shell and Exxon were the best water-pollution controllers. Texaco, followed closely by Amoco, had the worst air-pollution–control record, while the worst overall pollution-control performance (both air and water) was also turned in by Texaco. See Figure 2.

We found that a refinery's pollution-control performance was the result of a complex interaction among technical factors, company pollution-control policy, and regional pollution-control requirements. To determine the extent to which local regulations and enforcement affected the pollution-control performance of refineries, CEP examined the average performance in seven regions that contained four or more refineries in the study: Illinois, Washington, New Jersey, Louisiana, Texas (Gulf Coast), northern California (San Francisco), and southern California (Los Angeles).

This analysis revealed wide regional variations in control performance. For example, every Los Angeles refinery had a much better air-pollution–control record than any Illinois refinery. In water-pollution control, the excellent performance of Washington and Illinois refineries contrasted sharply with that of refineries in New Jersey and Los Angeles.

The laws that regulated pollution control and their enforcement were the most influential determinants of a company's policy in a given region. Under strong regulation, the penalties for noncompliance were great enough to force all companies to perform well. In a very weak regulatory climate, all companies tended to relax and perform poorly. A firm's attitude toward pollution control found its fullest expression when regulations were applied with only moderate force: each firm had its own way of responding to a regulatory push at this level.

---

[3] Greg Kerlin and Dan Rabovsky, *Cracking Down,* Council on Economic Priorities, New York, 1975.

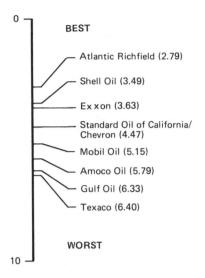

FIGURE 2   Petroleum-refining industry pollution-control performance: the top eight firms ranked from best to worst.

State and regional regulations varied (and still vary) widely. Some regions, like southern California, concentrated first on controlling certain regional air-pollution problems. As a result, Los Angeles had the best refinery air-pollution control (but not the cleanest air) and the worst refinery water-pollution control in the country. Other regions pushed first for improved water quality. Washington and Illinois, for example, began to regulate water polluters long before federal laws were enacted.

Only two of the twenty-four companies surveyed in our 1970 study of pollution in the pulp and paper industry[4] had records of sustained interest and effort toward achieving excellent pollution control at their mills: Owens-Illinois, Inc., and Weyerhaeuser Co. All four Owens-Illinois mills had adequate air-pollution and water-pollution controls. In 1970 Weyerhaeuser operated eleven pulp mills, nine of which had been constructed with state-of-the-art pollution controls after World War II. Weyerhaeuser also instituted many techniques for control, such as the first kraft-mill odor-control system, because it recognized the problem and had a desire to control it. On the other end of the spectrum in 1970 were the St. Regis Paper Co., Potlatch Forests (now Potlatch Corp.), and Diamond International Corp., all

[4] Leslie Allan and Eileen Kohl Kaufman, *Paper Profits,* Council on Economic Priorities, New York, 1970.

of which exhibited little if any concern for environmental protection. In a 1972 update[5] Owens-Illinois continued to be top-rated, while St. Regis had risen to fifth place and Weyerhaeuser had dropped to ninth (see Figure 3).

In 1972 CEP published its first analysis of the environmental impact of fourteen of the nation's major investor-owned electric utilities covering the calendar year 1970.[6] The study assessed air and water pollution at 124 major fossil-fuel plants and rated each plant and company according to the adequacy of its controls. Subsequently federal legislation on air and water quality was enacted, and CEP did an update of the study for the period through 1975, which was published in 1977.[7] The update covered 119 plants operated by fifteen utilities, ten of which were in the original study. Among the findings for the fifteen companies were that overall environmental performance had improved significantly for only one of the four major pollutants studied: thermal discharge. Sulfur dioxide and nitrogen oxide emissions showed little improvement, while overall particulate emissions had deteriorated mainly because of fuel conversions from gas to oil and oil to coal. In both studies Pacific Gas & Electric Co. received the top rating, which was attributed to its extensive use of clean natural gas to fuel its power plants. The Tennessee Valley Authority, a federal agency, had the worst pollution record in the update. Of the ten companies retained in the update from the original study, Florida Power & Light Co. had the most improved environmental record, while Baltimore Gas & Electric Co. showed the least improvement during the 1970–1975 period covered in the update. See Figure 4.

FAIR-EMPLOYMENT EVALUATIONS

In 1972 the council completed a study of the employment of women and members of minority groups in eighteen commercial banks in six cities.[8] Only 10 percent of the banking industry's officials and managers were female. Even more discouraging, the number of high-ranking women had actually dropped from 164 presidents for the country's 14,000 commercial banks in 1960 to only 40 female presidents 10 years later. The number of female vice presidents had dwindled from 688 to 164.

The study also showed that in 1960 employment of blacks averaged fewer

---

5 Eileen Kohl Kaufman, Leslie Allan, and Joanna Underwood, *Paper Profits: Pollution Audit 1972,* Council on Economic Priorities, New York, 1972.

6 Charles Komanoff et al., *The Price of Power: Electric Utilities and the Environment,* Council on Economic Priorities, New York, 1972.

7 Ronald H. White, *Price of Power/Update,* Council on Economic Priorities, New York, 1977.

8 Rodney Alexander and Elisabeth Sapery, *Shortchanged: Minorities and Women in Banking,* Council on Economic Priorities, New York, 1972.

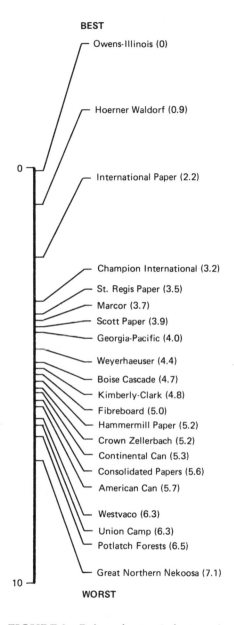

FIGURE 3 Pulp and paper industry pollution-control performance: twenty-one major companies ranked from best to worst.

163

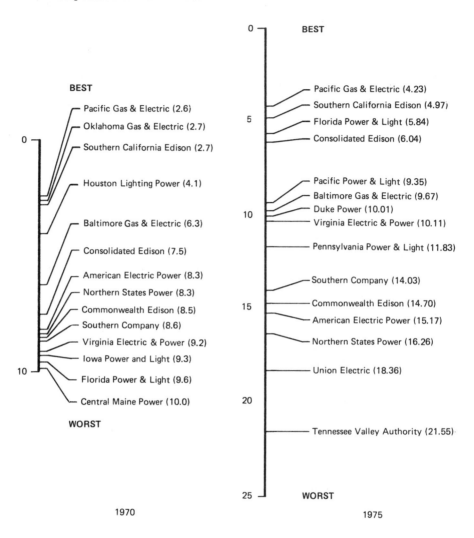

FIGURE 4 Electric utilities industry pollution-control performance: major utilities ranked from best to worst.

than one per banking establishment and that 10 years later banks still had the worst record of hiring and upgrading members of minority groups of any white-collar institution. In 1970 members of all minority groups accounted for only 2.7 percent of bank employees in the officials-and-managers category, compared with a 3.6 percent average for all white-collar industries, and for 13.7 percent of the nation's workforce. While minority men and women constituted 25 percent of all employees, they were restricted primarily to office and clerical work; only 6.7 percent held jobs above that level.

As in our pollution-control studies, we found wide variation in the performance of individual banks. The council's key measure of performance was a bank's utilization of women and minority members as compared with their availability in each bank's local labor force. Two basic categories—officials and managers; and professionals, technicians, and sales employees—were used in our rankings. These categories were established by the Equal Employment Opportunity Commission (EEOC), and information was drawn from 1971 EEO-1 reports filed with the Treasury. The National Bank of Detroit and the Bank of America had the best records in employment of minority-group members as officials and managers. The Wells Fargo Bank and the National Bank of Detroit ranked best in the employment of women in the officials-and-managers category.

In an expanded update of the study published in 1976,[9] the council evaluated twenty-four banks in eight cities and found that the banks had made substantial progress in the increasing utilization of women, especially minority women, at the management level. Women still did not, however, fare very well in the officers category despite some improvements since 1971. Overall, the study showed that minority men were still encountering extreme difficulty in obtaining jobs at any level in large banks. The job classification of minority women had improved more than that of any other group. The best banks were the Bank of America, the National Bank of Detroit, Wells Fargo, and the Security Pacific National Bank. The poorest performances were found at the Girard Bank, the First National Bank of Chicago, the Continental Illinois National Bank and Trust Company of Chicago, and the Chase Manhattan Bank. Two of the three biggest New York banks had improved their already-good relative positions with respect to their use of members of minority groups in top jobs. Manufacturers Hanover Trust Co., which had ranked fourth in 1971, ranked third in 1975; and Chase Manhattan, which had ranked fifth in 1971, ranked fourth in 1976. Citibank, on the other hand, had fallen from third to thirteenth place (out of twenty-two).

When Crocker National Bank was sued in 1975 for discrimination against women, the bank used CEP's good ranking in its defense. Subsequently it cited our evaluation with pride in its letter to shareholders published in its 1976 annual report and signed by Chairman Thomas R. Wilcox and President Robert K. Wilmouth:

> Naturally we were pleased when at year-end Council on Economic Priorities, a nonprofit research organization that studies corporate performance in matters affecting the public interest, rated us at the top of all banks they surveyed in our employment of minorities in upper level positions. We do

---

9 Tina Simcich, *Shortchanged/Update,* Council on Economic Priorities, New York, 1976.

believe in and actively practice the utilization of individual talent from all segments of society. Indeed, it is this blend of ethnic and racial backgrounds in Crocker that provides us the means to understand and adapt to the changing environments in which we do business.[10]

In our study of employment practices in the largest general-merchandising chains—Sears, Roebuck & Co., J. C. Penney Company, Montgomery Ward & Co., W. T. Grant Co. (no longer in business), and S. S. Kresge (now K Mart Corp.)—we found minorities continuing to be underrepresented in all except the most menial sales, clerical, blue-collar, and service categories. The retail-sales job market is very accessible for unskilled workers. In 1974 we found that the general-merchandise industry had a slightly lower percentage of minority workers (13 percent) and a much higher percentage of women (67 percent) than were found in the United States labor force overall (15 and 38 percent respectively). Despite the overrepresentation of women in sales, their numbers decreased significantly in the big-ticket sales category: items that carry commissions for the seller. Even when women and members of minority groups had obtained positions equal to those of white males, the retail industry paid them lower wages.

The best firm overall in the employment of members of minority groups was Sears, and in the employment and promotion of women J. C. Penney ranked best. Kresge scored worst in both employment areas and also in product safety. In considering Sears' Number 1 status on minority employment, it should be noted that Sears is the only retail chain studied that has federal contracts and is thus more deeply affected by government and private enforcement of equal-opportunity programs. Kresge's extremely poor performance in both product safety and fair employment had yet to take its toll on profitability. This is the sort of instance which often brings the public to the conclusion that regulation is needed. But even with regulation, uneven or unfair enforcement can remain a problem. For example, while the Environmental Protection Agency (EPA) follows the sensible procedure of identifying particularly bad polluters for enforcement actions, the EEOC does no such thing. It either follows up on individual complaints, or it moves against the largest firm in an industry. While it is evident that virtually all major institutions in our society exhibit patterns and practices of discrimination, I maintain that it would be far more fair and effective to take advantage of an incentive system and to focus on the major firms in an industry with the poorest performance records. Instead, the EEOC took action against high-ranking Sears but ignored the abysmal performance of Kresge. Perhaps that

---

[10] Thomas R. Wilcox and Robert K. Wilmouth, "Letter to Shareholders," *Crocker National Corporation 1976 Annual Report*, pp. 2, 3.

is why the relationship between social performance and profitability breaks down here.

CEP found that written affirmative-action programs were productive in increasing the number of minority applicants hired but were not as effective in promoting them to higher-level positions. Long-term policy goals for the firms are based on projected local population and labor force statistics. Because women already form the majority in retail-sales personnel, the policies are geared toward training them for higher positions.

One might imagine that the presence of women or members of minority groups on the board of directors of a firm would reflect or result in a reasonably good employment pattern for women or members of minority groups, or both, but CEP has found no correlation between such a presence and a firm's fair-employment performance.

WHY A LINK BETWEEN POLLUTION CONTROL AND PROFITABILITY?

The council's in-depth studies of pollution control in major industries have shown a wide range of ways in which proper pollution controls reduce costs and even produce revenue. Of course, firms with higher profits are better able, and thus more likely, to invest in cleaner plants, but CEP has found this proposition to be more valid on an interindustry than an interfirm basis. Good managements are likely both to earn higher profits and to be more careful in protecting the environment.

Probably the most important way to offset the initial expense of installing pollution controls is through revenue from the recovery of by-products. This system deserves so much attention not only for its financial advantages but for its further contribution to the cleaning of the environment. Much industrial pollution is caused by the discharge into air and water of a product that is essential for manufacturing but is ecologically hazardous.

Oil refineries present an excellent example of how by-products can be lucrative. From the emissions of hydrogen sulfide and hydrocarbons, sulfur can be reclaimed and reused. Crude oil and related products are no longer pollutants when equipment such as floating roof tanks is employed. Carbon monoxide boilers are a good example of recycling pollutants within a refinery to make partners of energy conservation and pollution control. The refinery process gives off by-product gases, which when recaptured are a very cheap source of fuel and when ignored are a major source of pollution. Since recycling equipment is equally important as pollution-control and regular investment machinery, many companies consider only a percentage of its cost in the pollution-control category.

The council's study of 130 paper mills owned by twenty-four companies[11] found that it was common practice to recycle wood chips because of new state laws against burning them and because of the increased cost of wood. Owens-Illinois had by 1972 overcome the major obstacles to evaporating the "liquor" to recover chemicals in a recyclable sodium sulfite form.

A widely cited study by Jay Bragdon and John Marlin ranked seventeen of twenty-four paper companies according to five measures of profitability and three measures of pollution-control performance as established by CEP and found that "the cleaner pulp and paper companies show higher profits than those with worse pollution control records."[12] With reference to this study, *Business Week* ran an editorial in which it concluded: "There is not necessarily a fundamental conflict between profitability and pollution control. The manager who does good may also do well. Nice guys can finish first."[13]

Manufacturers have often claimed that installing pollution controls means higher costs for the consumer. In many cases this may be true, but according to the CEP studies this price increase is usually a great deal smaller than assumed and should cause a negligible decrease in the quantity that consumers purchase. The authors of CEP's *Cleaning Up*[14] report that in the petroleum industry the customer will almost certainly pay the lion's share of the increased costs that result from pollution control. If the price of the product increases by as little as 1 percent, the company will recover 75 percent of its initial costs. And with this 75 percent recovery, only one of eight major oil companies (the firm slowest to clean up) would lose as much as 1 percent profit, while others would lose as little as 0.1 percent.

In all four CEP pollution-control studies, analyzing and ranking oil refineries, paper mills, steel mills, and electric utilities, it was found that the pollution-control equipment installed at various plants varied widely within a particular firm. In the majority of cases, this variation can be explained by the great variations in the strictness of the laws from one geographic region to another. The older the plant, the more difficult and expensive it is to add the new equipment. If pollution controls must be installed quickly because of pressure, they can cost a firm as much as three times more than if the cost had been absorbed gradually. Depending on how much catching up is needed to meet government regulations, some companies will have to spend

---

[11] Eileen Kohl Kaufman, *Paper Profits: Pollution Audit 1972,* Council on Economic Priorities, New York, July 1972.

[12] Joseph H. Bragdon, Jr., and John A. T. Marlin, "Is Pollution Profitable?" *Risk Management,* April 1972.

[13] *Business Week,* Aug. 7, 1971.

[14] Joan Norris Boothe, *Cleaning Up: The Cost of Refinery Pollution Control,* Council on Economic Priorities, New York 1975.

much more money than their competitors, leaving them at a disadvantage. The best-performing firms were seldom those with a top-rated plant, which often concentrated all the control investment at one site, leaving other plants woefully neglected. Consistent across-the-board upgrading tends to result in better companywide ratings. Good management is instrumental in realizing the benefits of pollution controls. Companies that are concerned about the efficiency of their plants know the importance of the health and safety of their workers and of a good relationship with other businesses and with inhabitants of the area. Installing pollution controls lessens the financial burdens of management by lowering the premiums for health insurance, cutting taxes by using tax write-off provisions for equipment, and diminishing the chance of legal suits and fines because of lack of controls.

We work toward the day when corporate compliance with legal standards will be the prevailing norm and CEP's comparative-performance evaluations will be able to concentrate on degrees of excellence above minimum requirements. We have found considerable interest in objective assessments of comparable social performance of firms from those directly affected by corporate actions, from investors, and from managers who have found that irresponsible firms often eventually pay a price. Many believe that a company's social performance may be an indicator, perhaps even a leading indicator, of the quality of management and of future profitability.

DISCLOSURE

The council has found many companies that are willing to disclose adequate, comparably gathered, precise data in areas like pollution control and employment. Their very existence demonstrates that the information is neither competitive nor prohibitively costly to gather and report. As in other areas, however, we find great unevenness within the corporate community and within a single industry. The council has therefore developed the technique of rating each company studied on its disclosure of information requested and on its willingness to be open and honest about its problems, attempts at solutions, and related issues beyond the narrower confines of the specific data requested. For example, in our 1972 update of our study of pollution in the pulp and paper industry, International Paper Co. and Crown Zellerbach Corporation were the least cooperative in providing data, whereas Georgia-Pacific Corp., Weyerhaeuser, and Kimberly-Clark Corp. were among the most cooperative. In our study of pollution control in the oil-refining industry, four of the eight companies studied—Amoco, ARCO, Exxon, and Shell —were rated excellent in disclosure, whereas Standard Oil of California, Texaco, and Mobil provided limited cooperation, and Gulf refused to cooperate in any way.

Because the state of the art of social-issue analysis is still primitive, a well-coordinated voluntary or mandated program of disclosure would speed the development of generally accepted accounting principles in these new areas. That would make information more timely, less expensive to gather, and more useful, to say nothing of eliminating overnight the bugaboo that full and honest disclosure would put a firm at a competitive disadvantage. Furthermore, corporate costs would be further minimized by eliminating the need to respond to requests for data in different forms.

LAND DEVELOPMENT AND WORKING CONDITIONS

JOANNA UNDERWOOD

Joanna Underwood is the founder and executive director of INFORM, a national nonprofit research organization established in 1973, that analyzes and reports on the influence of United States corporations on the environment, their employees, and consumers. Before setting up INFORM, from 1970 to 1973, she was codirector and editor for the Council on Economic Priorities in New York. Her earlier work included research and reporting for Time-Life and organization and direction of a national audiovisual service for Planned Parenthood–World Population. She received her B.A. degree from Bryn Mawr College.

Ms. Underwood is a member of the board of Planned Parenthood of New York City, the Energy Conservation Alliance of New York State, and the New York State Energy Research and Development Authority. She is also a member of the Consumer Affairs Advisory Committee of the U.S. Department of Energy and the United States Association for the Club of Rome.

Since the 1960s we in the United States have been deeply involved in redefining our social and environmental goals. We have been reassessing the role of our public and private interests in the allocation and use of human and natural resources. United States corporations have been the focus of particular attention as the impact of their policies and practices is felt throughout the fabric of our society. Legislation since the mid-1960s has created many federal regulatory agencies whose mandates include setting standards for industry to protect our land and mineral resources from wasteful use, safeguarding the quality of our air and water, ensuring fair and equal treatment of our citizens, providing for a safe and healthful workplace environment for industrial workers, and assuring honest consumer practices.

In response to this seemingly sudden onslaught of regulation, corporations have reacted in three ways. Some have made desperate attempts to protect themselves from the forces of change by maintaining a wall of silence, withholding information on their activities and social impacts, and surrounding themselves with a barricade of legal counsel. Others have moved reluctantly, meeting the demands of the law only to the letter. Still others have grappled seriously and diligently with the spirit of the law; they are attempting to comprehend the deep public concerns that lie behind the new performance demands and are seeking within their own resources—technical, personnel, research, management, and economic—new ways to alter their impacts on society by improving their methods of doing business.

Since 1973 INFORM's research has explored particularly significant problem areas in industry's treatment of its environment and its employees. In comparing the responses of companies within an industry to changing and evolving public requirements and concerns, a broad range of performance has been consistently visible. And just as consistently visible in our research has been this result: those firms that balk at regulations and long for the old days when business was left to its own devices pay a heavy price for their shortsightedness. They often must make expensive and technologically difficult changes in their operations when they adapt suddenly, under regulatory pressure, to new requirements, whereas a slow process of change would have been infinitely easier and cheaper. At the same time their public images suffer. Indeed, not only do such companies pay the price of their errors, but their behavior damages the reputation of the whole business community.

A look at the records of several companies in two of the industries on which INFORM has reported since 1974 illustrates the range of responses we have seen. The evidence in both the land-development and the copper-smelting industries not only suggests the tolls paid by firms that fail to face evolving social and environmental values squarely but also illustrates the benefits accruing to companies willing to explore those evolving concerns and face them as new business challenges. While such companies are usually ready to debate the virtues of some requirements, their compliance can force the competition to improve the efficiency of its performance.

THE LAND DEVELOPERS

Between 1974 and 1977 INFORM studied and compared the consumer sales and land-use practices of large-scale residential development companies in the United States and also evaluated the federal and state laws that regulate these companies' activities. (The findings of this research were published in *Promised Lands.*[1]) More than 6000 such companies operate in the United States, controlling over 2 percent of the continental land, or an area larger than the state of Florida. They have sold enough lots to accommodate 60 million people, a number equivalent to the total combined current populations of Los Angeles, San Francisco, Chicago, Detroit, Boston, New York, Philadelphia, Washington, D.C., and the entire state of New Jersey. Exploring the range of industry performance, our research focused on a sample of nine development companies. These represented some of the largest and most widely known companies in this industry, including such conglomerates as Dart Industries in California, better known for its Tupperware and Rexall Drug & Chemical Co. products, and ITT Community Development Corp., a Florida subsidiary of the International Telephone and Telegraph Corporation, as well as companies specializing in the retail land-sales business, such as GAC Corp., General Development Corp., AMREP Corp., and Horizon Corp. All these firms define their business as that of creating new communities at locations relatively distant from existing urban concentrations and free of urban ills. All operate by buying up large tracts of rural land, creating a master plan for their use by commercial, industrial, and residential sectors, building a central initial core, and selling lots to consumers primarily on the installment-contract basis.

Three of these companies' subdivisions are selected for comparison here: AMREP's Rio Rancho development in New Mexico, Deltona Corp.'s Marco Island development in Florida, and General Development's Port Charlotte subdivision in Florida.

AMREP Corp.

AMREP Corp., of all the companies studied in INFORM's sample, is clearly one of those most oblivious to the public's interest in its treatment both of its consumers and of the environment. Responding solely to the profit motive, AMREP proved entirely willing to sell raw and uninhabitable land at its Rio Rancho subdivision to more than 60,000 purchasers across the coun-

---

[1] Leslie Allan, Beryl Kuder, and Sarah L. Oakes, *Promised Lands 1: Subdivisions in Deserts and Mountains,* INFORM, Inc., New York, 1976; id., *Promised Lands 2: Subdivisions in Florida's Wetlands,* INFORM, Inc., New York, 1977; Leslie Allan, Beryl Kuder, J.D., Jean Schreier, J.D., and Patricia A. Simko, J.D., *Promised Lands 3: Subdivisions and the Law,* INFORM, Inc., New York, 1978.

try. It boasted that this land was part of a "glorious place to live with dramatic views of the skyline of Albuquerque."

Actually, the Rio Rancho site, located in Sandoval County, New Mexico, consists of about 91,000 acres (36,800 hectares) of dry, low-yield cattle rangeland, about 1 mile (1.6 kilometers) above sea level, land that is criss-crossed with arroyos (large, deep gullies) formed by flash-flood waters rushing through to the Rio Grande. Only 2 percent of the site is actually developed and inhabited; the rest consists of more than 90,000 acres (36,400 hectares) of dry grasslands cut up into thousands of ½- to 1-acre (0.2- to 0.4-hectare) lots whose boundaries are defined by miles of bladed dirt roads.

Environmentally, the site is appropriate for a certain amount of residential development. It contains no valuable water-related resources, no habitats of endangered species, and no prime agricultural lands. However, arroyos on the site should be withheld from development because of their flood potential. In peak summer floods, the major arroyos in the Albuquerque area draining into the Rio Grande have at times carried more water than the river itself. Yet AMREP largely ignored these constraints, platting and selling lots in arroyos and other flood-prone areas. In addition, AMREP stripped topsoil from hundreds of miles of roads and hundreds of acres of building areas to reach the impenetrable hard underlayers, a practice that had the effect of increasing runoff and erosion and flood problems.

Indeed, the company's planning reflected not one sophisticated planning concept. AMREP made no effort to fit roads, lots, or open space to natural terrain. It superimposed predetermined grids of roads over rolling hills and gullies alike and located parks not where they might be needed to serve neighborhood areas, but often on small, irregular, or rough parcels, i.e., on land that couldn't be marketed.

Since 1975 AMREP's practices, which abused both the environment and the consumer, have come back to haunt the company. In that year the town adjacent to its subdivision suffered the consequences of Rio Rancho's poor drainage plans when floodwaters washed hundreds of cubic yards of silt down from the top of the Rio Rancho Mesa to the town downslope. The silt clogged and then collapsed a major culvert, creating a dam which diverted the floodwater to streets, yards, and homes. Homeowners sued AMREP for damages.

Also in 1975, both the United States Attorney and the Federal Trade Commission (FTC) began investigating the company's practices. They uncovered unfair high-pressure sales practices at sales dinners and false inflation of lot prices. Their legal actions against this company claimed that its sales and advertising intended to misrepresent, conceal, and defraud the public; it was particularly noted that there was not, and had not been in the 14-year history of the site, *any* resale value to the land at Rio Rancho outside the core areas. Thus, AMREP's practices, adhering to few principles of honest marketing, finally produced a federal criminal indictment in the United States district court that led to the conviction and imprisonment of four members of the company's management.

These investigations also uncovered fraudulent representations about both the immediacy of Albuquerque's growth and the availability of water to Rio Rancho residents, one of the most serious problems of site conditions. Not only does AMREP provide no central water supply outside its tiny developed core area, but the alternative of drilling an individual well on each lot will be legally denied to most lot owners. A New Mexico law prohibits the use of individual wells together with septic tanks on lots less than ¾ acre (0.3 hectare) in size, and the vast majority of lots at Rio Rancho are ½ acre (0.2 hectare) or less and rely on septic tanks. Perhaps even more serious in the long term is the possibility that water may not be available either via a central water system or in wells. The water in the Santa Fe aquifer which underlies the Rio Rancho property and which AMREP mentions in its literature would be enough for the site, but that water, according to the strict allocation system in the state, has already been assigned to other users. And there is no assurance that these users will be willing to sell these rights.

Deltona Corporation

When Deltona Corp. launched a development project called Marco Beach on Florida's Gulf Coast in 1964, it was heralded for initiating a sophisticated and well-planned new-community effort. The quality of its plans and the initial sensitivity to the environment that they reflected placed this company a world apart from such a firm as AMREP. Nevertheless, over the years Deltona adapted its policy in only the most minimal fashion to changing environmental consciousness and regulations, recognizing no more than the letter of the law—a policy that has cost the company its reputation and many millions of dollars.

Today Deltona's 19,500-acre (7890-hectare) site consists of 3900 acres (1575 hectares) of dredged and filled land on and around Marco Island and 15,600 acres (6315 hectares) of largely swampy wilderness: mangrove swamps, salt marshes, and open lagoons, including the habitats of rare birds. When planning for the site began in 1964, Deltona's work was praised by Florida conservationists. The company cooperated with state agencies, dedicated land for public use and preservation, and developed new techniques to limit environmental change.

However, the company did not adapt its policy well to subsequent advances in environmental attitudes and knowledge. Over the next 15 years it clung stubbornly to its original development objectives. For many reasons, within a few years of its initial planning much of the Marco Beach site was generally recognized to be inappropriate for residential development. A large part of the land is underwater during high tide, necessitating extensive dredging to drain it. Much is a vital aquatic habitat which supports endangered species, including roseate spoonbills and bald eagles. Moreover, the site lies almost entirely in a hurricane flood-hazard zone.

Finally, and most unfortunately, only after Deltona's initial planning was complete during the late 1960s and early 1970s, did it become clear that the plan ignored the environmental and economic importance of estuaries in Florida. Deltona's plan was described critically in May 1973 by an official of the U.S. Department of the Interior as requiring "the largest single commitment of estuarine resources to any single public or private enterprises ever undertaken in Florida."[2] Mangrove swamps, dismissed in 1964 as noxious and mosquito-laden, by 1970 were understood to be key parts of a complex ecological system that nurtures and protects a majority of Florida's commercial and sport fish. Florida's coastal wetland regions were increasingly recognized to be not just developable land but essential components of the state's economy and ecology. Their destruction threatened the long-term prosperity of the state.

Florida's laws and requirements did not change overnight, and the rumblings from the environmental community and the creation of new state agencies to protect Florida's land resources gave warnings that Deltona's plans should be altered and adapted. In the mid-1960s the Army Corps of Engineers, in a landmark case involving environmental factors similar to those at Marco Beach, had denied a permit to a developer to dredge and fill land. Yet despite such multiplying signs of changing values and requirements, Deltona was technically allowed under law to continue selling lots on its site. Until mid-1973 it went on doing so, in the face of increasingly evident risk that the governmental permits needed to turn its underwater plots into dry, buildable land might never be granted. Then, in 1976, the Corps of Engineers, in a decision almost without precedent, refused Deltona permission to dredge and fill more than 2000 acres (810 hectares) of mangrove swamp that it had planned to convert into 4300 homesites. Deltona went to court, and a compromise was finally reached between the company and the state regulatory agencies: because laws had not clearly prohibited the sale of lots, the company was allowed to continue development of some of its sold property.

Nonetheless, Deltona's nearsighted practices and its failure to confront openly the fact that public requirements were changing cost the company dearly. They cost it the support and respect of an environmental community that had once praised its efforts as innovative, and they created tensions with

---

[2] Quoted by Jerry Drake, "Will Marco's Final 5,000 Acres Be Developed?" *Naples Star,* Mar. 22, 1974.

government agencies. Deltona's practices also cost it millions in reparations to its own customers. In 1976 many of the thousands of purchasers of Deltona Marco Beach lots had to be offered the opportunity either to trade their underwater land for land which the company had already dredged and filled at Marco or at a Deltona subdivision elsewhere or to receive, over a 3-year period, a full refund of principal and interest paid toward the purchase of their lots. Some 32 percent of Deltona's customers requested a refund, 56 percent agreed to exchange their lots for other Marco Island property, and the rest (12 percent) decided to wait for the outcome of Deltona's suit against the Corps of Engineers. Deltona's 1976 write-down for anticipated losses was $14.7 million.

General Development Corp.

Quite a different response to the changing environmental and legal climate was made by General Development Corp., which found itself trapped with a major subdivision site that had been planned in the 1950s in an environmentally obsolete fashion. Initial planning at the development site, Port Charlotte, a 185-square-mile (479-square-kilometer) subdivision on Florida's Gulf Coast, had included a layout of streets in a monotonous gridiron of straight lines and rectangular lots with little land left in its natural state. Lots, many of them in flood-prone coastal areas, were marketed across the country to people seeking a better life in the sunny South. Dredge and fill of low-lying land was, as was the case at Deltona's Marco Beach site, an important part of the development picture. As of mid-1978 almost 85 percent of the site's approximately 194,000 lots had been sold, though only 16,000 dwelling units had been built.

It was only after the original owners of the Port Charlotte site, the Mackle brothers, had sold their company to new management in the early 1960s, that significant modification of General Development's business methods occurred. During the same period in which Deltona Corp. waged an increasingly prolonged and bitter struggle to continue policies that threatened to eradicate a priceless natural environment at Marco Beach, General Development pursued a very different course. It made an unusual effort to stay abreast of emerging environmental knowledge and to cooperate with newly formed state governmental agencies and new regulations.

What is more, the company worked in notable ways to undo the mistakes of the past. For example, not long after management of the company changed hands, corporate policy was altered to prohibit the platting and selling of lots in marshes and swamps along the site's rivers. General Development not only ended up by preserving 7000 acres (2830 hectares) of valuable mangroves but since that time has transferred parts of these lands to conservationists.

This constructive move, however, did not solve all the company's environmental problems. Several years later, in 1971, an order by the United States District Attorney served as a stern warning that dredge and fill of any ecologically significant areas in anticipation of permits would not be tolerated. And the company was forced to restore a 150-acre (60-hectare) portion of its site that had been dredged and converted from swampy terrain into lots salable as high-priced waterfront homesites. To restore the site to its natural state, the company had to fill in the canals and plant mangrove seedlings.

Other alterations of the company's Port Charlotte plans were voluntarily negotiated. Plans for extensively dredging and filling canal systems in two parts of this site (south Gulf Cove and Muddy Cove) were radically changed to prevent the creation of water bodies which, it was becoming increasingly evident, might soon turn into stagnant pools polluted by runoff from streets and lots and choked by growths of aquatic weeds. (In many of Florida's artificial canal systems such weeds have prevented boatowners from using their boats and have forced them to employ herbicides which kill fish.) General Development modified its already-constructed upland canal systems to improve the flow of waters there and to minimize pollution with newly recommended techniques.

Finally, to ensure a continuing environmentally sensitive program at all its sites, General Development hired an environmental director, who over the past few years has constructively debated and negotiated the company's policies and practices with personnel in the state's environmental agencies and organizations, all of which have lauded the responsiveness of the firm.

Summary

The nature and variety of corporate responses in the residential development industry reflect similar responses of companies in other industries. Planning perspectives range from the most closed and narrow to the most open and inclusive. When the planning effort fails to consider changing social, environmental, and political values, business decisions are seen as primarily a one-way process, not a two-way dialogue and agreement between business and society. That is when plans often go badly awry, as did those of AMREP and Deltona Corp.

THE COPPER INDUSTRY

Turning now to the copper-smelting industry, which has also been the object of INFORM research over the past few years, we found again distinct differences in company performance. These differences were seen in response to changing public requirements relating to occupational safety and health. The copper-smelting industry, like the steel industry and other basic industries, until recently has had little contact with the public and has no broad consumer market creating a context which requires the development of sensitive corporate public relations responses. As a result, defensiveness and resistance to pressure for greater corporate social and environmental responsibility are the rule rather than the exception.

The industry includes large firms such as Anaconda Co., owned since 1977 by the Atlantic Richfield Company (ARCO); Kennecott Copper Corp. and Phelps Dodge Corporation, whose operations include a broad range of mining, smelting, and refining activities; and small companies such as White Pine and the Inspiration Copper Company, which operates just one smelter. A total of nine firms operate the sixteen United States primary smelters. Seven of these smelters are located in Arizona; the rest either are in the Southwest (Utah, New Mexico, Texas, and Nevada) or are scattered in other parts of the country (Michigan, Tennessee, and Washington).

Smelters are dangerous places in which to work. The 5000 United States smelter workers daily risk damage to their health from exposure to arsenic, a known carcinogenic agent; sulfur dioxide; the dust and fumes from other metals and chemicals; and physical hazards, such as noise and heat. They work near smoky furnaces whose internal temperatures reach 2000°F (1093°C), transport ladles containing up to 50 tons of molten copper, and carry out many hazardous tasks involving huge and heavy machinery. Accident rates in this industry are much higher than those for most manufacturing companies.

From 1970 to 1978 the copper industry experienced profound changes in both technology and regulation. Recent technical advances have displaced smelting processes which had been essentially unchanged since early in the twentieth century. Air-pollution regulation has created enormous tensions between copper companies and government by requiring the installation of expensive pollution-control equipment. Moreover, after 1974 economic performance was poor, as this typically cyclic industry experienced a downswing. Until early in 1979 world copper prices were low and company earnings weak.

In addition to these pressures on the copper industry, with the passage of the Occupational Safety and Health Act in 1970 the Occupational Safety and Health Administration (OSHA) began to oversee conditions affecting workers inside the smelters. Tightening standards and increasing inspections, OSHA recently made one of its most important moves: it promulgated a strict new standard regulating the exposure of workers to airborne arsenic, a ubiquitous and most dangerous smelter contaminant.

INFORM evaluated the efforts of copper companies to respond to the national mandate expressed in 1970 that workplaces be made safe and healthful. Our staff examined occupational safety and health conditions at each of the sixteen domestic smelters and also evaluated programs in five areas: safety, medical services, industrial hygiene, workers' rights, and use of engineering controls (essential equipment that reduces health hazards at their source). The practices of two of the nine companies we studied, those of ARCO (with its subsidiary, Anaconda Co.) and those of Newmont Mining Corp. (and its subsidiary, Magma Copper Co.) illustrate the different types of responses we found in this industry. Reviewing those responses here helps to clarify many implications for the firms themselves.

Newmont Mining Corp.
(Magma Copper Co., subsidiary)

Newmont Mining Company's practices and programs are representative of the least responsive attitudes we found—attitudes which unfortunately were reflected to a great degree by most of the companies in the industry. Newmont's smelter in San Manuel, Arizona, which produces 10 percent of the nation's copper, employs 3300 people, 800 of whom are in production work. The smelter managers here exhibited a uniform policy: they shared minimal information on conditions or programs in the workplace with any outside public sources, with government, or even with their own workers.

Newmont's firm refusal to share data with INFORM was not unusual: five of the nine firms we studied also refused. But the degree to which it failed to communicate with its workers or to involve them in the process of exploring better ways to make the smelter safe and clean was unusual. Few of the workers' rights found at other smelters are provided here. Workers are not allowed to participate in investigating accidents, nor are management's findings on accidents made available to them, although the smelter has more than six times the industry average rate of recordable injuries and illnesses (between 1974 and 1976 eight of every ten workers suffered such an injury or illness).

Workers, furthermore, do not have access to either their medical records or information on their exposure to dangerous workplace substances, even though explaining the causes of accidents or the levels of risk that workers face is a first and essential step in involving their positive thinking in problem solving. The workers at the San Manuel smelter do not have the right to refuse unsafe work, a right which is afforded workers at ten of the sixteen smelters which INFORM studied. Indeed, in 1973 the firing of a worker who refused to work on a power line while it was electrified caused a wildcat strike, which continued until the worker was finally rehired. San Manuel is also practically the only smelter site without a workers' safety and health committee of its own.

As a result of the secretive and backward policies at San Manuel, management and labor were found, not surprisingly, to be sharply divided. United

Steelworkers Local 937 at the plant made a greater number of formal complaints to safety and health regulatory agencies than did any other union local which INFORM studied. OSHA alone inspected the smelter sixteen times between 1972 and 1977, a rate well above that of most other smelters; twelve of these inspections were prompted by worker complaints.

Under pressure from OSHA, some important program improvements have occurred at San Manuel. The smelter has a good respirator program, and it has even designed some of its own engineering-control systems to reduce air pollution and noise levels in the plant. However, in many instances the company has tried to keep confidential the information which it has had to release to the government. Unlike the managements of any of the other nine companies surveyed, Newmont's management refused to allow the U.S. Environmental Protection Agency (EPA) to release specific data on the arsenic content of its concentrate, the raw material in the smelting process. These data were finally obtained by INFORM under the Freedom of Information Act. Newmont further requested that OSHA not disclose to anyone the facts regarding the engineering-control systems designed and developed by the company so that it would not lose the competitive advantage which it held in meeting regulations.

Insofar as workplace safety and health are concerned, not only machinery but also management policy, the sharing of information between managements in the industry and with government agencies, and the attitudes of involvement and mutual concern by workers and managers all are intricately interrelated and essential ingredients in achieving an effective program to protect workers. When workers' lives and health are very much at stake, such a response as Newmont's is unfortunate indeed.

ARCO (Anaconda Co., subsidiary)

At the opposite end of the scale in terms of corporate initiative and response is Anaconda, ARCO's fully owned subsidiary. The Anaconda smelter in Montana employs 1000 people (270 in copper production) and produces 12 percent of domestic copper. Since ARCO took over the company in 1977, relationships between the company, government, and the public have been expanded to create a much freer flow of detailed information. This development reflects management interest in openly exploring Anaconda's problems and in trying to acquire the feedback needed to devise new and better ways to protect workers.

When INFORM's report on the industry was released in April 1979, an Anaconda official's public response was, "If we find new ideas in this report on how to better safeguard our workers, we will certainly consider them." Newmont's response, in contrast, was to place last-minute calls to INFORM asking us not to release the study before meeting with their representatives—a curious request after almost 4 years of denying INFORM any cooperation.

Even before ARCO took Anaconda over, the company had exhibited significant initiatives. The Anaconda smelter smelts copper from concentrates with an unusually high percentage of arsenic, and to its credit Anaconda was one of the first companies to try to measure this hazard. It found that from 1938 to 1963 its workers were exposed to dangerously high levels: between 290 and 11,270 micrograms per cubic meter. Workers at the smelter were found to be dying of lung cancer at from three to eight times the rate of other state residents.

Though the smelter may still be one of the most hazardous in the industry, over the past years ARCO's management has moved ahead to introduce engineering-control systems which have reduced contaminants significantly. By the time of INFORM's research this smelter and Kennecott Copper Corp.'s smelter in Garfield, Utah, were the only two of the sixteen smelters to use 80 percent of the widely available engineering-control systems that should form the backbone of any effort to create a more healthful smelter workplace. Anaconda recently took on two independent consultants to analyze possibilities for further improving engineering-control systems to meet federal and state standards.

While such control systems are the first line of worker protection, respirator programs constitute an important backup. Anaconda's respirator program was found to be one of the best in the industry. The company not only provides excellent respirator equipment to its workers but takes responsibility, when many other firms do not, for properly maintaining the equipment and instructing workers in its use.

At the same time, the company could make many further improvements in its hygiene, safety, and medical-service programs. These include stepping up safety research to help define the causes of accidents, improving inspection of engineering-control equipment, and providing a rehabilitation program for injured workers. However, the likelihood that effective changes will occur at Anaconda is increased not only by the openness of the management to outside comment but also by the strong participation of the Anaconda smelter workforce. Perhaps because of the strength of the local union and perhaps also because of a more receptive management attitude to worker input, the local has secured for its members many important rights that are far above the average for this industry. Since 1970 ARCO has had a joint safety and health committee which participates in inspections related to all accidents at the smelters and in discussions of evolving programs to reduce industrial hazards. It also pays its workers for the time they spend on committee business and gives them access to their own medical records, though not yet to health-hazard records, which would be a significant step forward.

Anaconda workers, like those at nine of the other fifteen smelters, may refuse unsafe or unhealthy work with specific grievance procedures for disputes. However, the workers at Anaconda are the only workers in the industry with an important additional right: they retain their wage rates if they must be relocated to new jobs for reasons attributable to workplace conditions.

As a result of active worker participation at Anaconda, some significant problems have come to light and been effectively addressed. In 1968, for example, worker concern about exposure to beryllium, a highly toxic metal, and about the failure of the company to monitor levels of this substance led to a series of meetings of company, union, and regulatory officials. These meetings resulted in a list of recommendations to improve conditions. Union pressures over the years have also markedly increased the impetus of management to improve its engineering-control and respirator programs.

CONCLUSIONS

From the examples offered here in both the land-development and the copper industries, it becomes clear that, in a self-reinforcing fashion, companies seriously injure themselves when they do not grasp the two-way concept of communication, which includes sharing information with and listening carefully to their many publics, including consumers, customers, and others whose lives and environment are affected by their operations. Companies that see these publics and regulatory agencies as obstacles to be skirted as adroitly as possible may pay a great price. In the land-development industry, as the AMREP case illustrates, careless land-use planning takes its toll not only on the company's land and water resources but also in the wrath of thousands of consumers who one day find they have paid for land that has neither investment value nor value as livable homesites. In costly lawsuits, administrative expense, and a poor public image, such companies pay heavily in the long run. In the copper industry, as the Newmont case illustrates, the price of management secrecy especially is paid in terms of both a lack of more creative programming and an unnecessarily adversary relationship with its workers.

The process of good communications and the complexities of two-way planning may appear expensive, but they generally prove rewarding. As was true of General Development Corp. and Anaconda, these strategies helped ensure early recognition of environmental and workplace problems, the timely development of important corrective programs, and the fostering of highly constructive relations with communities, workers, and government regulators.

Beyond these benefits, a corporation that energetically responds to evolving social requirements may win the kind of testimonial that adds immeasurably to its public image. For example, the vice president of Florida's Audubon Society, which at one time opposed General Development's land-use activities, publicly praised the company for its farsighted environmental stance and commended its "earlier support for Florida's Dredge and Fill Rule which curbed the excesses of some developers—even though the position was not popular within the business community at the time."[3] That kind of recognition is almost certain to evoke positive reactions from the public, regulatory agencies, and workers. And it is such reactions to constructive corporate efforts that in turn serve to lessen the remaining defensive postures and to reinforce the dynamic impetus of two-way planning.

---

[3] Letter from Charles Lee, vice president, Florida Audubon Society, to L. Fisher, president, General Development Corp., Apr. 4, 1975.

A CONSUMER AGENDA FOR CORPORATE LEADERSHIP

SANDRA L. WILLETT

Sandra L. Willett is executive vice president of the National Consumers League (NCL), a membership organization founded in 1897. She is responsible for the direction of NCL's legislative program, consumer-education programs, and research projects on credit, insurance, product safety, food, energy, health, and consumer representation, as well as NCL's fund-raising and staff management.

Ms. Willett received a master's degree in public administration from Harvard University and an undergraduate degree from Wellesley College. Prior to her work with NCL, she served as Director of Consumer Education, Office of Consumer Affairs, U.S. Department of Health, Education, and Welfare. She is a commissioner on the Minimum Wage Study Commission, serves on the Travel Advisory Board to the Secretary of Commerce and on the Board of Overseers of the Institute for Civil Justice, and is active in national and local public-interest organizations.

These are neither the best of times nor the worst of times. The opinion polls of Yankelovich, Skelly and White and others indicate that public confidence in business continues to plummet:

> On the case of business, public confidence has fallen from the 70% level in 1968 down to 15% in 1977[;] . . . there is a strong sense among the public that business will put profit ahead of its broader responsibilities to take into account environmental goals.[1]

An AP–NBC news poll showed that 54 percent of the public believed that the energy crisis was a hoax. Corporate leaders may have cringed again to read in the *Harvard Business Review* that "business should be alarmed at the amount of unresolved dissatisfaction that apparently exists in the market-place."[2]

As grim as these signs may be, however, polls also suggest that a growing segment of the public is better informed before making consumer purchases, more willing to take responsibility for individual action, and substantially supportive of the American enterprise system. While the Lockheed Corp.'s bribes, Watergate scandals, and illegal campaign contributions have de-throned many corporate and political heroes and while the threat of Chrysler Corporation's bankruptcy has shaken conventional economic theories, these occurrences have also stimulated many companies to put their own behavior under the microscope in a beneficial way.

Although the gap is still wide between what corporate executives see under that microscope and what they might then do to encourage forward-looking policies, several corporate leaders are indeed looking beyond the strict profit-maximization incentive to corporate accountability in a changing economy as a necessary and feasible goal for the 1980s. This shift in perspective, stimulated to a large degree by public dissatisfaction and consumer activism, signals new leadership and urges corporate executives to act on a new agenda.

Corporate leaders now have the opportunity to take certain practical steps to address some of the public's expectations and consumer concerns. Having worked with at least one major company or industry association which has implemented one or more of the items on the proposed agenda, I would argue pragmatically that these items can be made as acceptable to the corporate world as they are needed by consumers. Although stated as "options," they are intended as action steps for a corporate-responsiveness strategy—one that goes beyond the bottom line to broad corporate accountability.

---

[1] *A Report to Leadership Participants on 1977 Findings of Corporate Priorities,* Yankelovich, Skelly and White, Inc., New York, 1977, pp. 5, 9.

[2] Alan R. Andreasen and Arthur Best, "Consumers complain—Does Business Respond?" *Harvard Business Review,* July–August 1977, p. 100.

OPTION ONE

Corporate leaders must prevent their companies from always climbing on the special-interest, anticonsumer lobbying bandwagon. Leadership must be exerted in determining a legislative position which best fits an individual company's purposes.

Corporate lobbying has become a $1 billion industry. In 1968 only 50 companies maintained Washington representation. A decade later the number was well over 500.[3] On October 1, 1978, *The Washington Post* reported a volcanic outpouring of corporate money to members of Congress through newly formed political action committees (PACs). PACs had collected $54 million between January 1, 1977, and July 1978, the greatest part coming from industry.

Money talks. With the outpouring of corporate dollars to support anticonsumer slush funds and candidates, the corporate world is developing a quasi fourth branch of government, as James Reston has warned. Genuine efforts to understand the consumer interest before signing up with the consumer critics are essential to a strategy of corporate responsiveness.

It is imperative that corporate leaders steer business away from the emotional rhetoric and skewed statements of many trade associations, including the Chamber of Commerce of the United States and the Business Roundtable. It will benefit a company more in the eyes of the public and the Congress if it charts an independent path and does not hasten to join the special-interest hue and cry of organized industry lobbyists. For example, the major trade associations, unanimously opposing legislation to create an Office of Consumer Representation, frequently referred to outdated proposals of a previous congressional session, painted the bill to create the new office as something which would destroy the free enterprise system, and matched their prophecies of doom with slush funds of several million dollars. Although the bill was finally defeated for several reasons, the business lobby won a hollow victory and lost considerable respect because of its tactics.

Corporations which have fiercely defended their unique products, their distinctive services, and their independent reputations have begun to rush into the arms of trade associations that promise to "beat the bastards" on Capitol Hill. As a result, distinguished corporate executives keep company with the new Elmer Gantrys. Reputable businesses find themselves following the lowest common morality of the group.

There is no doubt in my mind that many corporate leaders would prefer to think for themselves rather than to lobby in a group in which they must relinquish control. I urge companies to follow an independent line of thinking, as the American Express Co., for one, is doing and as 110 corporations,

---

3 Walter Guzzardi, "To Win in Washington," *Fortune,* Mar. 27, 1978.

including Levi Strauss & Co. and the Cummins Engine Company, did when they broke with the trade associations to support the Consumer Representation bill.

No one disputes the right of the corporate world to represent its interests. That right belongs to everyone. Business in fact has a responsibility, as do we all, to make its interests known to Congress and the executive branch. However, I question whether the lack of reason and the hard-hitting, overkill manner, fast becoming a frequent posture on Capitol Hill, are truly in corporations' best interests.

OPTION TWO

Corporations need to improve their planning and design capabilities to reduce the volume of consumer complaints. Efficient complaint handling is important to consumer satisfaction and, even more so, as a barometer for corporate management. But it in no way substitutes for thorough research, sound engineering design, careful production, and straightforward marketing. Prevention of abuses wins hands down over any after-the-fact cure.

Having read the public-opinion polls, corporate leaders know that consumers worry about safety and that they are willing to pay a few cents more for protection. Contrary to what many companies were saying in the late 1960s, companies now know that safety sells.

Think of the benefits to the Ford Motor Co. and the Firestone Tire & Rubber Co. if management and engineers had been more concerned with safety and prevention. The manufacturers of home insulation, through their voluntary association, the American Society for Testing and Materials (ASTM), have invited consumers to work cooperatively to set voluntary standards regarding chemical additives and flammability. This is prevention, and this shows responsiveness.

OPTION THREE

Corporations can go directly to consumer advocates for research, speeches, and meetings with top management. Given our perspective, our membership, and the experience that we have had with many different industries, we know that, like NCL, most public-interest representatives can be useful to a business which is serious about treating consumer concerns. Public relations firms and the new breed of commercial consumer consultants cannot provide the same authenticity.

Johnson & Johnson, for example, was curious about consumer advocates. The Board of Directors of Johnson & Johnson's domestic operating companies, a group of twenty distinguished gentlemen, asked me to be the target of their curiosity. We discussed obvious areas of disagreement, such as those in proposals for drug regulatory reform and national health insurance. However, we also listened to each other and parted with the satisfaction that each had valid points to make and that together we could do valuable research where agreement existed.

NCL has participated in many similar meetings with, for example, two major oil companies. These meetings have been held at the companies' invitation. The corporate participants have been the companies' chief executive officers, vice presidents, and top managers. They have expressed genuine satisfaction with this direct approach to consumer advocates.

It is better to talk directly to the consumer movement than to gather impressions from the press, trade associations, or public relations firms.

OPTION FOUR

It is legitimate for business to join forces publicly with the consumer movement on issues on which the company and consumer organizations are in agreement. It is effective to lobby together.

James S. Kemper & Company was one of a handful of insurance companies which actively supported no-fault automobile insurance legislation. Chairman James S. Kemper and his staff made public statements, contributed to the Committee for Consumers No-Fault, and lobbied with consumers. Congress was impressed.

OPTION FIVE

Corporate leaders should support the research and education programs of various consumer organizations. Corporate resources should be committed to periodic meetings, to studies, and to seminars. A meager 1 percent of the advertising budget in most companies would go a long way to providing financial support for research by consumer organizations on issues of mutual concern.

A consumer-oriented direct-mail insurance company, for example, wanted to cosponsor a conference with NCL on life and health insurance. So interested was Consumers United Group in publicly exploring consumer needs for insurance that the company put up seed money to make possible what eventually became a productive, standing-room-only seminar. The 2-day session produced results, among them an increased understanding by consumers of the industry's regulatory problems; a heightened awareness by industry of consumer concerns over industrial insurance, archaic policy language, and inadequate cost disclosure; and a series of relationships between people who now talk regularly to each other, thanks to changes inspired by one insurance company.

It is better to talk together than to shout long-distance. It is better to emphasize similar concerns than to harp on differences.

OPTION SIX

Corporate leaders, sensitive to public expectations, know that they should address consumer concerns before government regulation becomes a distinct possibility. A company can initiate change before federal or state intervention becomes either necessary or politically attractive.

The National Coal Policy Project involves environmental leaders and executives from some of the *Fortune* 500 companies. Its purpose is to decrease the polarization that has characterized the national debate over energy and environmental policy and to identify and implement measures whereby cooperation will foster solutions that advance the national interest.

OPTION SEVEN

Corporate leaders have the authority to initiate or increase a company's consumer budget. If they are serious about the consumer interest, they can determine the amount of dues that a company pays to the Chamber of Commerce of the United States, the Business Roundtable, and other trade associations to which it belongs. An amount equal to 20 percent or more of those funds could be budgeted for serious consumer work within the company. The company might decide to reduce the fees paid to trade associations by that amount, on the ground that in supporting its own consumer programs it is advancing its best interests. Devoting a small percentage of trade association dues to consumer programs seems modest in light of corporations' lack of credibility and the imperative for constructive change.

OPTION EIGHT

It goes without saying that initiatives must be carried out. This, of course, is where a real difference can be made.

It has taken several years of trying, but something very constructive is under way between four chief executive officers of leading property and casualty insurance companies and a number of consumer groups. The chairmen or top officials of Aetna Life & Casualty, Allstate Insurance Co., Sentry Life Insurance Co., and Travelers Corp. are meeting with consumer representatives to find solutions to the problems of availability and affordability of automobile and homeowners' insurance. Candidly admitting their concerns, these corporate chief executive officers spent a day exchanging views on rate-classification criteria, residual-market subsidization, and the overall cost structure of their industry.

Such meetings are building confidence and respect between corporate and consumer leaders. They are stimulating different ways of looking at complex problems, strengthening the company bottom line, and building corporate accountability.

OPTION NINE

Chief executive officers must spread the word throughout corporations. In my experience, chief executive officers are often genuinely interested in the consumer viewpoint and concerned about rising public expectations. Usually they can afford to be: they have made it to the top. Middle-level managers and most second-level executives, expecting to be judged by the profit-maximization criterion, are far more resistant and closed to consumer activists.

After a candid discussion with the top echelon at an insurance meeting, one senior officer spoke truthfully in response to the chairman's agreement with many of the consumer suggestions. The official said, "The people who should really be hearing the chairman agree with the NCL are our field managers. They are on the firing line every day."

It is one thing for the top executive to espouse a forward-looking policy; it is another thing to assure its implementation throughout the corporation. Do not let the cream settle at the top.

OPTION TEN

Corporate leaders can introduce the board of directors to the consumer viewpoint. If the time is not right to elect someone familiar with the consumer movement to the board, a discussion with one or more consumer leaders can be scheduled during a board meeting.

Seeking to expand the vision and exposure of its directors, a former board member of a major United States corporation is designing a program to have social leaders outside the company meet with the board. The idea is still preliminary, but it is being considered. Such a program would go a long way to expose the board to the concerns and proposals offered by groups of consumers, women, environmentalists, and senior citizens for a more genuine and constructive corporate response.

Business executives, caught in the tension between self-aggrandizement and community concern, between profit maximization and corporate accountability, are aided in their choice by many voices from other corporations that have begun the transformation. These voices, from inside and outside the corporate sector, are likely to blend together to call for recognition of what Kenneth Boulding defines as the spaceship economy.[4] These voices are likely to chide corporations which refuse to recognize the irrevocable conditions evolving from an economy of limited rather than unlimited resources and of increasing corporate concentration and decreased sensitivity to consumers.

Limitations on resources require expanded responsibilities. A probable slower rate of economic growth makes obsolete, even offensive, Detroit's tradition of a new car every year. Recycling must take the place of careless waste. Human welfare must be viewed as a condition to be improved, not manipulated.

These factors necessitate replacing the criterion of profit maximization with that of reasonable profits and corporate responsibility. Social utility must be given considerably greater weight as a measure of corporate performance. To use a scientific reference, corporate self-interest is a necessary but not a sufficient ingredient of success. As Irving Kristol has pointed out with his analogy of the corporation as a dinosaur lumbering its way to extinction, corporations must adapt, become attentive to the public interest, and learn to govern, learn to "think politically" rather than just to "think economically."[5]

Innovation in the future may well fall less in the technical arena and more in the arena of social accountability. Corporations that chose to implement consumer-oriented strategies, for example, will be viewed as leaders of society. Chief executives who define costs in long-range terms to include environmental health, who reward prevention, and who strive for reasonable consensus rather than conflict should rightfully be heralded as the new pioneers.

The consumer wants in. Consumer participation in business and government decision making can guard against institutional inefficiency. Cooperation rather than confrontation will give rise to creative solutions of the tensions between wants and needs, between the get-ahead ethic and community concern.

Corporate leaders face an imminent choice. Several have taken the step. Many others need to take it. The choice seems analogous to the choice that the Catholic cardinals faced when selecting a pope twice in 1978. Do you vote for a traditionalist, a scholar, an expert in the liturgy, a defender of the faith? Or do you recognize that changing public expectations in a complex

---

[4] Kenneth Boulding, "Economics of the Coming Spaceship Earth," in Henry Jarrett (ed.), *Environmental Quality in a Growing Economy: Essays from the 1966 RFF Forum,* published for Resources for the Future, Inc., by the Johns Hopkins Press, Baltimore, 1966.

[5] Irving Kristol, "The Corporation and the Dinosaur," *The Wall Street Journal,* Feb. 14, 1974.

economy demand a willingness to face social problems as well? That is the tension. Consumers are turning to the corporate world for a response.

SOCIAL RESPONSIBILITY AT DOW CHEMICAL

PAUL F. OREFFICE

Paul F. Oreffice is president and chief executive officer of the Dow Chemical Company, a major international manufacturer of chemicals, and chairman of its Executive Committee, positions he has held since May 3, 1978. A Dow employee since 1953, Mr. Oreffice was first elected to the Dow Board of Directors in 1971.

Mr. Oreffice has a B.S. degree in chemical engineering from Purdue University. After beginning his Dow career in Midland, he held successive positions in Italy, Brazil, Spain, and Coral Gables, Florida, where he set up headquarters as first president of Dow Chemical Latin America. In 1970 he returned to Midland as financial vice president of the company, a position he held until being named president of Dow Chemical U.S.A. in August 1975.

Currently, Mr. Oreffice is a member of the Board of Directors of Junior Achievement and of the Chemical Manufacturers Association. Additionally, he is a director of the European-American Bank and Trust Co., the First Bank Corporation of Midland, the Dow Corning Corp., and the Connecticut General Insurance Corp.

The Dow Chemical Company's primary objective, to produce maximum long-term profit growth, is little, if any, different from that of most industrial corporations. If we have done a good job of meeting our social responsibilities, it is because we have been able to relate the profit motive to the solution of social problems and, of equal importance (and driven by the same profit motive), to steer a course that has avoided conflict with the changing interests and concerns of society. The question, then, is: Why have we been more successful than some other companies in meeting our social responsibilities? I believe that the answer lies in our history, and I would like to develop that premise for your appraisal and criticism.

History

The Dow Chemical Company was founded in the late 1800s by Herbert H. Dow in Midland, Michigan. The location was selected because of abundant underground brine deposits and available cheap energy in the form of wood slabs abandoned by the then-expiring logging industry.

History Lesson Number 1. The supply of wood slabs, used to fire the salt-brine evaporators, was soon exhausted, and the company experienced rapidly escalating energy costs. Thus Dow was faced in its formative years with a critical economic squeeze that forced innovation in process technology and product diversification.

History

Herbert H. Dow, chemist and inventor, came as a stranger to the Midland community. He married a local schoolteacher and built a home at the end of Main Street. He was enough different from what the local citizens had known in the lumbering days that he was called (behind his back) "crazy Dow."

History Lesson Number 2. It is not easy to be different. Engineers and chemists moving into a turn-of-the-century logging community were social pioneers, forced to rely on their own judgment and values. Being different was a way of life, and being tolerant of the rights of others to be different became second nature to early Dow employees.

History

The city of Midland, Michigan, is situated at the confluence of three small rivers. This was a necessary attribute in logging days but a rather serious handicap for a developing chemical company. The river was big enough to float logs but not big enough to absorb chemical pollutants or to supply process water for a growing company.

History Lesson Number 3. Proper waste treatment and resource management must be an integral part of plant design.

History

As observed by Don Whitehead, distinguished journalist and author, "In Midland, the homes and golf courses are hardly more than a ten minute drive from the factory gates for most executives and employees." He further noted, "Those who seek anonymity after working hours and who wish to build a wall between their business lives and their private lives find the small town a difficult place. Such walls are not easy to build in a small town. The town's life is not a separate thing from the life of the company."[1]

History Lesson Number 4. There is no place to hide. The decisions made in the boardroom will be critically discussed at the ball park, at the farmers' market, and in the local churches.

The early experiences of Dow's management became a part of the company's fabric: openness and candor were and are the order of the day, concern for the environment and conservation of resources were and are necessary for our survival, and self-sufficiency and independent thought were and are the mark of our management thrust.

As society became increasingly demanding of corporations on matters of the environment, worker safety, energy conservation, and fair employment practices, it required only an adjustment in emphasis to put us in a leadership position in responding to these changing public expectations. I believe that our small town and our small river have been two of the key influences in guiding our company along a socially acceptable path.

CORPORATE SOCIAL RESPONSIBILITY

The lessons that we have learned as a consequence of our unique situation were nicely summarized by former Board Chairman Carl Gerstacker in a lecture he delivered at Columbia University a few years ago. He referred to his five postulates for creating a management environment for socially responsible corporate performance. They are:

> *Postulate No. 1.* Social responsibility must be a firm, deep-seated belief of the management. It must be soundly and deeply a part of the ongoing goals and strategy of the corporation, and unless there is a deep commitment on the part of the management this is not going to happen.
>
> *Postulate No. 2.* The management must be consistent in its support of social

---

1 Don Whitehead, *The Dow Story,* McGraw-Hill Book Company, New York, 1968, p. 10.

responsibility. Consistency is the cornerstone when you are trying to build an environment, whether you are trying to create an environment for social responsibility or for growth or quality or any other management objective. If you change directions too often your people will simply turn off their hearing aids.

Postulate No. 3. It must be a long-term commitment. This seems to me to be self-evident, but it is vitally important. You cannot go into any major management commitment, whether it is a social responsibility activity or something else, with merely short-term goals, if you expect to be successful. If you go into an Equal Employment Opportunity program, for example, with short-term goals, or decide that you are going to launch a program to upgrade your use of women's talents, or whatever, and don't set yourself long-term goals in this area, then you aren't really committed to these programs. If earnings are down and you say, "Well, we can't do these things this year, business is down," then you aren't really committed for the long term.

Postulate No. 4. You must never underestimate the power of non-verbal communication. You cannot preach one thing and do another; it must be "do as I do," not "do as I say." In establishing a climate for social responsibility you ignore this rule at your peril.

Postulate No. 5. You must always frame your approach in terms of the carrot, not of the stick.

If you want to establish your company as socially responsible you won't get very far by announcing that every employee who shows signs of being socially irresponsible will be horsewhipped or given early retirement at his option. Coercion is not the route to anywhere anymore. Does that mean I believe you ought to pay bonuses to socially responsible employees? Perhaps, in isolated cases, and Dow does. But I have a different type of carrot in mind, and that carrot is the self-interest of the employee and the identification of his self-interest with that of the company.

The chairman concluded his lecture with this final comment:

The five postulates or principles that I have discussed are in my view necessary to the establishment of a management climate in any organization that is going to exhibit socially responsible performance. You must have a deep management commitment to social responsibility; it must be an integral part of the business, and the management must be consistent in its communications about the subject, and willing to stick with commitment through thick and thin. Further, the management must avoid doing one thing and saying another, and it must tie rewards in with success.

But these rules, important as they are, must always be subordinate to the most important principle of all. Let me repeat, or rephrase, this overriding principle for you once again, one final time, because it is the most important point of all: because the corporation's first responsibility is long-term profit growth, all its efforts to solve social problems will fail, or be only shallowly successful, if they are not integrated into the primary objective of long-term profit growth, and understood in this fashion by management and the other employees.

In other words, solving social problems must be good business as well as good citizenship.[2]

Now, if we look at the potentials and limitations of responsible corporate conduct and keep Gerstacker's postulates in mind, the potentials seem limitless as long as we rigidly apply the discipline of good business.

ECOLOGICAL PROGRAMS

To realize maximum benefits it will be necessary for all of us to think in broader terms than we have in the past. For example, in assessing the value of new ventures, we have tended to look almost exclusively at the primary benefit of the activity and to ignore the less obvious consequences, in which some of the major values often lie. Several examples come to mind.

The Dow Chemical Company has had an active waste-control program since the 1920s and a toxicology laboratory to verify product safety since the 1930s. Our environmental action has intensified through the years. Two developments will illustrate an increasing concern for involvement in environmental improvement: the use of ecological base-line surveys at manufacturing locations and the formation and operation of a company Ecology Council.

Ecological base-line surveys have been conducted at all major Dow plants in the United States and in a number of other countries. Surveys are also being made at all new plant sites. The surveys consist of detailed physical, chemical, biological, and hydrological studies of the soil, water, and air surrounding the site of a manufacturing plant. They serve as a bench mark to measure the effect of changes in the environment caused by human activities. They also serve as a guide to plant operation.

The Dow Ecology Council, organized in January 1970, was composed of key Dow officials including the president and the chairman of the board. It met regularly to establish objectives, determine guidelines, identify resources, catalyze action, and ensure communications for environmental improvement throughout the company.

A key to making things happen was the formation of ecology subcouncils in all of Dow's manufacturing divisions and product departments. These groups also are composed of the organization's top executives.

Here are the top priorities established by the Ecology Council:

---

[2] Carl A. Gerstacker, "Creating a Management Environment for Socially Responsible Performance," Garrett lecture, Columbia University, New York, Nov. 21, 1972.

● Authorize new facilities only if they meet or better tomorrow's pollution standards. Subject existing plants to pollution inventories to identify problems (water, air, solids, odors, noise), rank them in order, and develop plans for solution with timetables and auditing mechanisms.

● Build in fail-safe mechanisms and facilities to avoid ecological disasters (for example, diversionary sewer systems and dikes to contain accidental spills from storage tanks).

● Set up early warning systems to identify and control serious hazard potentials. This program involves such approaches as surveys of all metals or toxic elements appearing in the manufacturing processes. It also involves product end-use surveys with immediate work on those products presenting serious hazard potentials. The remainder of the products can be rank-ordered on a no-hazard or hazards-unknown basis.

● Seek and develop improved technology. This program refers to process technology emphasizing recycling, increased yields, and waste prevention and waste-treatment technology featuring chemical and biological degradation or incineration, or both, to replace limited disposal techniques such as landfills or even hiring a contractor to haul wastes away to an unknown destination.

All these programs obviously call for assessments not only by chemists, engineers, and managers but by biologists, biochemists, and toxicologists.

As examples of action steps on these priorities, I would like to list several illustrations involving our headquarters plant at Midland, Michigan:

● To avoid accidental spills in the river, a new water-diversion system was installed at a cost of $800,000. Total-oxygen-demand analyzers, invented by Dow, provide automatic analysis of the water flow in clean-water sewers at 3-minute intervals. Alarm systems allow the diversion system to take contaminated water directly to a shot pond instead of the river following any accidental spill.

● Curbs and dikes are located around tanks throughout the plant site to isolate and contain chemicals that might leak from storage tanks.

● The general manager of the Midland Division plant has told production and research managers that no new plants will be built unless waste problems are under control. He has also challenged people in existing plants to solve their own waste problems rather than rely on the division's $25 million waste-control facility. As a result, the division's 500 operating plants have reduced by more than 25 percent the total amount of wastes sent to the general waste-treatment plant.

● Twenty-eight cooling towers have been installed to prevent thermal pollution of the Tittabawassee River. They cost $7.2 million to install. Better operating efficiency and lower water costs gave us a 10 percent return on this investment. While this return was not great, it was not bad.

● A new chloro alkali complex has no outlets to the river.

● An interdisciplinary environmental research laboratory has been established to provide a technical base for the elimination of waste and the know-how to clean up wastes until new technology is developed.

● Midland provides 24-hour supervision for its environmental-quality–control activities.

In the first 3 years of special emphasis on waste prevention (1968–1971), the Midland Division saved $6 million in materials that previously had been lost to the sewers. The savings, of course, continue. As these programs have been extended to our worldwide operations, we have proved again and again that there is profit in pollution control.

EQUAL-EMPLOYMENT PROGRAMS

Measuring the profit contributions made by pollution control is an easier job than measuring short-term profits derived from an effective affirmative-action program. However, the fines and penalties provided under Title VII of the Civil Rights Act of 1964 for failure to pursue such programs diligently provide more than enough incentive.

Dow was faced with several situations that complicated our moving rapidly on programs to provide increased job opportunities for members of minority groups. For example, approximately 45 percent of our professional workforce have degrees in chemical engineering or chemistry. Only 5.7 percent of the 1976 graduating classes in these two disciplines in United States colleges were members of minority groups. To increase the number of members of minority groups in our workforce it was obvious that we had to compete more aggressively for available qualified minority candidates, and it was equally obvious that we had to do something that would increase the number of members of minority groups graduating in the disciplines that we need. The latter is necessarily a long-range program. To be effective, a program attacking this problem must start at the junior high school and high school level. Young students must be encouraged to take the basic mathematics and science courses necessary to prepare them for the pursuit of a technical degree in college. Dow was a prime mover in founding Chemical Industry for Minorities in Engineering (CHIME), a group of twenty chemical companies working together to provide encouragement and incentives to young minority students.

Participation in other organizations targeted at increasing the number of minority students studying for technical degrees has become a way of life at Dow. We are active in the National Advisory Council for Minorities in Engineering (NACME), the Committee for Minorities in Engineering (CME), which is part of the National Science Foundation, the Minority Engineering Educational Effort (ME), the Texas Alliance for Minorities in Engineering (TAME), and other organizations. Programs designed to help minority students already in college are of real importance. We approach this need from several directions. Scholarship funds are provided to students and schools to assist those requiring financial aid. We are involved in alternate-term cooperative education programs which emphasize minority participation. These programs provide students with an exposure to the industrial world of chemistry during their academic careers; they are an excellent way to help students grasp the practical aspects of the technology that they are learning. Summer jobs supplement these programs and are especially helpful at schools at which cooperative programs are not available.

Of course, not all jobs in our workforce require college degrees. Achieving a broader base of minority employees among our operating personnel posed different problems. A good example is our experience with affirmative action at Plaquemine, Louisiana. The plant there had few if any minority employees prior to 1963 even though the population in the area was 35 percent black.

Dow responded to increasing public and government pressure by instituting a companywide program for actively searching out qualified minority employees. At Plaquemine progress was slow; turnover was high. Minority employees felt that promotions came too slowly and that white supervision was not sensitive to their needs. There were no blacks in the front office. After a series of meetings between the plant manager, his industrial-relations staff, and representative minority employees, a seven-step program of action was undertaken:

1.   A black equal-employment-opportunity (EEO) counselor was appointed to communicate with minority employees.

2.   Blacks were moved into key supervisory jobs as they became qualified. The appointment of the first black shift supervisor was a major forward step; he provided an effective role model that had been absent.

3.   Meetings were held with all employees to discuss EEO commitments and to seek inputs.

4.   Blacks were appointed to serve on committees and in employee activities like the credit union. The result was to draw blacks into the mainstream of company activities.

5.   Local parity hiring goals were established.

6.   Career days were established at local schools. Dow keyed its presentations to black students and to job opportunities. This information was further spread by word of mouth.

7.   Dow representatives spoke at civic clubs, to church groups, and at science fairs, talking mostly about jobs and company philosophy.

The net result of these activities was to establish Dow as a good place to work. The percentage of minority employees in the workforce increased from a negligible figure prior to 1963 to 23.8 percent in 1978. Progress has been steady, as illustrated by the accompanying table.

Minority Operators' Program, Plaquemine

	January 1974	January 1975	January 1976	January 1977	January 1978	January 1979
Number of blacks	73	134	153	188	217	234
Percentage of blacks	14.6	19.7	21.6	24.1	23.8	24.6

Perhaps the best evidence of our success in moving forward in EEO activities was the recognition given to our programs by the government regulatory agency responsible for monitoring our compliance when it singled us out for self-audit. Rather than agency representatives, our own personnel were permitted to audit our various locations for compliance with EEO regulations. These auditors were given special training and worked as teams in auditing and preparing reports on their observations. The net result was a tougher auditing stance than that which the government itself assumed. The training program also brought in a wide spectrum of Dow employees and thus broadened the awareness of our many programs. A secondary benefit was the reduction of forms and paperwork that seem to accompany most government programs. We did not reduce the amount and quality of the data, but the data we developed were compatible with our own system rather than an addition to it. Although a change in government responsibilities (all EEO compliance activities are now within the Labor Department) has eliminated our self-audit relationship, we have maintained our program as part of an internal commitment to continued excellence. We make information on this program available to other companies that have an interest in it.

Fair employment practices have also paid dividends. Hiring and promoting the best available people is bound to be advantageous. A less obvious benefit has developed at Dow. In the United States discrimination based on skin color has only recently been vigorously challenged. In England racial prejudice is less prominent, but historically a young man has found it difficult if not impossible to rise above his father's station in life. Other countries have similar prejudices. A few years ago Dow chose a Canadian employee of Hungarian birth to be its chief executive officer. This decision did not go unnoticed by our employees around the world. I am happy to say that when the time came to promote another employee to the position of chief executive officer, that employee's Italian birthplace played no role in his selection. While EEO may be seen as a United States program, its consequences reverberate around the world.

OCCUPATIONAL HEALTH AND SAFETY

IRVING S. SHAPIRO

Irving S. Shapiro is chairman of the board and chief executive officer of E. I. du Pont de Nemours & Co., a major international manufacturer of chemicals, headquartered in Wilmington, Delaware. He came to Du Pont in 1951 as an attorney in the legal department after serving in the U.S. Department of Justice during the Roosevelt and Truman administrations. He is the first person in the history of the world's largest chemical firm to rise to the top through a career in law. In 1965 he was appointed assistant general counsel of the company. He became a vice president and a member of the Executive Committee in September 1970 and was designated a senior vice president in January 1972. On July 16, 1973, Mr. Shapiro was named vice chairman of the board, a new position that made him the second-ranking officer of the company behind Chairman Charles B. McCoy. On December 17, 1973, he was named Mr. McCoy's successor and elected to the Finance Committee, effective January 1, 1974.

Mr. Shapiro holds degrees from the University of Minnesota and the University of Minnesota Law School. He is a director of the International Business Machines Corp., Citibank and Citicorp, the Bank of Delaware, the Continental American Life Insurance Co., and the Greater Wilmington Development Council and serves on the Board of Trustees of the University of Minnesota Foundation and the University of Delaware. He is also a member of the Board of Directors of the Associates of the Graduate School of Business Administration of Harvard University, the Visiting Committee of the John F. Kennedy School of Government of Harvard University, the Board of Trustees of the University of Pennsylvania, and the Board of Governors of the University of Pennsylvania Law School.

Mr. Shapiro is an American director of the U.S.-U.S.S.R. Trade and Economic Council and a member of the Advisory Council on Japan–United States Economic Relations. He is a founding member and a member of the Board of Governors of the Jerusalem Institute of Management in Jerusalem, Israel. Mr. Shapiro is a trustee of the Conference Board and the Ford Foundation. He was elected chairman of the Business Roundtable in June 1976 and served in that capacity for 2 years. He was a vice chairman of the Business Council from January 1977 through December 1978.

It may sound like a homily, but corporate responsibility does begin at home. No matter what tests of responsibility are eventually devised, the first criterion will probably be the way in which an organization treats the people who are directly and most seriously affected by its activities. If a company's relationships with employees and the communities surrounding its plants or offices are flawed, no amount of papering over (by an extra gift to a local charity or by Thanksgiving turkeys to the faithful) will be acceptable as excuse or ploy.

Perhaps there is no better method of evaluating a company's sense of responsibility than to look at its programs in occupational health and safety. Few subjects affect people's lives more directly or arouse greater interest. The appearance of harmful effects from exposure to previously commonplace substances, along with technological changes which allow scientists for the first time to detect parts per billion and to analyze their effects, have led all of us to reexamine that which was previously thought to be safe.

How can lives be saved and businesses improve their programs in this area? Although it is risky to generalize from a sample of one, Du Pont's experience indicates that an emphasis on safety-conscious management, medical surveillance, and toxicological research, combined with a prime directive to make only those products which can be manufactured, transported, consumed, and disposed of safely, can make a difference.

SAFETY-CONSCIOUS MANAGEMENT

The total management commitment to safety at Du Pont is reflected in everyday activities, large and small. Safety posters and safety meetings are requisites in all departments. Safety glasses are worn in all laboratories even when nothing dangerous is going on, and "Four on the floor" refers not to cars but to the legs of a chair. Extreme? Perhaps *The Wall Street Journal* was right in noting that "Concern about safety and health takes on a slightly manic air at Du Pont,"[1] but attention to detail is a necessary element in the reduction of the accident rate.

Individuals, knowing that their possibility of accident may be 1 in 100,-000, sometimes get careless; managers who are responsible for preventing the 1 in 100,000 have a different perspective, and it is their job to lead the way. Direction from top management is essential to our policy that *all* accidents and illness from exposure to known hazards can be prevented. Every supervisor, for instance, learns quickly that Du Pont is not prepared to accept any predictable level of injury or illness in any manufacturing unit; he or she learns that the supervisor's job is to see to it that employees do not get hurt. We are extremely demanding and serious about this: a supervisor learns that

---

[1] Thomas J. Bray, "Hunt for Hazards: Protecting the Health of Du Pont Employees Is a Costly Proposition," *The Wall Street Journal,* June 28, 1976, p. 1.

if he or she cannot maintain a safe shop, Du Pont will get somebody who can. Similarly, every employee quickly learns that responsibility for his or her own safety is a condition of employment and that assuming unnecessary risk is unacceptable behavior.

Safety-conscious management, of course, cannot guarantee zero risk, but everyone learns through constant safety training that management is committed to minimizing risk.

MEDICAL SURVEILLANCE

In 1915 Du Pont became one of the first firms to institute a regular medical-surveillance program on a formal basis. As knowledge and awareness of chronic occupational health hazards have developed, tests have become more frequent. Now employees have physical tests when they first come to work at Du Pont and every year or two afterward, or more frequently if they are assigned to an area where hazardous substances could present a problem.

Du Pont has also been a leader in industrial epidemiology, in part because of a policy of continued medical monitoring and commitment to the health of employees even after they have retired. Epidemiological data accumulated since 1956 have added to Du Pont's ability to maintain a close watch on the employee population for the effects of subtle hazards.

TOXICOLOGICAL RESEARCH

A commitment to toxicological research and disclosure is also essential to any thorough occupational safety program, since some potential hazards are still unknown. To reduce the extent of the unknown, Du Pont and two dozen other companies support the Chemical Industry Institute of Toxicology, which will concentrate on the hazards of long-term, low-level exposure to commonly used chemicals. Sharing of information is also aided by the use of chemical "hot lines" which allow rapid checking of suspect compounds. But our first line of toxicological defense, and that which has allowed us to gain a leadership position in this area, is the Haskell Laboratory for Toxicology and Industrial Medicine, with a staff of about 200 on a 386-acre (156-hectare) site near the Maryland-Delaware border.

It is worth noting that the Haskell Laboratory was established in 1935, long before the Occupational Safety and Health Administration (OSHA) was even a gleam in the regulatory eye, and that the corporate decision to spend funds on toxicological analysis during a depression was far from universally hailed. As President Lammot du Pont said at the laboratory's dedication:

> We will run up against difficulties. For instance, the operating department will want to know "why the laboratory doesn't produce something." The sales

department will want to know "why the laboratory works up data that might make our customers believe our products are unsafe." But we are embarked on our campaign with determination and it is only a question of time before the world recognizes that a very constructive thing has been done.

THE BOTTOM LINE
AND COMMON SENSE

The acid test of a corporation's resolve is the financial bottom line. Talk is cheap, and anyone can make noises about a commitment to safety; the test comes when safety costs dollars in terms of lost production, potentially profitable products which are never produced, and the risk of criticism in the wake of frank disclosure.

Du Pont continues to demonstrate its willingness to spend money for safety and to forgo potentially profitable products when there are serious unresolved doubts about possible hazards. For instance, when Du Pont found that a compound was effective as a fire retardant for synthetic fibers, Haskell tested the chemical and recommended that it not be used because its combination of acute toxicity and persistence in the environment presented unacceptable risks. Du Pont dropped the compound as a candidate for this use and presented the results of its studies at a Society of Toxicology meeting and in several journals.

There are often difficult decisions to make in those gray areas where implications of hazards are present but proof is not. Du Pont's general policy here is to err, if err it must, on the side of safety, by taking into account the degree of irreversibility and the severity of consequences when deciding which immediate action should be taken concerning a suspect chemical. If, for instance, there were a slight chance that a particular substance could be causing minor skin irritation and if it were known that the irritation could be stopped simply by eliminating contact with the substance, it would be reasonable to wait a short time until more definite test results were in. But if there were significant scientific evidence that a compound could be causing severe or irreversible damage, the company would move without hesitation: exposures would be reduced or eliminated through changes in procedures or equipment. Common sense argues against one-way trips into blind canyons.

Common sense is also needed when companies are faced with some exceptionally hard trade-offs in the area of known but avoidable hazards. Does a pharmaceutical company, for instance, offer a pain-easing, life-prolonging drug with adverse side effects for some small fraction of its users? I have no better answer to that type of question than the one framed by Dr. William W. Lowrance in his book *Of Acceptable Risk.* Dr. Lowrance concluded that "a thing is safe if its risks are judged to be acceptable."[2] In other words, a product is to be deemed safe if people who understand its risks to themselves or to those in their care are willing to take the risks.

This means that all makers or users of a product must be informed of the attendant risks. It also means that it is the responsibility of management and others to be very sure that safety hazards sometimes perceived as givens actually are. No one should argue, for instance, in favor of the notion that *x* number of workers have to die to build a bridge or *y* number must be injured to complete a tunnel. Specious law-of-averages arguments like that are unacceptable, because with proper safety management no one needs to die on such projects. Similarly, although in dealing with chronic health hazards it is impossible to say that no one will ever get sick, a company should accept *only* that level of risk at which it is reasonable to predict that employees will not be harmed. Unavoidable risks are *only* those which come with commensurate benefits (e.g., the pain-killing drug) and are impossible to eliminate without forgoing the benefits.

RISK AND RESPONSIBILITY

Top attention from management, a willingness to spend money to avoid harm, and the refusal to settle for averages—these are policies which seem to work. They can be compared with policies advocated by some that do not seem to work: simply implying that dangers should be accepted, simply going back to nature, or simply saying that corporations should be trusted regardless of past records.

1.   It is wrong to say sanguinely that "Everything in life is dangerous," with the implication that occupational hazards are simply par for the course. The appropriate course of action is to contain and reduce all risks and to make sure that all persons involved receive *all* the facts that bear on the situation.

2.   It is wrong to acquiesce in movements to push society backward. Just as we cannot take great risks to promote even great benefits (since lives, not just dollars or national objectives, are at stake), we also cannot simply stand pat, because a world with more people each year needs progress just to stay even. In any case, returning to a preindustrial economy of scarcity is no guarantor of safety. As Erik Eckholm pointed out, "Workers in pre-industrial societies face special health risks just as workers in technologically advanced societies do. Farmers and fishermen in many tropical countries, for example, are especially liable to contract schistosomiasis and other infections spread by

---

[2] William W. Lowrance, *Of Acceptable Risk,* William Kaufmann, Inc., Los Altos, Calif., 1976, p. 8.

waterborne parasites."[3] Nor are less advanced technologies an answer: small shops with antiquated equipment have consistently been found to be less safe than larger ones with more advanced machinery and process design.

3.   It is wrong for corporate leaders to ask for public trust without having first made a commitment to safety and backed up that commitment with practice reflected in good performance. Since there *have* been cases of corporate irresponsibility in the area of occupational health and safety, corporate preachments in this area are suspect. The best and wisest course for companies with information about potential hazards is to present the facts to those who can make use of the information, either to take action in the interest of greater safety or to conduct additional research to expand knowledge about the hazards.

GOVERNMENT, INDUSTRY, AND SCIENCE

People who are looking for additional checks and balances on corporate leadership often turn to government for help. I can sympathize with that tendency in part. Certainly, we must work to develop an atmosphere of greater understanding and communication between industry and government, and we must realize that both sides have erred in the past: business has at times exaggerated the economic penalties of meeting exposure-level and safety standards, and government has sometimes gone overboard in one area while ignoring others. Certainly, we need laws on the books concerning safety and health, and we need inspection provisions to ensure that those laws are being carried out. But few of us want regulatory agencies to gain so much control that innovations are made impossible and freedom is stifled.

There are, in short, no paternalistic panaceas. But there *is* a constant scientific search to extend our knowledge about the challenges which face us, and it is on science (along with improved management techniques, better communication, and sincere commitment) that we must rely if we are to identify unseen risks and reduce hazards. We must learn to share knowledge freely and improve our performance through listening to the criticisms of:

● Professional organizations such as the American Occupational Medical Association, the American Conference of Governmental Industrial Hygienists, and the American Industrial Hygiene Association.

● Hospitals, medical schools, and research institutes. Two examples of note are the Kettering Laboratory at the University of Cincinnati, which has

3 "Unhealthy Jobs," *Environment,* August–September 1977, pp. 29–30.

evaluated the toxicity of lead and mercury, and the M. D. Anderson Hospital and Tumor Institute of the University of Texas at Houston.

● Standard-setting organizations such as the American National Standards Institute, which has developed scores of standards voluntarily adopted by industry.

Independent and professional organizations are in a unique position to mediate among business, government, and various interest groups. The exact mechanisms of extended cooperation need to be further developed, but it is clear that mediating structures of this type will be necessary if we are to avoid the optimism of reliance on individual morality and the pessimism of subservience to government. Above all, business, government, and other groups need to avoid getting into shouting matches with each other; this issue is too important for us to waste time on anything but the most diligent research and the most thorough practice. We need more knowledge so that we can make judgments based on the full extent of workplace hazards and their potential consequences. We need better communications so that employees know about the risks that affect them and agencies outside the corporation have the facts on which to act. And we need commitment from the executive committee of a company on down.

The issue of corporate responsibility for occupational health and safety, in summary, is a complicated one. A company such as Du Pont cannot stop searching for innovations: we have a responsibility to our society and to the world to make better products through science to meet people's needs. Corporate responsibility still begins at home, however, and companies have a responsibility to consider the potential risks as well as benefits to employees, customers, and communities. That obligation is central to our way of thinking in Du Pont and is interpreted to mean this: if a product cannot be made and used safely, it ought not be made at all.

Part 4

THE INTERNAL PROCESS OF CORPORATE DECISION MAKING

The Organizational Implications of Corporate Responsibility

Many contemporary observers of business have become increasingly interested not only in the substantive output of management decision making but also in the way in which the decisions are made. Since the late 1960s such issues as the role and composition of the corporate board, the value of the social audit, and the rights of employees have been the subject of considerable controversy both within the business community and among the public at large.

The first two essays in Part 4 deal with the issue of corporate governance. In a wide-ranging essay, Donald E. Schwartz, a professor of corporate law who has written extensively on this issue, argues that strengthening the participation of stockholders in corporate decision making would enable a corporation to more effectively balance economic and social objectives. He suggests that the area of corporate governance offers executives an ideal opportunity to exercise private initiative and particularly urges that the independence of the corporate board be strengthened. Schwartz, however, cautions against judging a corporation's social performance on the basis of its adoption of suggestions of corporate reformers like himself. While corporations vary in their attitudes toward shareholder participation, some of the most socially responsive firms have done little to change their governing structures.

J. Wilson Newman, who served as an outside public director of the Lockheed Corp. from 1976 to 1978, essentially echoes Schwartz's recommendations. While stressing the fundamental soundness of our business system, Newman believes that the traditional system of corporate governance is no longer adequate. He believes that a strengthened corporate board can play a critical role in improving the responsiveness of the corporation to economic and social changes. Newman particularly emphasizes the importance of an effective public issues committee as a way for management to become more sensitive to the corporation's social role and impact.

The need for voluntary changes by the profit sector also informs Harvey Kapnick's essay, "Improving Corporate Social Responsibility: The Role of the Accounting Profession." Kapnick argues that unless executives define the social role of business both "generously and expansively," additional government regulation will undermine the vitality of the private sector. He suggests that the accounting profession has a particularly valuable role to play in establishing practical guidelines that can help management find "the proper balance among *all* corporate objectives." While criticizing the concept of the social audit as impractical, Kapnick does propose a framework to enable managers to monitor the social programs of their companies more effectively. Kapnick especially stresses the need for executives better to inform both government officials and the public about the way in which corporations define their responsibility to society.

David W. Ewing urges voluntary changes in corporate behavior with respect to another issue, that of employee rights. Ewing is troubled by the substantial degree of authority that executives exercise over their employees. He argues that this degree is incompatible with the Western tradition of respect for civil liberties. Ewing wants corporations to establish procedures that protect the privacy of their employees, provide them with the opportunity to challenge corporate policies with which they disagree, and enable them to object to requests that they judge either immoral or unethical. While Ewing is disappointed with the lack of interest in these reforms on the part of most business executives, he does describe several firms, including International Business Machines Corp., Cummins Engine Company, the Bank of America, Atlantic Richfield Company, General Electric Co., Pitney-Bowes, Dow Chemical Company, American Airlines, Polaroid Corp., and Donnelly Mirrors, that have taken the initiative in providing some mechanisms of due process for their employees.

Our final contributor is John H. Filer, the chairman of Aetna Life & Casualty. In his essay, "The Social Goals of a Corporation," Filer urges corporations to pay more attention to the social impact of their activities and to examine ways in which they might apply their characteristic skills and strengths to the solution of pressing social problems. Filer emphasizes the critical importance of involving executives throughout a company in the formulation and implementation of corporate social goals but concludes that the ultimate responsibility for social goal setting by corporations must rest with the chief executive officer.

CORPORATE GOVERNANCE

DONALD E. SCHWARTZ

Donald E. Schwartz is a professor at the Georgetown University Law Center. He was educated at Union College, the Harvard Law School, and New York University Law School. Professor Schwartz has worked for the Securities and Exchange Commission; served as counsel and secretary of the Columbian Financial Corporation; and worked as an associate and partner with the law firms of Brinsmade and Schafrann and Hill, Betts, Yamaoka, Freehill and Longcope. He is counsel to the law firm of Williams & Connolly.

He is the author of more than thirty-five articles and reviews in law journals on various aspects of corporate law. He has also participated as a panelist in numerous forums sponsored by the Practising Law Institute.

The claim of many corporate reformers since the late 1960s has been that the corporation so closely resembles a political entity that it requires "legitimacy" if it is to be allowed to dominate our lives and affairs. The question of legitimacy focuses on the governance structure of the corporation, and this has led critics to pose two central questions: Do the governed select the governors? Are the governors accountable to their constituencies?

PROBLEMS OF ACCOUNTABILITY

These reformers have noted that the governed are not the stockholders of the corporation, at least not the stockholders alone, but include all those significantly affected by large corporations. Thus, the proper constituencies include employees, customers, and indeed the public as a whole who breathe the air and drink the water contaminated by corporate activity—the group sometimes referred to as the "neighbors" of the corporation. The critics, believing that neither the economic force of competitive markets nor the regulatory controls of government are effective or at least are not sufficiently so to prevent private decision makers from imposing their unaccountable decisions on the public, have claimed that it is necessary to politicize those decisions to protect the commonweal. The side effects of business activity are the externalities that largely escape the control of either the market or the government. It is the recognition of the severe social cost of these externalities, pollution being the most obvious and worrisome example, that has encouraged the search for other controls to ameliorate their effects. To pursue the illustration, the competitive marketplace may encourage the cost savings accomplished by pollution, yet the regulatory control of government cannot be so far-reaching as to bring under surveillance and control the day-to-day ordinary business decisions that give rise to pollution, at least not without an unacceptably high cost and loss of freedom. The precise cure prescribed by some respected critics has been to make the corporation conform more nearly to an acceptable political model.

Precisely how to do this has not been carefully delineated, but critics have spoken of requiring boards of directors to include representatives selected by various constituencies; of politically appointed directors, of codetermination in the selection of directors, and of similar schemes to broaden both participation in the process and the groups to which managers would be held accountable. Presumably, the standard of accountability would be affected by the selection of the groups to which the directors would be held accountable.

There is at least a superficial appeal to this approach because it is doubtless true that large corporations possess considerable power. In turn, this means that the managers of corporations, who by and large are self-selected, individually wield considerable power. Our society has a long tradition of mistrust of large concentrations of power.

Nevertheless, closer analysis erodes some of the initial attractions of politicizing corporations. Proper perspective makes us realize that the considerable power of corporations and their managers is far from absolute. Competitive forces can still make unsound decisions like those that produced the Edsel car and Corfam poromeric material quite costly. The growing power of government to affect the lives of both companies and individuals has prompted demands for deregulation from both liberals and conservatives. Furthermore, politicization does more than constrain the corporation; it menaces its future.

The critics have succeeded in diagnosing the problem, but their prescriptions for a cure are notably less successful. This is due mainly to their failure to take account of the dominant economic characteristics of corporations or, in some cases, because they lack sympathy for that method of allocating resources.

By and large, corporate managers tend to respond to market forces out of a recognition that their central mission is to produce goods and services at a profit. By and large, market forces dictate the allocation of resources. Those with the most direct interest in the corporation—managers, owners, and employees—share a common goal of economic growth, which produces both profits and employment. A political restructuring of the corporation would introduce into the decision-making process persons who disagree not only over the means but, more fundamentally, over the purposes of the business. The allocation of resources would then be subject to the pulls and hauls of varying criteria, and the different objectives would be resolved by a show of political force rather than by a single criterion of maximization of economic growth. Rather than bringing the externalities under control, it is more likely that the corporation would be incapable of achieving any goal whatsoever.

It still remains desirable to reconcile the political impact of the corporation with its economic character. Reconciliation does not mean that all our economic and social aspirations can be fully satisfied; indeed, it necessarily means that they at best can be brought to tolerable levels of accommodation. It is my own view that this accommodation requires some restructuring of the corporate governance arrangement together with continued government regulation and greatly increased disclosure about corporate activities. I believe that more than likely change will come about only as a result of some form of federal corporation law that mandates a revamped governance structure.

Both the traditional corporate pursuit of profits and the achievement of other social goals that limit profits must be recognized as social values if reform is to be achieved within the existing framework. This is an immense challenge to any reform effort that seeks to accomplish change by altering the internal structure. Unbridled growth imposes social costs; limits on growth deter the accumulation of capital. Moreover, loss of profitability promotes takeover bids by aspiring managers who will attempt to promote economic growth at the expense of social goals. This vicious round-robin persists as long as the stockholders remain the exclusive voting constituencies of the corporation. Yet at the same time giving the vote to any constituency other than the stockholders makes it almost impossible for the corporation to achieve its economic goals. Such may be the dilemma of capitalism, and yet it is probably the most widely shared view that some form of economic capitalism is integral to our system of a free society. The dilemma deepens.

However, the achievement of economic success by a corporation must be viewed in a proper time frame and made to take account of all the costs. Further, success does not require that managers possess virtually absolute power and be free from close scrutiny by independent monitors. This scrutiny can be accomplished by changes within the existing governance structure. Over the years the boards of directors of corporations, as bodies of independent significance, have tended to wither away, so that the full-time managers of our largest corporations have been self-selecting, self-perpetuating, and self-policing. In the largest of our corporate enterprises, those that have the most significant impact on the greatest number of people, the stockholders have been able to exert little power over the affairs of the enterprises. The stockholders themselves have not been much concerned about this loss of power because they have retained their individual power to sell their stock and to escape the effects of poor management. While the so-called Wall Street rule, which enables investors to vote with their feet, protects individuals, it tends to have little effect on altering the performance of the managers of the largest enterprises.

The inability of others to affect management's power is most acutely felt with respect to the social performance of the corporation, the sphere of activity in which investors have the least interest. It is fair to ask whether an increase in stockholders' power and the requirement of greater accountability to stockholders and to a strengthened board of directors chosen by stockholders would have any effect at all on the social performance of the corporation. I believe that it would, particularly when changes in the governance structure are accompanied by certain other changes that would serve to regulate corporate conduct.

Increased accountability by managers is necessarily an open process that serves notice to the larger community about corporate activities. Whether or not affected citizens have a formal opportunity to influence decisions that affect them, it is surely true that they have an opportunity through the political process to take away some of the freedom that corporate managers otherwise enjoy when the exercise of that power imposes costs on the community. Therefore, a governance structure that requires managers to account to stockholders allows nonstockholders to exert their influence on decisions. Of course, the process that renders managers accountable to stockholders also permits stockholders to protect their own interest, but if they do so with such zeal that unacceptable costs are imposed on nonstockholders, they incur the risk of costly retaliation. There must be continued interest by government in the activities of corporations if the possibility of such political redress is to be believable. Regulatory agencies are part of the control and accountability system, although it is hoped that they are not the fastest-growing segment. By forcing the accountability process into the open, rational behavior will lead to sensible accommodation—an optimality with all costs considered.

The foregoing presents the theme around which I suggest that we design a corporate governance structure. We must now consider what specific processes and mechanisms will help achieve the type of managerial accountability that will enable the corporation best to balance its stockholders' goals with its public responsibilities. We design systems because we do not want to rely solely on the good faith of individuals to do the right thing. While enlightened, imaginative leadership may be a far better solution than any system we can devise, we know that poor leadership is more common. Thus, we must opt for the second-best solution. Moreover, while we can probably proceed on the assumption that most managers conscientiously want to conduct their business with proper regard for the public interest and that this goal involves extremely complex judgments, we must also observe that managers, especially aspiring middle and junior managers, seek personal advancement and that they will do what they can to attain their goal. This leads them to resolve most of the complex, close issues in their own favor. In other words, junior and middle managers have an incentive to impose costs on society rather than on their company. A system of accommodation requires independent persons to monitor the performance of managers and those that report to them in order to see if they are really reducing costs or merely deferring them. This, in turn, requires an adequate flow of information to senior managers. The monitoring function must be structured so that it is capable of obtaining the necessary information and interpreting it. The availability of an adequate staff to carry out these assignments is needed.

Increasingly, American business leaders have perceived that there is a significant role for the board of directors of the corporation, as a body distinct from the management of the corporation, to carry out the monitoring function. Where once the board of directors was largely indistinguishable from senior management and hence could be said to be responsible for managing the business of the corporation (as was its legal mandate set forth in all corporation statutes until recent years), modern corporate managers no longer hold to that view. They see the value of a body of largely detached overseers who will not be responsible for day-to-day management but will have some responsibility for determining basic business goals, acting in a time of crisis, serving as a sounding board on policy issues, and, most important, acting as monitors of the performance of management. Critics of the corporation have also perceived the unique opportunity that the board has to reflect the broader social values by which the corporation must conduct its business as well as the social dynamics in which the corporation must function.

RECOMMENDATIONS OF THE AMERICAN ASSEMBLY

The Fifty-Fourth American Assembly of Columbia University, which met at Arden House, Harriman, New York, in April 1978, wrestled with the issues of corporate governance and tried not only to discover a general theme for the subject but also to delineate specific solutions. Its recommendations, most of which I believe are sound, represent a good starting point for analysis.

The American Assembly report[1] begins by emphasizing in its preamble that the concerns of corporate governors go beyond the welfare of stockholders. It expresses a dislike for centralized power and a search for internal methods within the corporation to achieve its varied goals.

After describing the board's functions, in which a monitoring role was stressed, the assembly stated that a majority of board members should be true outsiders. This means that most should be neither from management nor from outside organizations that have significant business relationships with the company. However, the assembly specifically rejected the idea that only one officer, the chief executive officer, should be a member of the board, as had been proposed by Chairman Harold M. Williams of the Securities and Exchange Commission (SEC) and, indeed, by Courtney C. Brown, the chairman of the American Assembly, who strongly urged his views at this gathering. It did accept the views of both Chairman Williams and Chairman Brown that the chairman of the board should be someone other than the chief operating officer.

The assembly also focused on means of creating a professional atmosphere within the board. Individually, the measures seem almost trivial, but collectively the institutionalizing of these procedures could transform a passive board into a creative one. These steps include the furnishing of adequate information to board members prior to the meeting, committee reports, regular and comprehensive board meetings, and interim reports and discussion of pending issues.

---

[1] William R. Dill (ed.), *Running the American Corporation,* Prentice-Hall, Inc., Englewood Cliffs, N.J., 1978.

The assembly also stated that there should be at least four committees: nominating, audit, compensation, and public issues committees. The first three should be composed entirely of independent directors, and the fourth should have at least a majority of independent directors. One of the most significant recommendations, largely because this was the first nonadvocate group to make such a recommendation, was the proposal that shareholders have the right to nominate directors and have their nominees included in the proxy statement paid for and distributed by the corporation.

The assembly urged disclosure of the board selection process as a device to improve the board's effectiveness. This recommendation was a significant recognition of the role of disclosure as part of the governance process and of the view that disclosure would be both informative and therapeutic.

The corporate committee that received the most attention from the assembly, naturally enough, was the audit committee. Commentators and the SEC have both placed great emphasis on the role of this committee in providing better controls and obtaining greater accountability of management. The assembly believed that the committee should be made up entirely of outsiders and that it should have broad responsibilities. The suggestion was much along the lines contained in the settlement that the SEC negotiated with Killearn Properties, Inc., in 1978.

The assembly recognized that the corporate structure itself must be a mechanism to be employed in dealing with social issues that stem from the conduct of a company's business. It was generally agreed that mere compliance with law was insufficient; the legal standard was seen as only a minimum standard. All agreed that a public issues committee of the board should be a part of the established procedure by which the board would sensitize itself to important social issues and monitor management performance on these issues. An innovative proposal of the assembly called for establishment by the corporation of quality-of-life advisory committees including representatives of employees, consumers, environmentalists, affected communities, and other interested groups which would advise management on social concerns and proper responses. Moreover, following lengthy debate the assembly recommended the development of evaluation systems for public issues, a concept similar to a social auditing process to help monitor social performance.

The assembly also dealt with the serious underlying problem of the pursuit of individual goals, mentioned earlier, which allows and may even encourage middle and junior managers to ignore social concerns. In brief, since middle managers are evaluated on the achievement of the subunits over which they have control and in which most of the details of management are implemented, they have an incentive to avoid incurring costs growing out of social concerns, to externalize whatever costs they can, and to pursue business objectives regardless of social costs. Unless social costs become part of the evaluation of middle management, then, regardless of the official policies pronounced by senior management and by the board of directors, the corporation may continue to inflict these costs on society and avoid positive actions that might reduce favorable short-term performance. The concern of the managers is not long-term profitability but the short-term objectives by which their own advancement is measured. The key is for the corporate governance structure to develop awareness and a response to this dynamic.

The assembly proposed that corporate executives require regular reports from middle and lower managers on the social and environmental consequences of their operations. Their reports should include an evaluation of alternatives for operations or for the design of products that have social and environmental consequences. Whether this proposal is adequate is not clear; perhaps a change in liability exposure is needed. But disclosure is the place to begin.

GOVERNANCE REFORMS

The full recommendations of the American Assembly are not reflected in practice by any large corporation, but there certainly has been progress on the part of major corporations in moving toward an improved governance structure. A board of directors composed of independent directors is now the norm among major corporations. An audit committee is now required of any company whose shares are listed on the New York Stock Exchange. A number of companies are providing far greater disclosure about their operations than they are required to furnish by law. In this respect, two examples may be cited. BankAmerica Corporation adopted a voluntary disclosure code in 1976 (it was revised in 1978), and now citizens are considerably better informed about the company's operations and their social impact than is required by law (see also essay "Voluntary Disclosure," by A. W. Clausen). BankAmerica had formed a task force which made a limited effort to solicit the views of outsiders about what disclosures were desirable, although the product was surely an inside rather than an outside document. General Motors Corp., beginning in 1970 and probably largely at the prodding of Ralph Nader's Campaign GM, began to circulate or make available a report of the impact of the company's activities in areas of social concern. Atlantic Richfield Company includes a brief social audit by an independent journalist in its annual report; some of the remarks are critical of the company, in fresh contrast to the self-serving declarations of good citizenship found in most corporate annual reports.

Most of the governance reform that has been proposed and that has been implemented has been oriented toward improving profitability. Of course, managers must regard stockholders as their first constituency, if for no other reason than survival. An interesting qualification on that point was one that was made by Control Data Corporation, which approved the following amendment to its charter at its 1978 annual meeting:

> TENTH: The Board of Directors of the Corporation, when evaluating any offer of another party to (*a*) make a tender or exchange offer for any equity security of the Corporation, (*b*) merge or consolidate the Corporation with another corporation, or (*c*) purchase or otherwise acquire all or substantially all of the properties and assets of the Corporation, shall, in connection with the exercise of its judgment in determining what is in the best interests of the Corporation and its stockholders give due consideration to all relevant factors, including without limitation the social and economic effects on the employees, customers, suppliers and other constituents of the Corporation and its subsidiaries and on the communities in which the Corporation and its subsidiaries operate or are located.[2]

Perhaps this amendment may be explained on the ground that the company's management would like to have all possible resources at its disposal in the event of a takeover attempt in order to protect its own jobs and has given itself the broadest possible mandate for countermoves. But the amendment may also be explained as a response by a management that has built up a business and does not want to see its efforts wasted in the name of the pursuit of short-term profits. In other words, the managers are concerned about the totality of operations and would consider it improper if someone sought higher profits at the expense of social concerns. That the shareholders approved this amendment would seem to sanction social responsibility as a value of the corporation alongside that of profitability, but the test will come when there is an actual clash between profits and social goals. To some extent the amendment causes confusion because it is likely that management already possessed the power spelled out in it. It would be a mischievous result if managers and courts came to believe that without such a charter provision management *must* ignore the social consequences of corporate action.

Sensitivity to changes in corporate governance is a relatively new phenomenon in large corporations. To a large extent it was promoted by the use of stockholder proposals following the adoption of an SEC rule in 1942. The traditional corporate activists, Lewis Gilbert and Wilma Soss, used proposals to urge management to show greater awareness and responsiveness to their stockholders by conducting the annual meeting in accessible places, furnishing postmeeting reports to stockholders, and making such substantive changes as providing for stockholder ratification of the selection of auditors and adopting cumulative voting in the election of directors.

Of course, none of the stockholder proposals submitted by Soss and Gil-

---

[2] Proxy statement, Control Data Corporation, Mar. 20, 1978.

bert were ever adopted by majority vote of the stockholders, but some companies voluntarily made the changes when a sufficient number of shareholders indicated their concern by voting for the proposals. About 3 percent of the votes by stockholders was usually enough to trigger a change. Most large companies responded by becoming more open in their stockholder processes, although few embraced cumulative voting. Nonetheless, some companies persist in holding their meetings in remote places like Flemington, New Jersey, that are inaccessible for most people. A growing number of companies furnish postmeeting reports in considerable detail to their stockholders, but others, for example, Fuqua Industries, Inc., respond to such a suggestion with a statement that they are not required by law to do so. Indeed, a number of companies, including both General Motors and Ford Motor Co., furnish a complete transcript of the annual meeting upon payment of a nominal fee.

Real reform of the governance process means changes at the board level, since stockholders can at most perform a peripheral role. Some companies have been especially innovative in experimenting with techniques for improving the performance of the board. Connecticut General Insurance Corp. has tried to define the board's monitoring role carefully and has issued a manual that serves as a model for others. Texas Instruments has created a permanent officer of the board who devotes full time to board service. This provision institutionalizes a type of professional director drawn from the ranks of management.

Governance reform is a relatively recent phenomenon. It has not been the focal point of concern about corporate responsibility, at least until the last few years. Now some old devices are receiving a fresh look. Audit committees, for example, have been known for a long time, but the existence of an audit committee proves very little; what matters is who composes the audit committee and what functions it performs. A number of companies have made sound use of their audit committees in highly special circumstances as a follow-up of a particular crisis, such as the discovery of improper corporate payments, and often as a result of a court order which has dictated its creation and composition. The New York Stock Exchange now requires such committees to be composed of independent directors, although one can quarrel with the definition of independence.

The nominating committee is a newer phenomenon, and its existence is not yet required. A number of companies have created such committees, but few data exist to show how independently these committees are functioning and what changes they are producing in the composition of the board.

A progressive and responsive governance scheme is but one indication of a socially responsible company. There are autocratically governed companies that boast splendid records of sensitivity to key social issues, such as pollution and discrimination. Ranking social responsiveness or social responsibility is an immensely complex task because so much depends upon the weight that the evaluator gives to the various factors. By tradition and attitude, some companies seem more sensitive to the social climate, and reform of their internal governance procedures can be expected to assist the development of greater awareness of public concerns. This is political wisdom.

Several illustrations demonstrate this sensitivity and awareness. In 1974 the Project on Corporate Responsibility, which I was serving as director and as counsel, submitted stockholder proposals to both General Motors and Eastman Kodak Co. The General Motors meeting was held in Detroit, and the Kodak meeting was scheduled for Flemington, New Jersey. I was scheduled to represent the project at the Kodak meeting, but a last-minute conflict prevented my appearance, and I arranged for several of my students in a graduate seminar to substitute for me. I advised the secretary of Kodak of the details and concluded my conversation by saying that I was sorry I couldn't attend the meeting but hoped that I would be able to do so the next year. His response was, "Why don't you pick on someone else next year?" Almost as soon as that conversation was concluded, I received a call from the secretary of General Motors asking about arrangements for his meeting, and I told him that I would not be able to attend but that we would be represented by someone else. His remark to me was, "I'm sorry you won't be there, but perhaps you'll be able to attend next year." If those corporate secretaries reflected the managements of the two companies, and every indication was that they did, the attitudinal gulf between the companies is a veritable chasm.

Nevertheless, it is difficult to single out governance issues as indicative of management's overall attitude toward social responsiveness. An experience with Levi Strauss & Co. is illustrative. In 1973 the project submitted a proposal to several corporations including Levi Strauss, asking their managements to devise a plan for improving the manner of selecting directors. The management of Levi Strauss thought that was an excellent idea and supported the proposal, which was then adopted. The chairman of the board of Levi Strauss, Walter A. Haas, Jr., then telephoned the project in Washington and said that he would like to meet with its representative in order to get some ideas that he could discuss with his board. He flew to Washington and spent an afternoon with members of the project and invited them to furnish a memorandum. Chairman Haas gave every indication that he was serious about implementing some of their proposals. These proposals, incidentally, were no more radical than suggesting that the company create a nominating committee, but in fact none were implemented, and Haas later explained that his board was unresponsive to making the kind of changes contained in the memorandum. No one can doubt the overall sensitivity and social responsibility of this company, which was even reluctant to become a public company because the management was fearful that public ownership would inhibit its traditional charitable activities. The episode is recounted to show the complexity and, indeed, the ambiguity of the issue concerning corporate governance. Dominant leadership of the progressive kind may be more likely to produce beneficial results than any systemic reform. But one-man benevolence is an unreliable tool of progress, and systems are needed.

I would recommend, therefore, that certain basic governance reforms be instituted without waiting for new rules from Congress, the SEC, or the New York Stock Exchange. Reform starts with management's examination of existing operations to see if the company has kept pace with the kinds of reforms that have been widely discussed in recent years. Open analysis with the directors and counsel must follow. The steps would simply be as follows:

1. To see whether the board of directors is management-dominated and whether greater independence is necessary.

2. To examine the committee structure to see whether, at a minimum, the company has an audit committee (it probably does if it is a big company), a nominating committee, a public policy committee, and a compensation committee. These are the minimal requirements. These committees should be as independent as possible. Moreover, the company should define independence so as to make sure that it is real and not merely apparent.

3. To resolve that all stockholder proposals be considered with an open mind, with the possibility that some will be adopted. The company would be well advised to take stockholder proponents seriously, engage in communication with them, and see if some things can be worked out even without putting matters to a vote. A number of companies over the years have done this with Lewis Gilbert and Wilma Soss. I experienced a fruitful negotiation with officials of the International Telephone and Telegraph Corporation over a stockholder proposal that resulted in the board's adopting a bylaw proposed by the project.

4. To examine closely its disclosure documents to see whether management provides adequate disclosure in the form of annual reports, postmeeting reports, and perhaps special reports about material facts of interest not only to stockholders but to other claimants for the company's attention.

My own view is that private initiatives in improving governance systems ought to be encouraged and that far-reaching legislation should be held in reserve until there has been greater opportunity to experiment with alternatives. In the long run, however, I am doubtful that far-reaching changes will come about except by some form of compulsion, of which the most logical in my opinion would be a federal corporation law. The main thrust of such a law would not be to impose additional regulations but rather to prescribe a more sensitive and responsive governance scheme that would eliminate the need for more detailed federal regulation.

CORPORATE ACCOUNTABILITY

J. WILSON NEWMAN

J. Wilson Newman is chairman of the Finance Committee and a director of Dun & Bradstreet Companies, Inc., an organization that provides a wide range of information and services to business management throughout the world. He was chief executive officer of the company from his election as president in 1952 until 1968, when he retired as chairman of the board to his present position. During that period the firm expanded its activities from its original credit-reporting services to include the first large-scale system of computerized data for sales and marketing purposes as well as other services in such fields as business education, plant-site location, and a variety of investor services.

Mr. Newman was educated at Clemson University and New York University Law School. Following a brief experience in banking, he went to R. G. Dun & Co. in 1931 as a credit reporter, shortly before that company's merger with the Bradstreet Company. After several years of reporting, he was given a wide range of assignments, leading to his election as vice president in 1946. He was elected president in November 1952 and became chairman of the board in May 1960, continuing as chief executive officer until October 1968, when he became chairman of the Finance Committee.

I have been invited, because of my experience as an outside public director of the Lockheed Corp. and chairman of its Special Review Committee (April 14, 1976–May 8, 1978), appointed pursuant to a consent and undertaking with the Securities and Exchange Commission (SEC), to contribute an essay on the role and responsibility of corporate boards. Quite naturally, my views are influenced by many years of experience (including 16 years as chief executive officer of Dun & Bradstreet and service as a director of numerous companies) in analyzing business operations and participating in business management as well as in undertaking several government and other public assignments. This background, mentioned in the interest of full disclosure, will enable the reader to endorse or impeach the views here expressed. They are solely my own.

FORCES FOR CHANGE

I must state at the outset that I believe that our business system is sound and that it is based on workable principles which can respond effectively to the interests of investors and of American society. But we cannot rest on that confidence. Business must constantly refresh its policies and techniques of governance to stay attuned to the demands of our constantly evolving society. We have seen evidence in recent years that the business community has failed to move forward at the same pace as social change, but I also see signs that the problem is being recognized and that we are heading toward solutions.

Certainly there are abundant signals of new forces at work which require change. Opinion polls show that the public holds large corporations in rather low esteem. We take small comfort from the fact that similar distrust is accorded major labor unions, the Congress, and other established American institutions. Society cannot survive over the long term in such an atmosphere of distrust, and it is encouraging to see many of these institutions taking steps to regain public confidence.

Much of the animosity toward the business world undoubtedly is founded on the stream of reports of bribes and other questionable payments from companies now numbering in the hundreds. These are serious matters, but I believe that the problem is broader. It includes the daily failure of many business products and services to meet public expectations.

Along with negative public attitudes, we have many regulators who point out specific errors and urge specific reforms. There are many proposals for additional layers of government regulation. If they were adopted, there would be more uniformity, more bureaucracy, and more concentration of federal control. This approach is a frequent response to problems of all descriptions, but in this case I believe it to be simplistic and destructive. As stated by SEC Chairman Harold M. Williams:

> What is necessary is that corporate directors and management be commit-

ted, in their own long-term self-interest, to making corporate accountability work. No legislation or rule can substitute for that commitment.

For that reason, the goal of those who believe in the efficiency and effectiveness of our present methods of private economic decision-making must be to stimulate the corporate sector to greater sensitivity to, and appreciation of, the need for it to address squarely the issue of corporate accountability. If too many business leaders insist that there is no problem or that the sole vehicle for corporate accountability is the bottom line, then I suspect that the political processes will ultimately take more and more of the control out of the hands of private managers and transfer it to the hands of government regulators. And that is a prospect that I would neither greet with enthusiasm nor expect to be, in the long run, consistent with a system of private enterprise.[1]

In my view the most effective way to bridge the gap between public expectations and corporate performance is through reform initiated within the corporate body itself. The responsibility for instigating this self-regulation lies with the corporate governing body, the board of directors. This view is reflected in the attitude of the courts, which have also taken a hand in this area, generally prodding the business community to change its ways and to evolve new attitudes and methods geared to meeting society's evolving standards. Court decisions relating to corporate governance have steadily increased the responsibilities of directors, both inside and outside directors, and held them accountable for what corporations do. Those decisions have held that directors are responsible not only for corporate actions about which they have known but also for any activities about which they should have known. This finding has stimulated a commendable increase in the attentiveness and curiosity of board members.

CORPORATE RESPONSE AND THE ROLE OF THE BOARD OF DIRECTORS

In this climate of change it is imperative that the corporate community respond to public demand for corporate accountability and reevaluate the traditional forms of corporate decision making. The failure to learn the lessons to be drawn from the public viewpoint may well lead to overreaction by government in the form of extensive and wide-ranging regulation.

The first lesson is that the old system of corporate governance is no longer adequate for the times. It has been traditional for boards of directors and their company managements to strive for personal compatibility and hand-in-glove cooperation. As could be expected, boards selected in this manner have

---

[1] Address before American Society of Corporation Secretaries, June 1, 1978, quoted in *Views,* Arthur Young & Company, New York, vol. II, no. 5, August 1978.

renewed themselves by choosing equally compatible and cooperative people as new directors. This style of governance has its virtues in terms of efficiency and smoothness of operation. The drawbacks, however, are more important than the virtues. Directors too often become captives of management, and there is not enough real measurement of executive performance. Such a system breeds insularity, a tendency to make comfortable decisions and to avoid confronting significant change in the surrounding world. It is an atmosphere in which directors reinforce rather than challenge each other's opinions and ideas. In short, there is too much potential for laxity.

The second lesson that should emerge is that business operates under a basically sound system of governance. It is grounded on democracy and has the flexibility to meet the needs of a diverse economy and an equally diverse society. The fault lies principally in the attitudes and methods which have developed over the years. The task before us is to get on with the renewal which will make a fundamentally sound system work as it was intended.

The board of directors is the key to renewal. Directors must begin serving their intended purpose and not simply act as pieces of parsley on a dish of fish. We must realize the democratic potential of the system and make directors stronger representatives of the shareholders who elect them. We must create a balance of power—of authority and responsibility—within each corporate system. The way to do that is to make the board of directors an independent force in corporate affairs rather than a passive affiliate of management.

This implies not an adversary relationship but a system of checks and balances. It implies that management's plans will be intelligently tested and debated and that management will receive sound and well-informed policy guidance from the board. It also implies that the directors will monitor results on an organized basis.

There are two fundamental elements which are vital if the system is to work properly. One relates to the quality of the people chosen as directors, and the second deals with the quality of the information they receive.

Corporations must take a fresh approach to the selection of directors. Greater attention must be given to finding people who can deal competently with business affairs and who have exhibited high standards of personal integrity. Directors also must have the independence to challenge the proposals which management has the duty to present and the courage to overrule management when necessary. A system of checks and balances is essential, but only the character and ability of the directors will make it work successfully.

The second vital element is information. The system must be structured so that all significant matters are brought before the board of directors in a timely fashion. All viewpoints and options must be presented so that the directors can examine each situation in whole before reaching a decision. With complete information the directors can do a proper job of perceiving directions in which to move, setting priorities, marshaling and allocating resources, and organizing the corporation to meet its goals. Then they must monitor progress and appraise the results.

This kind of open and balanced system, peopled by men and women of high character, will carry us toward the goal of eliminating the problems which have occurred in the past. Lord Acton warned that "Power tends to corrupt; absolute power corrupts absolutely." A balanced corporate system is the best defense against absolute power, and so we can expect it to be a strong defense against corruption.

Congress has a role in the national political system which is analogous to that of the corporate board of directors. Although the people select the chief executive, Congress makes policy through legislation and monitors the results through its oversight function. I believe that this system has worked with great success for almost two centuries, and I believe that the concept can be equally successful in the business world. I also have been interested to see that in its own efforts to update itself and restore public esteem Congress has chosen to improve attitudes and methods rather than change the basic system. The new codes of ethics and the evolution of the committee system are similar to the types of change appropriate for the business system.

EXPERIENCE AT LOCKHEED

Perhaps the most practical way to illustrate the kind of change I have in mind is to discuss what was recommended by the Special Review Committee of the Lockheed Board of Directors. As a result of recommendations of the committee relating to the composition and functioning of the board, the following framework for corporate governance was adopted by Lockheed. It indicates in part one company's response to some of the concerns to which I have referred.

1.   At least two-thirds of the board is composed of outside directors. No advisers to the corporation, such as legal counsel, may serve. Former executives can remain, but they must be counted as inside directors.

2.   Outside directors select and nominate all new and continuing candidates for election by shareholders.

3.   Key board committees (nominating, audit, compensation) are composed entirely of outside directors, and all committees have an outside majority. A majority of outside directors is required in any quorum for a committee or full board meeting.

4.   The membership of the audit committee is rotated periodically. Full

minutes of each meeting are distributed to the entire board, and the audit committee reports periodically to the full board. All financial matters of substance are brought to the committee's attention.

5.   The internal audit function has an independent budget. The director of internal audit reports at present to the chief executive officer and has direct access to the audit committee and the board. The director provides regular reports to the board.

6.   The outside auditors are nominated by the board and elected by the shareholders, and better methods of assuring the independence of the public accounting firm are being considered and developed.

7.   The compensation committee makes recommendations to the board on the compensation of management, including the director of internal audit. In addition, there is a system of performance review for senior management, including the chief executive officer. Not only is this valuable for compensation judgments, but it also enables the board to make intelligent choices for senior management positions.

8.   An organization review has been initiated to assure that lines of authority and communication are clear within the management structure. All managers are required periodically to make a written affirmation that they are following the principles of business conduct established by the board.

9.   A public issues committee monitors trends in society and helps the corporation operate in a way that is consistent with contemporary standards of conduct.

A public issues committee should be an effective force for constant renewal and updating in corporate governance. Many of my business friends regard such committees with suspicion, holding that a corporation should devote its attention to business, not to social issues. They miss the point. It is true that a business corporation exists to provide products and services and that it must strive for a profit to prosper in its role. But in addition to this primary responsibility to shareholders, any company is by definition a public corporation because it exists under law, and it is a social organization because it deals intimately with members of society. It pays wages, sets working conditions, provides pensions, and often affects the community environment in a variety of ways. For all these reasons, management must remain constantly sensitive to trends in society just as it must keep pace with the marketplace.

FUTURE DEVELOPMENTS

Various private groups—in business, law, the universities, and the investment community—also have turned their attention to the issues involved in corporate governance. It is my hope that one group, perhaps a special study commission organized for the purpose, will emerge as a leader in the private sector. We need a vehicle for focusing the debate and pulling together the practical recommendations which can set reform in motion on a broad scale. Encouraging business groups to evolve standards for responsible corporate governance would go far toward achieving immediate effects to accommodate various points of view currently being debated.

Our purpose at Lockheed was to establish the board of directors as a strong, independent, and effective force in the operation of the company. Several of the changes made at Lockheed can be found already in force at other corporations, and a trend toward substantive change in corporate governance seems to be under way. I believe that business leaders must work hard to accelerate that movement if the American business system is to continue to enjoy the freedom it requires, and must deserve, to operate successfully. I also believe that if people of strong character combine on a board of directors the seasoned abilities to set principled goals, to think out sound strategies, and to devise effective tactics for implementing them and if they act on the basis of full and timely information, we can look to the future of American corporations with great confidence.

IMPROVING CORPORATE SOCIAL RESPONSIBILITY

The Role of
the Accounting Profession

HARVEY KAPNICK

*Mr. Kapnick served as chairman of Arthur Andersen
& Co., from May 1970 until 1979, when he became
deputy chairman of the board of the First Chicago
Corporation and the First National Bank of Chicago.
As chairman of Arthur Andersen & Co., he was chief
executive of his company, an international firm of
accountants and auditors with world headquarters in
Chicago and Geneva, Switzerland, and offices in principal cities throughout the world. Mr. Kapnick was
graduated from Cleary College in Ypsilanti, Michigan, and the School of Business Administration of
the University of Michigan. He joined Arthur Andersen & Co. in 1948 in its Chicago office and became
a partner in 1956. In 1962 he became managing partner of Arthur Andersen & Co.'s Cleveland office and
served as a member of his firm's board of directors
from 1966 on.*

*Mr. Kapnick is a member of the President's Com-
mission on Pension Policy, the Advisory Committee
for Trade Negotiations, the Department of State's
Advisory Committee on International Investment,
Technology, and Development, the United States
delegation to the Ad Hoc Working Group on Ac-*

counting Standards, the Committee on International Investment and Multinational Enterprises of the Organization for Economic Cooperation and Development, the United States section of the ASEAN–United States Business Council, and the International Policy Committee of the Chamber of Commerce of the United States.

The social impact of business on the United States is undeniable. It is, after all, the central activity of our private-enterprise, market-oriented economic system. Most of what we Americans aspire to create and build, produce and market, we achieve through private economic activity. Yet we sometimes encounter a curious reluctance on the part of business and professional executives to admit freely that their economic efforts have social consequences and that they, therefore, have a social role to perform beyond their narrow economic function. There is a rather doctrinaire school of thought which holds that the social responsibility of business is to obey the law and to maximize profits—*period*. A company is said to fulfill its total social obligation by delivering goods to customers and dividends to shareholders. According to this line of thinking, any attempt to apply the talents and resources of a corporation to social objectives is a gross distortion of its function and a wasteful interference with the market mechanism, likely to turn business into a tool of government. Indeed, acceptance of corporate social responsibility is often depicted as surrender in advance to political and bureaucratic pressures for greater government regulation of business.

Unfortunately, this shortsighted business view is the mirror image of the opinions of righteous antibusiness critics who complain that business cares more about profits than about people and their problems. Of course, business *must* care about its profitability if it is to survive, bear the risks of innovation, and generate the funds to grow and to expand its output of goods and services. Profitability is the indispensable prerequisite to social responsibility.

I strongly dissent from these black-and-white concepts of business and its role in the American economic and political system because they are at odds with reality. If we do not define the social role of business generously and expansively, acknowledging clear-cut responsibilities to the public interest, we actually invite government to intrude further into the private sector and preempt even more private decision making. We cannot leave everything to government without in the end losing the vitality and perhaps the very essence of our democracy.

DEVELOPING A PROGRAM OF SOCIAL RESPONSIBILITY

Part of the price we must be prepared to pay to maintain our free society is to accept voluntarily the necessity of self-regulation and self-discipline in the public interest in order to keep the role of government limited. Happily, this argument has long since been resolved within the top ranks of United States corporate management. Without stepping out of character or ceasing to perform its economic function, modern business now recognizes that society expects it to be socially responsible, and it further recognizes the importance of satisfying these public expectations. The question is how far it should go, how fast progress is to be achieved, what priorities should be established, and how results are to be measured in terms of cost-benefit economics.

In a free enterprise economy, responsiveness to concerns of the general public is only one of the factors to be considered in establishing corporate policy. Finding the proper balance among *all* corporate objectives is the decisive task of management. Here I believe that the experience and analytic approach of the accounting profession can be very helpful in establishing practical guidelines.

The issue is not whether corporations have accepted their share of social responsibility as a corporate objective. On the whole, they clearly have, but with what priority? Certainly, most companies have as a minimum accepted their social obligation to obey the law and to follow a sound set of business ethics. However, each company needs to assess its total situation with respect to public expectations, the viability of the business, the severity of direct business problems to be resolved, and the collective social conscience of its own management and stockholder group. On the basis of this assessment, each company must decide how much of a leadership role it intends to assume in social responsibility.

In our firm, we are continually making such a self-appraisal. We concluded long ago that among our important responsibilities are the maximum effective development of the human resources at our disposal, including equal opportunity for all races, colors, creeds, and, even more important, nationalities of each country in which we operate. We also believe in intensive cooperation in activities leading to the improvement of our respective communities and the enhancement of the quality of life available in those communities.

As we define it, our basic social responsibility rests on our professional expertise. It is an unswerving dedication to improved financial reporting for the investing public. Many might not conceive this as a social goal, but it may well be the most important need in our economic system.

As auditors, we have looked carefully at many schemes for accomplishing an effective social responsibility program through a formal social-accounting system, including balance sheets and profit and loss statements. The results have been disappointing. To record the intangible values of such a program in financial statements of any kind defies comprehension.

We have also looked at the concept of the social audit. Frankly, we have found this approach impractical and have rejected it. The word "audit" is especially unfortunate. To audit demands preestablished standards and verification of data against such standards. In most cases, this would be impractical because of the subjective nature of social programs.

Therefore, to achieve an effective social responsibility program a company should (1) specifically assign executive responsibility for the program; (2)

develop a plan which will ensure maximum benefits to society consistent with the company's particular goals, capabilities, earning capacity, and available resources; (3) establish clear-cut priorities; and (4) communicate the results, including cost-benefit data, in a specific and meaningful way to those parts of the business which are actively engaged.

To assure sound management in a company's social responsibility activities, every member of top management must be involved. One way of accomplishing this is to establish a management committee on social responsibility. Such a committee should probably be chaired by the chief executive and consist of some or all of the officers who report directly to the executive or to his or her office. As with any other program, if a social responsibility effort is to be effective, the responsibility for achieving the program must be specifically assigned to an individual whose duties are spelled out. Selection of this executive is critical because he or she needs to be influential with the other members of management, not just happen to have the time to do the job. Initially, social responsibility may have to be given part-time attention, but it should not be considered less important than the executive's other duties. The adage "If you wish a job well done, give it to a busy person" should apply.

ASSESSMENT OF SOCIAL ISSUES AND CORPORATE RESOURCES

In developing a social responsibility program, the company should assess issues in which it has a significant interest or for which it has a unique ability to bring about concrete improvements. In most cases, the social issues with which the public, government, and others are concerned fall into six main categories:

1. *Energy and mineral resources.* The area of energy and mineral resources is concerned with the efficiency of energy consumption, alternative energy sources, and the conservation of scarce minerals and alternative minerals used to conserve those in dwindling supply.

2. *Human resources.* The area of human resources is concerned with efforts to provide equal opportunity for minority groups, women, handicapped persons, and citizens of all nations in which the company operates; increased job security and job satisfaction; avenues for upward mobility for all persons seeking self-improvement; improved occupational safety and health measures; and steps to foster the care and dignity of older people.

3. *Land resources.* The area of land resources encompasses such issues as whether a company's intended use of land conforms to a community's goals with respect to the development of its employment and taxation bases; the

preservation and enhancement of the land character and environment; uses of land which block or alter natural development patterns, particularly with respect to large tracts of vacant land; and the community's interest in enjoying the recreational potential of the land.

4. *Environmental protection.* The area of environmental protection has to do with the preservation or recovery of clean air and water, the abatement of noise and of pesticide and radiation pollution, and the satisfactory disposition or recycling of solid wastes. One of the more troublesome aspects of assessing these issues is to establish a bench mark against which improvement or deterioration will be measured. Is the proper standard the pristine environment of prehistoric times, the highest levels of pollution experienced during the last few years, or some intermediate point between the extremes?

5. *Civic participation.* Civic participation was probably the first social responsibility recognized by business and today is perhaps the one most commonly accepted. This subject encompasses the efforts of a business to maintain and enhance the environment in which it operates, including the construction of attractive, well-organized, and clean facilities, the effective control of employee and transportation traffic in and out of the plant, and the provision of open spaces, parks, swimming pools, and gymnasiums which supplement community recreational resources and, indirectly, make these available to company employees.

Another aspect of civic participation is involvement in community institutions such as youth programs, crime prevention, prevention of alcoholism and drug abuse, and programs to preserve and promote the community's facilities for transportation, communications, water supply, power supply, and waste disposal. Still another form of participation is involvement in special community programs to raise funds for worthy causes, to sustain projects, and to stimulate the quality of life through support of various artistic programs such as the opera, the symphony orchestra, and museums.

6. *Consumer protection.* The final area is consumer protection. A company should seek to maintain and improve standards related to advertising, sales promotion, packaging, labeling, guarantees, credit terms, product safety, product performance, durability, servicing, and attention to consumer complaints.

In developing a social program, this grouping of issues will usually cover all concerns that are reported when the public's concerns are surveyed. For example, Opinion Research Corporation, in a 1974 survey, asked more than 500 business executives to identify areas in which their companies had failed in social responsibility.[1] They identified these major issues: lack of awareness

---

[1] "Executives Appraise the Changing Role of the Corporation," July 1973.

of ecological problems, which falls in the area of environmental protection; failure to educate the public about business, which would be remedied by programs mounted in the areas of consumer protection and civic participation; neglect of employees and failure to recognize discrimination, both of which would be included in the human-resources group; loss attached to customers who have felt cheated, which, of course, falls in consumer protection; and criticism that business has been too narrowly profit-minded, which would be answered at least in part by the company's creation of a social responsibility program.

In addition to identifying the issues most relevant to a particular company, before a social program can be effective it must establish an inventory of corporate resources available to deal with the various issues. For example, to what degree can a company afford to forsake current profitability to achieve special goals? How much human resources, particularly at the management level, can be made available for civic participation and other worthy goals?

Given an understanding of the relative significance of issues and the availability of resources, a company should proceed with something closely akin to a business budgeting process. Specific priorities need to be assigned to the various issues, and resources allocated to sustain specific programs described for those issues. The benefits sought should be estimated to justify the costs of each program established. These benefits should be in specific terms, such as the number of permanent jobs which would be created for handicapped workers and the anticipated tenure of persons hired for those jobs. Establishing priorities is sometimes difficult, but it is essential if a program is to be translated into meaningful action.

MEASUREMENT AND REPORTING

After a company has established its social responsibility plan and assigned responsibilities and priorities for implementation, the next requirement is to create a measurement and reporting system so that effective communications can be achieved for all facets of the program. This requires identification of expenditures made for the various programs apart from those which are incurred for ordinary business activities. Also, effective reporting requires quantification of the benefits achieved as a result of the plan.

Some of the measurement processes required to achieve effective reporting will involve new and often difficult concepts. For example, at what point does a social-impact program become a normal part of the company's operation and thus no longer a suitable subject for reporting? It would be ludicrous, for example, for a company still to be reporting the costs and benefits of converting to an 8-hour day back in the early 1900s.

We have examined most of these reporting problems, however, and are confident that they fall within the present-day state of the art. Particularly encouraging is the fact that much of the information needed already is captured in various data processing applications, particularly those related to operating systems rather than accounting systems. The problem then becomes capturing the remaining unrecorded data and converting the presently recorded data to the purposes of effective social reporting. Accurate cost-benefit information will not be easily attained, but if real benefits are to accrue to society, government, and others from the program, this measurement process must be accomplished.

The final issue is to whom such information should be communicated. Certainly some form of internal reporting is essential. Any company which sets goals for itself, whether for growth, profitability, personnel recruitment, public image, or social responsibility, needs to know whether it has succeeded and what the costs of its efforts are.

Further, a company needs to review these data to determine whether elected officials, their aides, and government regulators should be briefed so that they understand cost-benefit relationships. Also, consideration should be given to how such information may be used to answer social critics' attacks or, what is an even better tactic, to preempt their criticism. At the very least, a company armed with these data will know the costs and limitations involved in attempting to achieve unrealistic public demands.

According to former Secretary of Commerce Juanita Kreps, "The past 15 years have seen corporations devote dramatically increased attention to social responsibility." As evidence she offers the following observation: "In 1977, 456, or 91.2 percent, of the *Fortune* 500 industrial firms published information about social performance in their annual reports, according to an Ernst & Ernst survey. This is nearly twice the number of firms that did so in 1971."[2]

We believe that it is important to communicate to the general public, as a matter of business credibility, what companies that assume a leadership role are doing to help improve the specific areas of social concern. Generalities and platitudes will not help, but specific examples will start to turn the tide of antibusiness sentiment. Many companies already are doing more. We must recognize that a credible public report is essential to effective leadership. To be credible, such reporting should generally be based upon quantified results, including costs as well as benefits, and results should be documented to assure maximum credibility if they are challenged. Accountants have a special role to play in gathering and providing this solidly factual information.

In my opinion, we business and professional leaders have a clear obliga-

---

[2] Speech given at Duke University, Oct. 19, 1977; referred to in *The New York Times,* Oct. 20, 1977.

tion to inform the public about our social programs. Whether we believe that corporate social responsibility is fulfilled by meeting minimum legal standards or should be expanded to include voluntary efforts, we must tell the public in specific terms what we are doing and why and the tangible results of our policies. Free enterprise has shown what it can do to solve social problems. With improved communication of our goals, efforts, and accomplishments, we may foster a dramatic change in public attitudes toward business and our free enterprise system based on our willing adherence to new standards of social accountability and responsibility.

CONSTITUTION-ALIZING THE CORPORATION

DAVID W. EWING

David W. Ewing is executive editor—planning, Harvard Business Review, *and a member of the faculty of the Harvard Graduate School of Business Administration. He attended Amherst College and Harvard Law School. He has been associated with the* Harvard Business Review *since 1949.*

Mr. Ewing is the author of The Managerial Mind, The Practice of Planning, The Human Side of Planning, Writing for Results: In Business, Government, and the Professions, *and, most recently,* Freedom inside the Organization: Bringing Civil Liberties to the Workplace. *He has published articles in numerous periodicals, including* Harvard Business Review, Fortune, Harper's, The Nation, The Civil Liberties Review, Challenge, Public Relations Quarterly, Management Review, Organizational Communications, The Wall Street Journal, Saturday Review, *and* Psychology Today.

An old Pennsylvania Dutch proverb admonishes, "Think what you please—but not too loud." However, George B. Geary, a salesman for 14 years in a large steel corporation in Pennsylvania, did not take this advice to heart. Geary was sure that a new tubular casing which the company was making was dangerous and unfit for customer use. When he voiced his fears to his superiors, he was told to stop worrying: after all, the new casing had been tested. But the testing had been inadequate, Geary insisted, and so he took his misgivings to the vice president in charge of sales. His reward for his efforts was a summary discharge.

The veteran salesman went to court. In 1974 the Supreme Court of Pennsylvania heard his case and decided that he had no right of action for wrongful discharge.[1] The decision has no precedential value (the courts have taken this line for centuries), but the case is remarkable in one respect: it was a 4 to 3 decision. Not long ago the vote would have been 7 to 0 against Geary.

The closeness of the decision is one of a growing number of signs of a gradual but momentous change in thinking about employee rights in industry. The traditional law of the master-servant relationship, which in the main holds that management can fire an employee for cause, for no cause, or for cause morally wrong, is being challenged as never before, not only by groups outside the corporation but also by groups inside it, including some top-management leaders. A momentous change in the corporate quality of life appears to be in the making.

What is the situation that a growing number of people want to change? In most corporations and for a great majority of corporate employees, civil liberties have been a will-o'-the-wisp. Union members are the major exception to this rule (not all of them, because some unions are totalitarian and reactionary), but unions cover only about 1 employee in 5. All the rest—managers, secretaries, scientists, engineers, salespeople, accountants, and many others—are subject to the traditional rule just mentioned.

For these many employees, the constitutional rights to which one has grown accustomed in family, school, and church life generally must be left outdoors, like cars in the parking space. As in totalitarian countries, from time to time a benevolent chief executive or department head may encourage speech, conscience, and privacy, but these scarcely can be called rights, for management can take them away at will. In the words of former Attorney General Ramsey Clark, "A right is not what someone gives you; it is what no one can take away."

---

[1] *Geary v. U.S. Steel Corp.*, 319 A. 2d 174 (1974).

BACKGROUND TO CORPORATE AUTHORITARIANISM

This situation is the curious, anomalous, and accidental product of two parallel trends, one legal and the other commercial. Since its beginnings, Western law has given the employer a fairly free hand in hiring and firing employees. Until a century or so ago there were good reasons for this. Businesses were small; the employer-employee relationship was close; commercial life, like personal life, was tenuous; and labor tended to be manual, simple, and interchangeable. But then came the era of the large organization, corporate power, and the so-called knowledge worker, that is, the employee whose value to the corporation lies not so much in his or her hands and physical energy as in learned abilities and know-how. The intimacy of the employer-employee relationship vanished; size made the corporation more stable and longer lived than any employee or management group; and technology and specialization produced employees who were not interchangeable among companies, employees who, though extremely valuable for *some* companies, might be of no value whatsoever to most. However, only in a few respects, such as collective bargaining, did the law change to accommodate this momentous change.

In the meantime a revolution was occurring in the operation and direction of business. The large corporation appeared and, with it, professional management. "In the past, the man has been first," said Frederick Winslow Taylor, often called the father of scientific management; "In the future, the system must be first." Taylor and the legions of industrial engineers and management experts who followed him looked at the organization as a system whose main function was to be efficient and effective. Individualism was something that, while precious in private life, was atavistic in work life, relevant only if its suffocation might conflict with the prosperity of the system. In work life, Taylor saw individualism mostly as a means to an end. If it seemed a valuable means, it would be stressed; but if it didn't seem valuable, it wouldn't be prized. Always the system—its efficiency, its productiveness— was the North Star in Taylor's hemisphere.

The consequence of these two trends, the organizational and managerial revolutions, each developing independently of the other, was a loss of civil liberties and a rise of authoritarianism that none of the Founding Fathers could have anticipated. It would not be fair to say that their dream of constitutionalism was eviscerated, for American political and social liberties expanded steadily in our first two centuries. On the other hand, it is fair to say that there has grown up an enormous corporate archipelago which, in terms of civil liberties, is as different from the rest of the United States as day is from night. In this archipelago, as Taylor mandated, the system comes first, the individual second (except when collective-bargaining, equal-employment-opportunity, safety and health, and similar regulations provide otherwise). Externally, the system operates at the sufferance of the consumer: no corporation survives unless it pleases a constituency in the marketplace. Internally, however, the employee works and behaves at the sufferance of the system as represented by his or her supervisors and managers.

DEVELOPMENT OF THE
EMPLOYEE-RIGHTS MOVEMENT

Until the 1950s the movement for employee rights was hypothetical. One could have traveled from Albuquerque, New Mexico, to Zilwaukee, Michigan, without seeing a trace of it. In the 1960s, without forewarning, it appeared here and there in tenuous form, but no one took it seriously. And then, early in the 1970s, employee rights abruptly began to materialize, and they have been spreading ever since. Why? A variety of feelings and beliefs about work and authority have been changing together, bringing about a subtle but momentous alteration in attitudes—what sailors might call a sea change in the economic weather.

One important change is the steadily growing conviction that top executives in an organization, whether private or public, have no monopoly on wisdom and understanding. While they must be free to make operating decisions and to demand excellent work performance, they are not entitled to impose thought control on subordinates. Watergate, the corporate payoff scandals, and other notorious cases of top-level bungling have contributed to this conviction.

Another part of the sea change is a growing feeling that there should be more to producing goods and services than narrowly defined efficiency. Human dignity has a role, too, and that means rights. In valuing the work system more than the individual, Taylor's school of scientific management was singing the ancient call of the totalitarian, with the corporation placed in the role usually reserved for the state. U.S. Supreme Court Justice Felix Frankfurter articulated the newer theme when he said, "I don't like a man to be too efficient. He's likely to be not human enough."

Still another reason for the new thinking is disenchantment with the notion of freedom of contract between employer and employee. The traditional reasoning of employers and jurists went something like this: "Employee, if you don't like it on your employer's terms, get out. He didn't have to hire you; therefore he can fire you. You can leave any time *you* want; therefore you must leave any time *he* wants." Such legal chauvinism once could be justified by arguing that a dismissed employee could waltz off to some rival employer on the other side of town. If this were ever true, certainly it is no longer. Let us suppose that the employee is a specialized engineer or chemist who cannot hope to find a new job except by uprooting his or her family and moving to another city or state. Let us suppose that the employee is middle-aged in a market that prefers younger people (equal-employment-opportunity laws notwithstanding). The typical employee is no longer a pair of hands that can be substituted readily for a missing pair of hands somewhere else. He or she is trained and equipped for a limited number of work opportunities.

Another kind of disenchantment that fortifies the employee-rights movement has to do with economic loyalty. The traditional attitude (no doubt born in the days when most owners also were managers) has been that only the chief executive and his or her top lieutenants know how to be truly loyal to the stockholders. Therefore, a lowly engineer, accountant, scientist, or even assistant counsel who disagrees with the boss has got to be wrong and, more to the point, dismissible by 5 P.M. the same day.

Now this notion seems workable enough in the area of economic matters and technical management. Here the so-called big picture possessed by the top executive does indeed (or should) entitle him or her to decide what is right. Not so, however, when it comes to matters of ethics and morality. Does anyone seriously argue, after our rich and mind-boggling history of top-management embezzlements, cover-ups, and other shenanigans, that corporate czars are more loyal and honest with the owners than are the kulaks (or, as one congressional punster said, the "czar-dines")? Too many dismissal cases in which facts have been aired suggest that it is the czars, not the kulaks, who should have been fired. The department head who fires the questioning accountant may be a neurotic, unscrupulous man who wants that green eyeshade out of the office fast for the sake of keeping his private embezzlement or political-payoff scheme under wraps.[2]

Finally, and perhaps most important, employee rights are being supported on grounds of accountability. There is a growing feeling, sometimes reflected in judicial decisions, that private industry no longer is private but is endowed with varying degrees of public responsibility. This being the case, more Americans are asking, don't we want employees to feel a *dual* loyalty, not only to the corporation but also to society and to the morality that holds society together?

This question brings us back at last to the Geary case. Dissenting from the majority view, Justice Samuel J. Roberts urged the Pennsylvania court to attach greater weight to the public's stake in responsible criticism by employees. "Geary's discharge is directly contrary to the societal interest in

---

[2] An absurd example of the traditional view is the case of *Campbell v. Ford Industries,* 546 P. 2d 141 (1975), in which an employee who came upon evidence of top-level embezzlement and requested a look at the books was fired outright even though he also was a stockholder. The Supreme Court of Oregon rebuffed his suit against the company for wrongful discharge.

preventing injury due to defectively manufactured products," Roberts argued. He felt that the sales veteran's action was more than an option; it was a "duty" and "in complete harmony with his employer's best interest." Mightn't Geary have been more culpable if he had *not* taken his worries to the top?

YANKEE DOODLE IN THE EXECUTIVE SUITE

Thus the argument for employee rights grows. At first it appears to be only a loose thread in a legal jacket, but when pulled, it causes the whole jacket to unravel. For two centuries our courts have concentrated, as they should, on protecting the individual from the oppression of political governments. But if rights against federal and state agencies are important, why not rights also against corporate economic agencies? "Let me add," Thomas Jefferson wrote to James Madison in 1787, when the two men were pondering the need for a constitutional bill of rights, "that a bill of rights is what the people are entitled to against every government on earth, general or particular."

Although Jefferson didn't know it, the state governments of that day were to be surpassed in size by corporate governments. The "population" of the American Telephone & Telegraph Co. is 939,000 employees, nearly twice the size of the population of Virginia when the American Revolution started. To be sure, AT&T's population is mostly daytime, whereas the people of Virginia were governed night and day; on the other hand, the telephone company controls its employees far more carefully than the Virginia statehouse ever dreamed of controlling its tradesmen and farmers.

The time-honored rebuttal to the suggestion that corporations should be constitutionalized is that without strict economic discipline our economic system would come apart at the seams. Any form of dissidence, any type of criticism of management prerogatives, however well motivated, is greeted as the most contemptible of crimes. To paraphrase Prof. Alan Dershowitz of the Harvard Law School, dissidence is considered a crime so heinous that even innocence is no defense against it. The unfortunate Geary, for instance, appears to have been innocent of any such ignoble motives as seeking to agitate fellow employees, tarnish the company image, or throw a monkey wrench into the machines making tubes.

"One of the tragedies of life is the murder of a beautiful theory by a gang of brutal facts," said Benjamin Franklin. The "Totalitarianism is necessary" theory would appear to be an easy victim. Looking around us, we can find numerous instances of organizations that have not come apart at the seams while establishing civil liberties. Which are these companies? What gaps in corporate civil liberties have they sought to fill? And why have they felt impelled to lead in the ways that they have?

Privacy

Corporate initiatives to develop a right of privacy for employees are important because traditionally managers have needed only the flimsiest excuses to search a subordinate's locker, desk, and files. Moreover, since managers alone have had access to an employee's personnel files, they have been able to clutter them, if they have wished, with irrelevant and inaccurate information. Another form of invasion is eavesdropping. For instance, in all but a few states company managers are free to monitor employees' conversations on company telephones without notifying the employees.

An employee's privacy is invaded in still other ways in organizations that exercise the full freedom given them by traditional law. It is invaded when an employer collects data about a worker. The company may employ exhaustive questionnaires about the person's life and habits, psychological tests, and electronic tests. Even enthusiastic supporters of such devices admit that they raise a legitimate question of unfair invasion of privacy, but they insist that the benefit to management and society outweighs the invasion. The employee's privacy may be invaded again when the information collected is put to use. Managers make decisions on the basis of information about which the employee may be ignorant, including hearsay and off-the-cuff opinions gleaned from quick interviews. The organization may use the same information to answer inquiries from social workers, credit bureaus, union officials, insurance companies, lawyers, government agencies, and other entities.

In changing this egregious situation, the International Business Machines Corp. has been the leader. This company has enacted for its nearly 300,000 employees a privacy code which may be the most advanced such code of any organization in the world. In addition to ruling out surreptitious monitoring of employee conversations and spying on employees' home lives, IBM insists on such principles as the following:[3]

1.   Management can collect and keep in its personnel files only those facts about employees that are required by law or that are necessary to manage operations. Thus, IBM's job application forms no longer request previous addresses or information on whether the prospective employee has relatives working for IBM. Nor does it ask about prior mental problems, convictions dating back more than 5 years, or more recent criminal charges that have not resulted in a conviction.

---

[3] For a more complete discussion of the IBM code, see Frank Cary's interview, "IBM's Guidelines to Employee Privacy," *Harvard Business Review*, September–October 1976, p. 82.

2.   Performance evaluations more than 3 years old must be weeded from an employee's file.

3.   Employees are entitled to know how filed information about them is being used. As IBM Chairman Frank Cary notes, employees should understand that "There's no great mystery about it."

4.   An employee is entitled to see *most* of the information on file about him or her. Only in this way can the employee share in the responsibility for accuracy. Of course, there may be some information that management is justified in withholding. An example is a confidential discussion of an opportunity for promotion that was never given or a boss's personal reactions to an unusual request made by an employee.

5.   Personality and general-intelligence tests are not permissible. However, aptitude and skill tests may be legitimate, for they give an employer relevant knowledge about an applicant's ability. For example, typing tests may be given at IBM.

The IBM approach is becoming the corporate Sermon on the Mount in the privacy field. Companies large and small have espoused it or are considering espousing it; Alan F. Westin, professor of public law and government at Columbia University, estimates that since the early 1970s about half of the *Fortune* 500 industrial companies have made a strong start in this direction.

What motivates a company to eliminate the Big Brother nightmare? IBM, by tradition a paternalistic company under two generations of the Watson family, has always attached great importance to morale. Also, IBM has been proud of its employees' continuing eagerness to reject unions; it wants its people to feel that unions are unnecessary. Last but not least, IBM has been sensitive to the possibility that its computers *could,* if business and government so desired, become the means to an Orwellian nightmare.

Cummins Engine Company, another leader in establishing privacy (among other things, Cummins provides its 10,000 employees with an annual printout of the content of their personnel files and encourages them to set the record straight if necessary), has been driven by a strong feeling of obligation to reinforce community values and to enhance the area physically (as by its donations to Columbus, Indiana, for hiring top-notch architects to design new public buildings). Bank of America, another advocate of employee privacy, sees a close and sensitive relationship between the ideals that move society and the aspirations of private enterprise. Anchored physically in certain communities, Bank of America may find it a little easier than many companies do to relate its fortunes to the ebb and flow of public perceptions about whether it is a good place to work.

Speech

One of the most daring and controversial trends in business is toward greater scope for employee criticism of a company, including whistle blowing. In years past, an employee who spoke out against a corporate policy or practice that he or she felt to be wrong was almost always penalized. Most business executives would have agreed with the legendary riding master in the British Cavalry who observed: "It's remarkable how a few days of reflection on his errors in the guardhouse can cause someone to keep his heels down and his elbows in." Actually, an employee who criticized management wrongdoing was lucky to get the guardhouse; outright dismissal was often his or her fate.

This tradition may be on the way out. In the spring of 1978 the president of the Atlantic Richfield Company, Thornton Bradshaw, sent a letter to its 50,000 employees, urging them to report to the government any instance of chemicals being used that might be a threat to health or the environment. While a great many business executives are appalled at the notion of encouraging whistle blowing, Bradshaw's lead already is being followed by a few other companies, and it seems clear that others will join them.

One big division of the General Electric Co. operates a hot line for employees who have questions, criticisms, or worries about wrongdoing to report. More than 100,000 calls were received and handled in a year. The New England Telephone & Telegraph Co. operates a similar system called Private Lines. An employee can remain anonymous, he or she can challenge management in sensitive areas like discrimination and dishonesty, and all questions are answered promptly, either by the Private Lines staff or by company officials.

The Dow Chemical Company and American Airlines open pages of their company publications to employee criticisms and questions. Embarrassing letters—accusations of management featherbedding, sham in labor relations, stupid supervisory practices—are published. While official responses may not always satisfy the critics, there is little doubt that the criticisms are heard, sometimes loud and clear. I know of no evidence that critics, when they give their names, are penalized.

Delta Air Lines holds regular meetings with its 28,000 employees in various locations where top officials ask workers, after supervisors and foremen have been excused, "What's bothering you?" Questions can be submitted anonymously by card. All queries are answered on the spot or as soon as possible after the meeting, sometimes on bulletin boards.

Pitney-Bowes, Inc., has a Council of Personnel Relations that includes thirteen employee representatives who are elected for 2-year terms from each company division. Meeting once a month, this group fields complaints and problems batted from workers to their representatives. Besides bringing employee criticisms into the open, the council arranges to solve a good many problems; in some cases, in fact, it has found a solution immediately. The company also holds what it calls jobholder meetings. At these meetings, held regularly at the main plant locations, top executives listen to employees speak out about troublesome problems, ranging from layoff policy to personal criticism of management practice.

The leaders in encouraging a limited right of speech are diverse in tradition, attitude, size, and technology. Invariably, however, they are *confident* companies. Their managements don't feel threatened by a little criticism; they are willing to learn. If they find that they are wrong, they don't feel that the sun will fail to appear the next morning.

But more than confidence is involved in the decision to encourage openness and inquiry. There must also be awareness that suppression of criticism, while it may eliminate the symptoms, does not eliminate the feeling of trouble or dissatisfaction. And so the managements of these companies have been willing to make a trade-off: a loss of calm for a gain in understanding. "If something is bothering people here," an executive in one of the companies explained to me, "we won't make it go away by refusing to hear it." And he added: "You know, I feel a lot easier when I hear complaints than when I don't. Because I know they're there. If I hear them, I may get unhappy, and I'll say to myself, 'Damn it, that's not right, they just don't understand.' But you see, I'm getting warned in time. It's a kind of early warning system, you might say."

Conscientious Objection

Developments in employee speech serve as a kind of paradigm for developments in the area of conscience. The right to object to an immoral or unethical order or request is particularly important to employees. Indeed, rightlessness in this area probably troubles more employees more often than does lack of free speech, judging from surveys by the *Harvard Business Review*.[4]

For unionized employees, the grievance procedure provides a sorely needed means of protection. A steel-company worker who was ordered to throw pollutants in a river, objected, and was suspended, took advantage of the union's backing and the grievance machinery to get his job back without loss of pay. Ralph Nader reports that on more than one occasion employees in automobile companies have been protected by their unions after objecting to violations of safety standards in production.

But for all the rest—the nearly 80 percent who do not belong to unions—

---

[4] For example, see Raymond C. Baumhart, "How Ethical Are Businessmen?" *Harvard Business Review,* July–August 1961, p. 6; Steven Brenner and Earl Molander, "Is the Ethics of Business Changing?" *Harvard Business Review,* January–February 1977, p. 57.

life is more totalitarian. One example of the traditional rule is the case of Shirley Zinman, a secretary in a Philadelphia employment agency, who had to resign when she refused to follow her boss's directive to monitor telephone conversations with outsiders without their knowledge. When she sought unemployment compensation from the local board, she was denied it on the ground that her resignation was not "compelling and necessitous." She appealed to the Pennyslvania Commonwealth Court and, in a 1973 decision hailed by civil rights leaders, the state board's decision was reversed.[5] This case is significant for what it does *not* say. The liberally inclined court does not suggest that Zinman should be reinstated in the agency.

In business circles, grapevine cases like the following are well known. A factory was making plans for expansion. The new general manager went over the details with the facilities engineer, an older man who was a few years away from comfortable retirement, assuming that he kept his pension. An eager-beaver type who wanted to make a good profit showing, the general manager insisted that the engineer specify footings and structural-steel specifications that were below the standards of good practice. When the engineer balked, he was told to choose between doing as he was told and losing his job.

In the great majority of companies, clearly, the rule for employees has been "To get along, go along." Few traditions have so polluted the quality of life between the hours of 9 and 5.

Any company that has some mechanism for criticism and protest, such as those mentioned in the section "Speech," offers a means of protection for the conscientious objector. A few have gone further, establishing procedures designed for this sort of problem in particular. One such company is IBM. Its open-door and speak-up systems both are well suited to the employee who, fearing to confront his or her boss, seeks some way of bringing an odious problem to the attention of senior people who desire and are able to see justice done.

Conscientious objection is a particularly troublesome problem for companies to deal with. In one sense, it spells defeat: who in management wants to learn that a supervisor down the line, perhaps one in whom seniors have placed great confidence, is taking illegal shortcuts or condoning immorality? The more that management sets a standard of perfection for itself, the more difficult it may be to face such a question. Only if management is willing to recognize and accept its imperfections—to "sin bravely," as the late Benjamin M. Selekman used to say—is it ready to take steps to establish a right of conscientious objection.

---

[5] 8 Pa. Comm. Ct. Reports 649, 304 A. 2d 380 (1973).

This brings us to the fourth new right, which is especially significant as a way of institutionalizing defenses for the conscientious objector.

Due Process

The emergence of due process is a momentous development in corporate society. It means that an honest, well-meaning critic can be protected from harassment or discharge despite the pressure on his or her superiors to increase profits. The veteran engineer who questions the safety specifications of a reactor is not at the mercy of some middle-management tyrant who has been counting on keeping costs down by cutting corners. The thoughtful supervisor who first questions the cancer danger of a new chemical process is not, like the early Christians, thrown to the lions because his or her message displeases someone in power.

A few pioneering organizations have experimented with informal, nonlegal "courts" for reviewing cases of alleged injustice.[6] These courts take the complaint before the aggrieved employee would have been been demoted or fired. To present his or her case the employee may be entitled to "counsel," not necessarily an attorney but at least an articulate executive who can represent the defense sympathetically.

This procedure has the advantage of speed. The aggrieved employee doesn't grow old waiting for a hearing, as may happen in the courts. The decision also is educational; it helps to define tolerable and intolerable behavior for the organization.

Polaroid Corp., with about 12,000 nonunionized employees, has a committee whose job it is to represent an employee with a grievance. This is done in a hearing before representatives of management. The committee members are elected from the ranks. Researchers A. R. Evans and Mark J. Thomas report that a fair number of management decisions are overruled in the hearings. If the decision goes against the aggrieved employee, he or she is entitled by company rules to submit the case to an outside arbitrator.[7]

Arbitration, traditionally associated with blue-collar unions and traditionally concerned with bread-and-butter issues, has an increasing potential for use in disputes over employee rights and for disputes involving professionals and middle management. Managerial unions received a setback when the U.S. Supreme Court in 1974 refused to place them under the collective-bargaining umbrella, but many observers are convinced that their growth is inevitable. And while unions have not pushed for civil liberties in their

---

6 See, for instance, "California Products, Inc.," EA-A 257, a case printed by the Harvard Business School in 1957. (The company name is fictional.)

7 Mark J. Thomas, "Employee Concern Review in the Corporation," unpublished working paper for the Mead Corp.

contracts, there is no reason that they should not do so. The Screen Actors Guild, for example, has written into its contract a clause prohibiting the interviewing of prospective actors and actresses outside an office—in a motel room, for instance.

In the unionized sector, arbitrators have overturned numerous discharges by supervisors who would have fired or suspended subordinates without just cause. Sometimes such Bill of Rights concepts as free expression, privacy, and conscience have been the basis of the arbitrators' rulings.

Why, says Clyde W. Summers of the University of Pennsylvania Law School, shouldn't all employees, unionized or nonunionized, be entitled to arbitration? It would be relatively simple for companies to extend the arbitration principle to all whom they employ, regardless of the presence and power of a local union. Summers writes:

> A body of arbitration law protecting against unjust discipline has existed for thirty years. But the harsh legal rule continues to leave a majority of employees vulnerable to the most arbitrary, oppressive, and vindictive actions. . . . We have arbitrated tens of thousands of discipline cases, finding nearly half to be instances of injustice, but we have closed our eyes to the tens of thousands of cases of unjust discipline suffered by employees who have no adequate forum for obtaining justice. It is time, and past time, to recognize these injustices and to provide statutory protection against them.[8]

Another form of due process is the ombudsperson. Like an arbitrator without portfolio, the ombudsperson can investigate promptly and hear out the principals to a dispute; unlike an arbitrator, he or she must count on persuasion or the backing of a senior executive to remedy a situation. In one recent case the ombudsperson of a large scientific organization investigated complaints that a manager was making sexual forays on his secretaries. After verifying the complaints by obtaining depositions from several secretaries who had been fired after resisting him, none of whom knew the others, the ombudsperson brought the evidence to the head of the organization, who talked with the manager the next day and obtained his resignation.

At Donnelly Mirrors in Holland, Michigan, an astonishingly successful David among Goliaths in the automobile-supply industry, due process takes the form of an employee board elected by the workers, each board member having his or her own "constituency." At Puget Sound Plywood, Inc., in Tacoma, Washington, the board of directors itself, all of whose members are elected by popular vote in the company, takes up cases of alleged unfair treatment, hearing "plaintiff" and "defendant" right in the boardroom if

---

8 Clyde W. Summers, "Individual Protection against Unjust Dismissal: Time for a Statute," *Virginia Law Review,* vol. 62, 1977, p. 481.

necessary. Both systems seem to have been successful in achieving their goals of fairness and justice.

Too few companies have experimented with procedures that give subordinates a fair chance to prove their complaints. Far too many have rested on such flimsy alternatives as a part-time personnel executive or a vice president "whose door is always open," methods that *may* be effective but generally are not because the investigator is allied, or appears to be allied, with the very bosses whose decisions are being questioned. Due process calls for highly committed investigators, usually full-time people, whose commitment is not to persons, or to authority, or even to corporate profits, but first of all to seeing that equity is achieved.

Most of the companies that have taken initiatives to establish due process are nonunion concerns. This seems surprising, for if a company has, say, 20 percent of its workforce under a due-process procedure, one would think that it would be logical to give the same benefit to nonunion employees. In actuality, I suspect that the union has little to do with the decision. Industry, location, technology, and corporate size may have little to do with it either. The big question is how management perceives the corporate purpose. Is the corporation seen exclusively as an economic agency committed to producing goods and services at a profit? Or is it seen as a socioeconomic agency for bringing people together, with all their foibles as well as their talents, to produce goods and services at a profit and in a personally satisfying way?

CONCLUSION

Organizations in our society have become "they," and individuals have become "we." Consequently, it has become possible to berate corporations as if they were lives unto themselves—a tendency that cannot be regarded as healthy. Many good explanations might be advanced for this division between we the people and they our organizations, but the phenomenon indicates that a serious value conflict exists between organizational and private life.

When we report to work at the average company, we, as employees, are supposed to leave our esteemed rights behind. Is it any wonder, therefore, that we suffer from a kind of national schizophrenia, from a lack of value communication between our organized institutional lives and our private lives? No matter how well-lighted, well-paying, safe, and efficient, the average plant and office become vaguely repressing and depressing in ways that cannot be explained simply by the unpleasantness of having had to get out of bed to go there.

By Americanizing our corporations, we may produce no magic increases in productivity and performance, although preliminary experience suggests that gains will indeed be made. But by erasing a subtle division in our culture which makes us rights holders at home and in the community and puppets in the plant and office, we could reduce an important cause of ambivalence in our outlook. We could become whole.

In addition, there is a practical logic for employee rights in a market economy that is hard to refute. It has never been stated better than by the late Zachariah Chafee, Jr., of the Harvard Law School. Speaking two decades ago, Professor Chafee was discussing the right of employee speech in particular, but his observations apply equally to due process, conscientious objection, and privacy. He said:

> Now, if into this delicate process [of decision making in a corporation] be injected threats of penalties for the expression of views which are unacceptable to superiors, the powerful emotion of fear impedes the process at every point. The multitudinous sources of impressions upon the minds of members of the enterprise begin to dry up. Ideas no longer come to them. Or if they do, their entrance into minds is impeded by the barriers of anxiety. Everybody down the line ceases to ask the vital questions, "Do I believe this as a fact?" "Is this course of action good or bad for the enterprise?" Instead, everybody asks, "Is this illegal or disloyal or liable to hurt me in some way which perhaps I can't precisely foresee?" The prevalent attitude becomes, "We must be neither good nor bad—we must be careful."[9]

---

9 Unpublished address, June Conference of the Management Training Program, Radcliffe College, Cambridge, Mass., June 11, 1955.

THE SOCIAL GOALS OF A CORPORATION

JOHN H. FILER

John H. Filer is chairman of Aetna Life & Casualty, the nation's largest publicly owned insurance and diversified financial corporation. Mr. Filer was graduated from DePauw University and Yale Law School. He served as clerk to U.S. District Judge Carroll C. Hincks before joining the law firm of Gumbart, Corbin, Tyler and Cooper in 1951. In July 1958, he joined Aetna as an assistant counsel, became general counsel in 1966 and, in addition, administrative assistant to the chairman and president in 1967. He was named executive vice president for administration and planning in 1968. In January 1972, Mr. Filer was appointed vice chairman, and in July 1972 he assumed the role of chairman.

Mr. Filer is a member of the General Council of Assicurazioni Generali and a director of the United States Steel Corp. He is a trustee of the Urban Institute, a member of the Board of Governors of the Nature Conservancy, and a director of the National Minority Purchasing Council. Mr. Filer is a director of the Insurance Association of Connecticut, a director of the Connecticut Business and Industry Association, chairman of the American Council of Life Insurance, and a trustee of the Committee for Economic Development. He is also chairman of the National Alliance of Business, and he formerly served as chairman of the Commission on Private Philanthropy and Public Needs.

I fall a very natural heir to a sincere concern about business's responsiveness to society. Henry Beers, who led Aetna Life & Casualty two decades ago, made one of the earliest statements of the doctrine of corporate social responsibility when he urged business people to give tithes of their time as well as their money for the public good. He was particularly insightful when he suggested that the survival of our economic system may well hinge on the extent to which business practices good citizenship. My immediate predecessor shared this conviction. Surrounded by some of the nation's most serious urban riots in the mid-1960s, Olcott Smith put our company among the leaders in a fight to correct social inequities and to revitalize the spirit and the face of our troubled city of Hartford, Connecticut.

Throughout this period our company and most others viewed social responsibility as an important but separate pursuit, to be taken care of largely by charitable gifts and community programs. Such programs have been valuable and have been welcomed by those who have benefited from them, but business must do far more. I believe that we must bring social responsibility into our day-to-day operations and make it a part of business decisions.

Charitable activities, while still vital, are a very small part of what most large corporations can and should be doing as responsible members of our society. The real test of the responsiveness of corporations to society is how they are doing in their basic business to meet the needs of society as well as of their customers.

Trying to bring corporate resources to bear on social issues is a matter of pressing urgency for each of us. We are likely to regret it bitterly in future years if we leave this job to others. As we do affect society, and by that I mean people, in a great variety of ways, we obviously have the power to impact on their lives if we wish to do so. Justice, equality, recognition, freedom, mobility, and self-determination are unevenly distributed in the United States today, and corporate America can either do something about the inequities or be required to do something. We, individually or collectively, cannot solve all these problems, but there are some aspects of most of them that we can influence for the better.

I am not suggesting that we focus the total power of the corporate community on curing all our nation's social ills. I suggest, rather, that each corporation give attention to the social consequences of each of its activities and, further, that each corporation examine its own special characteristics, strengths, and particular areas of interest and plan how it may best contribute to the fulfillment of one or more unmet public needs.

I'm not talking about the very big-ticket items, such as environmental protection. These must be handled in large part through the regulatory process as long as ours is a competitive business economy. Rather, I'm talking about the myriad other issues, ranging from the redesign of training programs to the imaginative employment of the corporate contributions budget, to making sure that our customers receive what we promise, and to participating in community development projects.

SETTING SOCIAL GOALS

If we are to do all this successfully, corporations must set social goals just as they set business goals. Setting business goals has never been simple, but setting corporate social goals is far more difficult. With traditional corporate goals, participants have a common understanding of overall objectives. They agree that such things as market share, cash flow, profit growth, quality of product or service, return on invested capital, and the like are legitimate values to seek. The differences of opinion among our managers in these areas are likely to have reasonable boundaries. We are experts dealing with experts, and fortunately the more senior we are, the more expert we are believed to be, so that disagreements get resolved and decisions are reasonably well accepted.

When it comes to social goals, none of us has much qualification or experience. There is no common understanding of what social values corporations should seek. And those set on doing something for the public good seldom have enough conviction that they are right to overrule the objectors, the doubters, and the potential second-guessers, not to mention the vigorous proponents of other corporate goals that seem, on occasion at least, to conflict with social progress.

Because social goal setting is so new, so different, and so difficult at this point, I believe that for now it must be primarily a role of the chief executive. The average manager is conditioned by training and incentive programs to view profit as the solitary goal. Few managers view the pursuit of social goals as necessary to personal success. Therefore, it is up to the chief executive to move the message downward, first through senior management and then into the middle and lower levels of the organization. This must be done as an exercise not of autocracy but of leadership.

Effective social goal setting cannot be mandated in any organization, just as we found that legislating civil rights did not go very far toward changing the attitudes of a vast majority of people. I do not believe that we can tell managers that they must place a set number of social goals in their business plans each year and expect those goals to be pursued. It is more effective, instead, to create a climate in which managers willingly and thoughtfully place such goals in their plans. It has recently been my role to encourage our senior people to see that the social problems they can address creatively through their operations are considered when preparing annual plans and that a like amount of thought be given to addressing people problems as is given to addressing profit problems. Anyone reading our company's annual business goals today would find a sprinkling of social goals mixed in with the traditional profit objectives. We have not, of course, addressed all the social problems that we are able to affect, but we are doing more than we were a few years ago, and we will be doing still more in the years ahead.

AETNA'S PROGRAM

To set and carry out social goals, managers must become educated and sensitized to the needs of the community. In our company we have a formal program which tracks the community and social service activities of our top sixty or so people, those at the vice-presidential level and above. We know who is or has been involved in which activities. If the community needs the particular expertise of one of our executives, we are able to find someone with the necessary knowledge or interest to do the job. In a sense, we act as a broker to get the right people into the type of community service in which they can make the greatest contribution and reap the greatest benefit.

This activity meets community needs, but it helps our organization as well. Very often such assignments are good developmental opportunities for our executives. The executives are prepared for higher-level positions in which they will have increased contact with the public. But more important, these outside assignments sensitize them to the community and its needs. We don't want our senior people sitting in comfortable offices thinking that they know what the public wants from us. We want them out there once in a while, hearing about problems from the people themselves.

One of the most recent and important examples of how such a program works concerns the issue of personal privacy, one of vital importance to an insurance organization. In 1975 our company president, William O. Bailey, was asked to serve on the Privacy Protection Study Commission in Washington. Bill Bailey was selected because of his interest in the privacy issue. He came away with heightened awareness of the erosion of privacy in our information society and with the firm belief that our company should take a leading position in doing whatever it can to assure the privacy of employees and customers.

As a result of Bailey's service on the Commission, our company expanded its privacy-protection principles for employees, and it implemented a program to protect the privacy of our 4.5 million individual policyholders. In this program we voluntarily complied with nearly all the Commission's recommendations regarding insurance.

This program, which we believe to be the first in our industry, is costing us time and money, but we consider that the advantages of adopting it and of doing so voluntarily far outweigh the negatives. These privacy measures give us an opportunity to shape the direction of change, to demonstrate that voluntary compliance can occur and that it can be more desirable than government regulation. Further, we believe that voluntary actions of this type demonstrate to the public and to legislators that business will take a responsible leadership position on important issues when it can make a meaningful contribution.

I referred earlier to the fact that one reason that social goal setting is so difficult is that few of us have the expertise to determine the direction for appropriate social goals. In an effort to develop this type of expertise within our organization, we have created a staff to analyze public-policies issues. Its assignment is to improve our ability to anticipate emerging issues, to analyze them, and to recommend a response before the initiative is taken from us.

One doesn't have to be a student of our industry to know that the affordability of automobile insurance is a serious social issue. Therefore, the first effort of this staff, undertaken before it was formally constituted, was to examine the affordability problem from an independent perspective that questioned the assumptions of the industry, its critics, and the public. We are now studying the staff report on affordability. It is being discussed and refined, and recommendations in some areas are being implemented. What is most important is that our company now has a clearer understanding of who is hurt most seriously. We know as the result of opinion surveys what the public dislikes about our practices. In short, we have direction. We have a better idea today than we did a year ago as to how we can go about alleviating this problem. If we are to stay in the automobile insurance business as we know it, we will have to do something.

It is important to realize that the setting of social goals is done with mixed motives. Goal setting is not merely a moral or an altruistic pursuit, but it seems to me that it is perfectly legitimate to try to accomplish some worthwhile social goal even though at the same time we bring about some favorable influence on our corporation. We must not overlook the fact that our primary function of producing quality goods and services while producing a reasonable profit cannot long be ignored. By the same token, we cannot make this objective our sole purpose and expect to continue earning a reasonable profit.

EQUAL EMPLOYMENT OPPORTUNITY AND CAREER DEVELOPMENT

I've dealt thus far with the voluntary setting of social goals. Sometimes we are not so fortunate as to choose our social goals, usually because we fail to pursue them ourselves. An example is the enactment of civil rights legislation and the ensuing equal-employment-opportunity standards under which we all operate. Equal employment opportunity was imposed upon us, but this does not mean that business cannot voluntarily find creative ways to achieve equality as quickly and as genuinely as is possible. I might add that failure fully to develop and utilize all employees is a waste of a corporation's resources. Such a course satisfies neither morality nor economics.

To assure that our company's affirmative-action objectives are met and, most important, are met willingly, we began in 1974 a series of workshops. The first was a day-long session for managers and supervisors that tried to make them aware of their erroneous assumptions about women and members of minority groups. These workshops tried to deal with the lack of dialogue between managers and their female or minority-group subordinates. They encouraged managers to focus on developing these people in the same way in which they had developed white males in the past.

The following year we introduced a program to complete the dialogue. It consisted of a series of 3-day workshops for women and a similar series for minority employees that were designed to help them evaluate their own attitude toward their careers and set personal and business goals, even if this meant the setting of goals that did not include Aetna Life & Casualty.

These workshops received an overwhelmingly favorable reception from the participants, but progress is perhaps better measured by the fact that almost half of the minority employees and approximately 40 percent of the women who attended have since been promoted. Another interesting statistic is that termination rates are much lower for the 1500 employees who have participated thus far than for those who have not.

While the workshops have been effective, they have also shown us that good intentions are not enough without a working knowledge of equal-employment-opportunity laws throughout the organization. To provide this for our managers, we began in 1979 another series of workshops with emphasis on the law as well as on managerial attitudes. Every manager and supervisor in our company was scheduled to participate in this program.

Corporations have given considerable care to equal employment opportunity largely because government abruptly brought management's attention to the matter. However, we must be equally concerned about all our people. As corporations tend to become more complex and monolithic, it has become easier for individuals to feel powerless in the face of unknown or changeable forces. The individual has primary responsibility for his or her future, but corporations also have a responsibility to create an environment conducive to career growth, to provide realistic information about opportunities and career paths, and to offer opportunities for training.

Recently we took some steps in this area with a series of career-development workshops for all employees, thus rounding out the program. We have a special session for supervisors to assist them in helping their employees plan rewarding careers. With career planning we hope to give our people an opportunity to take charge of their lives. I believe that this program strengthens them. It also benefits the company because helping people take care of themselves is far less costly and more rewarding than taking care of people throughout their working lives.

SUMMARY

In these and other ways our company has strengthened its commitment to making social goals a part of our business practices. We have found it a terribly complex and frustrating task that will not be completed over the short term. However, along with the frustrations there have appeared encouraging signs that may make the going somewhat easier in the future. Among these signs is our company's satisfactory level of earnings, which places us in a very respectable position within our industry. I believe that over the last few years we have proved at least that social and financial goals can be pursued together. While there are those who may disagree, I believe that our company's pursuit of social goals has had a measure of influence on attaining its financial goals as well.

INDEX